THE A-Z OF PAYMENTS

With over 1,600 entries, *The A-Z of Payments* provides readers with a comprehensive, practical, easy-to-read listing of payment terms.

The financial services industry is full of terms and abbreviations that can appear confusing or easy to forget (e.g. ACS, 3DS, RTP, PCI DSS, POS, PoS, A2A, P2P, and BaaS). This handy glossary, written in a plain and accessible style, is the perfect desktop companion for experienced practitioners wanting to check the latest terminology, fintech students starting out who want to navigate the world of payments quickly, or those curious about terminology. It will also appeal to those wanting to understand terms related to parts of the industry with which they are unfamiliar, whilst those new to the industry will use it as a reference to understand documentation they access, or better equip them for conversations they might have.

The A-Z of Payments is the ideal companion to anyone undertaking training in payments or on finance courses. It is particularly relevant to private sector corporations, regulators, and their employees.

Neira Jones has more than 25 years' experience in financial services and technology, and advises and coaches organisations of all sizes on payments, FinTech, RegTech, cybercrime, information security, fraud, and regulations. She also provides payment security expert witness services and is a panel member for the UK Payment Systems Regulator. Amongst her many listings and accolades, she is a Retail Technology Innovation Hub 2023 Top 100 Influencer; 2021 Fintech Weekly 100 Most Influential People in FinTech; SC Magazine Women of Influence: 30 Top Cybersecurity Leaders 2021; IT Security Guru 2020 Most Inspiring Women in Cyber, and Planet Compliance Top 50 RegTech Influencers.

THE A-Z OF PAYMENTS

A Modern and Practical Glossary for the Curious and the Forgetful

Neira Jones

Routledge
Taylor & Francis Group
LONDON AND NEW YORK

Designed cover image: Getty Images

First published 2025
by Routledge
4 Park Square, Milton Park, Abingdon, Oxon OX14 4RN

and by Routledge
605 Third Avenue, New York, NY 10158

Routledge is an imprint of the Taylor & Francis Group, an informa business

British Library Cataloguing-in-Publication Data
A catalogue record for this book is available from the British Library

ISBN: 978-1-032-94517-0 (hbk)
ISBN: 978-1-032-90313-2 (pbk)
ISBN: 978-1-003-57113-1 (ebk)

DOI: 10.4324/9781003571131

Typeset in Joanna
by codeMantra

CONTENTS

INTRODUCTION

Payments are complicated. A Google search on the word "payments" returns 6.7 trillion results. A further search on "what are payments?" reduces this number by two-thirds. If you narrow it down to "payments glossary", you get about 367 million results, the first of which is from the Bank of International Settlements,[1] first published in 2001 and revised in 2003 (a lot has happened since then), containing 569 entries. The second entry on Google comes courtesy of Adyen[2] and contains 89 entries and only relates to card payments. The third entry comes from the European Central Bank[3] and is as comprehensive as the BIS one. As they appear as the top three entries on Google, these three glossaries are obviously still popular today. It is, therefore, surprising that none of them will tell you what an account-to-account payment is or give a definition of Open Banking. The BIS glossary doesn't even list Payment Service Providers (PSPs), real-time payments, recurring transactions, or card schemes, but it does tell you about tri-party repo, subcustodian, netting by novation, and the minimum standards of the Lamfalussy report (!). Of course, some people need to know about these things, but payments professionals at large

DOI: 10.4324/9781003571131-1

don't, and those new to payments, or with a casual interest in them, have no use for this. If we continue to examine the Google search, we see that several companies provide "ultimate" glossaries for payments, such as acquired.com[4] (31 entries, card only, 2022), global payments[5] (59 entries, mixed terms, 2022), and Link Money[6] (26 entries, Open Banking only, US-focused, 2023). Whether something is "ultimate" is like beauty, and only in the eyes of the beholder.

Payments evolve fast. Fifteen years ago – at least in the UK, one of the most advanced markets – we wouldn't have dreamt of payments being so convenient, instantaneous, and ubiquitous. We thought nothing of bank payments taking three days or more to process. We still had cheque books, and much cash in our wallets. Today, we may still have a cheque book somewhere, just in case, probably a few years old, and we may carry some cash to pay the window cleaner. But increasingly, even the window cleaner may carry one of those devices enabling them to take card payments, or even just use their own mobile phone. Payments have evolved to fulfil a consumer need driven by technology, especially mobile phones. Don't you find it surprising that the most popular glossary of payment terms at the time of writing was published in 2003? Whilst the fundamentals of centralised payment ecosystems don't move that fast, the world has moved on at a staggering pace since then, and a lot of new vocabulary has been introduced.

Payments terms explained in plain English. The payments industry has never been as fascinating as it is right now. From traditional financial services institutions jumping on the digital transformation bandwagon to innovators and new entrants creating new business models and capitalising on new technologies to regulators trying to cope with it all and maintain some sort of integrity whilst fostering innovation in increasingly complex ecosystems that facilitate the exchange of value. I included a comprehensive glossary of payment terms in my first book, *Understanding Payments*, providing the reader with simple explanations for about 600 terms and acronyms used in the payments industry, as well as a comprehensive index. I also included a comprehensive glossary in my second book, *Beyond Payments*, with more than 800 entries.

But I wanted to go further in my mission of democratising payments knowledge, and I set out to produce this standalone over-arching glossary. It contains **more than 1,600 entries** (1,697 to be precise), with a practical, easy-to-read listing of the most used payment terms, with simple definitions, and more than 250 online references. It also lists some of the most prominent players in the industry, referring to the role they play in the industry. It may not list everything – no mention of Lamfalussy or Herstatt anywhere 😉, after all, this is a payments glossary, not an economist compendium – but readers will quickly be able to find terms they have heard or read, refresh their memory about the meaning of a particular abbreviation, and check out prominent organisations (what type of organisation is Mastercard?). For each letter of the alphabet, before delving into the full list, the reader will be greeted by the John and Suzie cartoon I introduced in my first book. John & Suzie will highlight three terms: two that I find particularly interesting and a third one for the ducks  (for the meaning of the duck, you'll have to read my books but suffice to say that they look serene on the surface whilst a lot of paddling goes on underneath).

This glossary is unique. It is written in plain English in a style accessible to all. It is suitable for novices and experienced practitioners alike, hence the subtitle "A modern and practical glossary for the curious and the forgetful". This glossary will appeal to those needing a refresher on terms and abbreviations: all too often, acronyms are used so much in the payments industry that whilst we might know what they mean, we forget what they stand for (e.g. ACS, 3DS, RTP, PCI DSS, POS, PoS, and A2A). It will also appeal to those wanting to understand terms related to parts of the industry with which they are unfamiliar, whilst those new to the industry will use it as a reference to understand documentation they access or better equip them for conversations they might have. Like my two books, this glossary will continue to democratise payments knowledge. After all, if the BIS glossary, published in 2003, is still the most referenced today, I may be filling a gap… I won't be pretentious and brand this glossary "ultimate", but I will be as bold as saying that it is comprehensive, modern, and practical. I dedicate it to all my payments friends.

Neira Jones, September 2024

Notes

1 A Glossary of Terms Used in Payments and Settlement Systems. Bank of International Settlements, March 2003. https://www.bis.org/cpmi/glossary_030301.pdf (Accessed 21 November 2023)

2 Payments Glossary. Adyen. https://docs.adyen.com/get-startedwith-adyen/payment-glossary/ (Accessed 21 November 2023)
3 European Central Bank. https://www.ecb.europa.eu/services/glossary/html/act7e.en.html (Accessed 21 November 2023)
4 The Ultimate Payments Glossary. Acquired.com, 7 September 2022. https://acquired.com/the-ultimate-payments-glossary/ (Accessed 21 November 2023)
5 The Ultimate Glossary of Payment Terms. Global Payments, 29 August 2022. https://www.globalpayments.com/en-gb/insights/commerce-andpayment-terms (Accessed 21 November 2023)
6 The Ultimate Open Banking Glossary. Link Money, 9 March 2023. https://link.money/blog/open-banking-glossary (Accessed 21 November 2023)

A AND A FEW NUMBERS

A IS FOR...

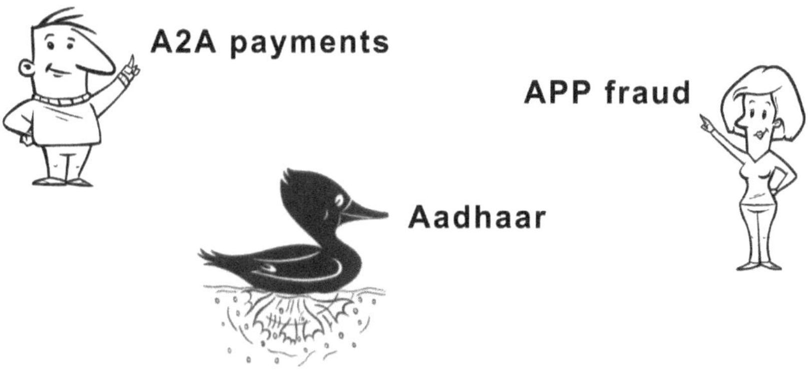

2FA See *two-factor authentication*.

3DES Triple Data Encryption Standard. A *symmetric cryptography* algorithm.

3D Secure (3DS)[1] An *EMV* standard for the *authentication* of *e-commerce* transactions. Deployments include Mastercard's "SecureCode" and "Identity Check", Visa's "Visa Secure", and American Express' "SafeKey". 3D Secure stands for "3 Domain Secure" and refers to the three *ecosystem*

DOI: 10.4324/9781003571131-2

domains involved in the process: the *acquirer* domain (acquirer and *merchant*), the *issuer* domain, and the interoperability domain (the *card scheme*).

3D Secure Server (3DSS) The *3D Secure* infrastructure deployed by a *merchant*. Used to be known as the Merchant Plug-In (MPI). This technology is usually provided by the *Merchant's PSP*, usually a *payment gateway* provider, but some *Access Control Server (ACS)* providers also supply the 3D Secure Server technology. This functionality provides the bridge between the *cardholder* (e.g. a pop-up window) and the *acquirer* during the *authorisation* process.

3DSS See *3D Secure Server*.

51% attack A 51% attack, also known as a "majority attack", occurs when a malicious actor or group gains control of over 50% of a *blockchain* network's *hashing power* (in *Proof-of-Work* systems) or *total stake* (in *Proof-of-Stake* systems). This majority enables them to potentially manipulate transactions, double-spend coins, reverse transactions, prevent new transaction confirmations, and disrupt normal network operations. By controlling the majority of the network's power, the attacker can undermine the decentralised nature and security of the blockchain, posing a significant threat to its integrity. See also *double-spending*.

5G technology The fifth generation of cellular network technology, offering significantly faster data transfer speeds, lower latency, and increased network capacity compared to previous generations. It uses higher-frequency radio waves and advanced antenna technologies to deliver peak data rates up to 20 Gbps, latency as low as 1 millisecond, and the ability to connect up to one million devices per square kilometre. For the payments industry, 5G enables faster and more secure transactions, supports the growth of *Internet-of-Things (IoT)*-based payment systems, enhances *mobile banking* experiences, facilitates real-time *fraud detection*, and allows for more sophisticated data analytics. Its low latency and high reliability also make it ideal for supporting emerging payment technologies like augmented reality shopping and autonomous retail systems.

A2A payment See *account-to-account payment*.

Aadhaar[2] A *digital identity* framework developed by the Unique Identification Authority of India (UIDAI)[3] on behalf of the Government of India. It consists of a 12-digit individual identification number and a set of rules governing the framework. The Aadhaar number serves as proof of identity and residence for any Indian resident, irrespective of age, and is valid for life. Through the Aadhaar deployment, the Indian government intends to promote *financial inclusion* for a largely rural and underbanked population by facilitating access to banking, mobile phone connections, and other government and non-government services. In March 2023, Aadhaar authentication transactions increased to 2.31 billion, and the UIDAI claims that its digital *KYC* (eKYC) deployment has significantly reduced customer acquisition costs for financial services institutions, telcos, and others.

ABA routing number An ABA (American Bankers Association) routing number is a nine-digit code used to identify banks in America. Similar to a UK *sort code*, it is sometimes referred to as a "check routing number", ABA number, routing transit number (RTN), or Fedwire number.

Access to Account (XS2A) A term widely used in the early days of the EU *Second Payment Services Directive* (PSD2), but not so much now, where the concept has generally been replaced with *Open Banking*.

Access Control Server (ACS) *3D Secure* infrastructure deployed by an *issuer*. Most issuers outsource this to an *Independent Software Vendor (ISV)*.

accidental fork An unintended split in a *blockchain* network that occurs when two or more blocks are mined simultaneously, creating temporary parallel chains. This situation is typically resolved quickly as the network converges on the longest chain, discarding the shorter one(s) as *orphan blocks*. See also *fork*.

account-based CBDC A *Central Bank Digital Currency* (CBDC) access model by which users access the CBDC through a *digital identity* scheme. Both *retail CBDCs* and *wholesale CBDCs* can use this access model. These CBDCs can run on either centralised (centralised CBDC account) or distributed (DLT-based CBDC account) infrastructure, and user identification may be provided by the private sector.

Account Information Service Provider (AISP) A *Third-Party PSP* (TPP) that accesses information from a payment account (card account or bank account) on behalf of a *Payment System User* (PSU) on a read-only basis. In Europe, an AISP that has registered with their regulator is called a Registered AISP, or RAISP.

Account Servicing PSP (ASPSP) The payment *ecosystem* actor who manages the account belonging to the *Payment Service User* (PSU) account throughout its lifecycle, from creation to closure. This can be a *bank*, an *issuer*, or a *non-bank Payment Service Provider* (PSP).

account-to-account payment (A2A payment) A type of payment that allows funds to move from a *payer's bank account* to a *payee's* bank account. There are two types of A2A payments: *push payments*, where the payer moves the money directly from their account to the payer's account (e.g. a bank transfer), and *pull payments*, where the payee moves the money from the payer's account with the payer's prior agreement (e.g. a *direct debit*). A push payment is also referred to as "giro payment", "giro", and *credit transfer*.

account takeover fraud (ATO) A type of *unauthorised fraud* where a fraudster compromises a genuine payment account and conducts transactions fraudulently with that account. This is generally linked to *identity theft* crimes and is a particular issue in financial services (but also in other industries). As data breaches continue to plague our lives, large volumes of stolen credentials are continuously being dumped on underground forums and offered for sale to criminals, facilitating this type of crime.

account updater A service that may be provided by *card schemes* or other *Payment Service Providers* (PSPs), which enables *merchants* to automatically update the stored card details of their customers. This is particularly helpful for merchants accepting card *recurring transactions*.

Accredited Scanning Vendor (ASV) A third party that provides *e-commerce* merchants with *Network Vulnerability Scans* (aka ASV scans), as dictated by the *Payment Card Industry Data Security Standard* (PCI DSS) validation requirements for that merchant. The *Payment Card Industry Security Standards Council* maintains a list of ASVs on their website.[4]

ACH See *Automated Clearing House*.

ACH payment A payment transaction conducted through an *ACH scheme*.

ACH scheme A legacy bank *payment scheme*. An ACH scheme is a network that enables payers to send money to payees on the bank rails with longer settlement times than modern *real-time payment system* (*RTP system*). Also referred to as an "ACH system".

ACH system See *ACH Scheme*.

acquirer A *Payment Service Provider* (*PSP*) that enables a *merchant* to connect to a *card scheme*. Commonly referred to as an "acquiring bank", "merchant bank" (if they are also a bank), "Merchant Services Provider" (MSP), "merchant acquirer", "acquiring PSP", or "processor". Acquiring services are also referred to as "merchant services".

acquirer agreement A contract between third parties (e.g. ISO, ISV, PSP, and payfac) and an *acquirer*. This agreement is negotiated to determine a variety of aspects, including processing rates, transaction fees, value-added services, liability, and service-level agreements.

acquirer margin A negotiable fee levied by an *acquirer* on a *merchant* for each card transaction and is supposed to cover the credit risk and overheads that the acquirer has, as well as the profit that the acquirer makes. This is charged to a merchant on top of processing fees and varies by the acquirer as it can be based on transaction volumes, industry, and other factors. Also referred to as "markup fee" or "acquirer markup".

acquirer markup See *acquirer margin*.

acquirer processor See *processor*.

Acquirer Reference Number (ARN) On the *card rails*, this is a unique identifier that is assigned to a transaction when it travels from the *acquirer* through the *card scheme* to the *issuer*. The ARN can be used to track a payment or refund.

acquiring The process of acquiring card transactions from *merchants* to enable those merchants to take card payments for cards issued on a given *card scheme* (e.g. Visa and Mastercard). Acquiring connects merchants with card schemes. Also referred to as "merchant services".

acquiring bank An acquiring PSP that is also a bank. See *acquirer*.

acquiring clearing files A file containing all of the *acquirer*'s card transactions for that day. Each acquirer will produce as many acquiring clearing files as the number of *card schemes* of which they are members (e.g. one for Visa and one for Mastercard). Acquirers submit their clearing files to the schemes in batch, usually at the end of the day, in line with the card scheme *clearing cycle*, and these files are specified in the card scheme *operating regulations*.

acquiring PSP See *acquirer*.

acquisition card See *purchasing card*.

ACS See *Access Control Server*.

active staking wallets A metric expressing the number of unique *blockchain* wallet addresses that are currently delegating tokens to validators in a *Proof-of-Stake* network, contributing to network security and consensus.

Address Verification Fee (AVF) The fee charged for the verification of a cardholder address, typically performed by an *Address Verification Service (AVS)*.

Address Verification Service (AVS) A *fraud prevention* facility enabling *merchants* to verify that the address given by the cardholder matches the billing address associated with the cardholder's account. Can be used in the *Card Present* (CP) and *Card Not Present* (CNP) channels.

AES Advanced Encryption Standard. A *symmetric cryptography* algorithm.

affiliate fraud A term used in the context of marketing where a fraudster poses as an affiliate marketer and uses manufactured traffic and/or fraudulent purchases to obtain a higher commission. Usually involves the usage of bots and scripts that can repeatedly click on ads. Affiliate fraud may generate high levels of *chargebacks*.

affiliate member On the *card rails*, an affiliate member of a *card scheme* is an *agent* of a *principal member*. An affiliate member can perform the following activities: issuing, acquiring, cash disbursement, and BIN licensing. The principal member sponsors the affiliate and is accountable to the card schemes for reporting, settlement, and ongoing fee payment (including for their sponsorees). An affiliate member of a card scheme cannot settle directly with the card scheme and uses the services of the principal for settlement and reporting. An affiliate member must comply with card scheme *operating regulations*.

Affirm[5] A *Buy-Now-Pay-Later* (BNPL) service provider.

AFL See *American Fuzzy Loop*.

agency banking See *indirectly connected participant*.

agent An entity that acts on behalf of, or is sponsored by, another entity (the *principal*) to conduct business activities. In payments terms, there can be settlement agents, agents of *Payment Institutions*, agents of *Electronic Money Institutions*, *affiliate members* of *card schemes*, and many more. The term "agent" is also used in a contact centre context, where its meaning is "contact centre assistant" or "telephone assistant".

aggregated payouts A payment processing method that consolidates multiple individual transactions into a single, larger *payout* to a recipient. This approach streamlines the payment process, reduces transaction fees, and simplifies accounting for businesses dealing with frequent, small-value payments to the same payee. Commonly used in *marketplaces*, *gig economy* platforms, and affiliate programmes, aggregated payouts allow companies to batch payments over a set period (e.g. weekly or monthly) before issuing a single, combined payment. This method can significantly reduce administrative overhead and costs associated with multiple small transactions, whilst providing recipients with more substantial, less frequent payouts.

aggregator A generic term used to describe any business that would aggregate functions, processes, or services to serve an *ecosystem*. Examples of aggregators in the payments world are *payfacs*, *API aggregators*, and *ISOs*.

AI See *artificial intelligence*.

airdrop Also called "crypto airdrop". A marketing process used by *blockchain*-based projects and developers to raise interest in their initiatives by sending out free *tokens* to their community members. This concept is similar to receiving a free discount to encourage you to buy something or visit a new shop. Sometimes, a crypto airdrop is issued to users in exchange for completing a certain task, which may involve following an account on social media, sharing or retweeting one of their posts, sending or receiving a transaction (using a particular crypto platform or *crypto wallet*), or creating an account and agreeing to receive updates.

Airtel Money[6] A *mobile money* service popular in East, Central, and West Africa. Owned by Airtel Africa, which is majority owned by the Indian telecommunications company Bharti Airtel.

AISP See *Account Information Service Provider*.

Algorand[7] A *blockchain* using the *Proof of Stake consensus protocol*.

algorithmic stablecoin A type of *cryptocurrency* designed to maintain a stable value relative to a target asset (usually the US dollar) through automated supply adjustments controlled by *smart contracts* and algorithms, rather than being backed by collateral. These stablecoins use mechanisms such as *minting* and *burning* tokens to regulate supply and demand in an attempt to maintain price stability. See also *collateralisation*.

Alipay[8] An *e-wallet*. One of the world's largest payment platforms, serving customers primarily in China and the broader Asia-Pacific region.

altcoin A term used to describe any *cryptocurrency* other than *Bitcoin*. Altcoins are often created to improve upon or offer alternatives to Bitcoin's features, and they can serve various purposes, such as enabling smart contracts, enhancing transaction speeds, or providing unique functionalities. Examples of altcoins include Ethereum (ETH) and Litecoin (LTC). See also *meme coin* and *privacy coin*.

altered card See *counterfeit card.*

Alternative Finance (AltFi) Alternative Finance is a catch-all term for almost any source of business funding other than traditional bank loans and overdrafts. Abbreviated as AltFi.

Alternative Payment Method (APM) Any payment solution that differs from traditional credit and debit card transactions. APMs include digital wallets, mobile payments, cryptocurrencies, bank transfers, *Buy-Now-Pay-Later* (BNPL) services, and other non-traditional payment options that provide consumers with flexibility and convenience in making purchases.

alternative payments A term coined by the cards industry that is generally used to describe payments that are not traditional card payments. See *Alternative Payment Method.*

alternative remittance See *barter system.*

AltFi See *Alternative Finance.*

Amazon One[9] A *payment method* developed by Amazon that allows customers to pay for their purchases using only a palm print. See also *biometrics* and *invisible payments.*

Amazon Pay[10] An *e-wallet* provided by Amazon. A *staged digital wallet.*

American Express[11] A *card scheme* that operates according to the *three-party model.*

American Fuzzy Loop (AFL) An *open-source* fuzzing tool that uses genetic algorithms to automatically discover bugs and vulnerabilities in software. It generates test cases by mutating existing inputs and monitors code behaviour to identify crashes or unexpected results.

AML See *Anti-Money Laundering.*

AML/CFT See *Anti-Money Laundering.*

AML/CTF See *Anti-Money Laundering.*

AMM See *Automated Market Maker.*

Anchor A *blockchain* development framework specifically designed for the *Solana* blockchain, providing a comprehensive suite of tools for creating secure and scalable *smart contracts.*

anonymity The state of being not identifiable within a set of subjects, allowing individuals to act or communicate without revealing their identity. In digital contexts, anonymity protects users' personal information and *privacy*, enabling them to engage in activities without fear of being tracked or recognised. This concept is crucial in various fields, including online communication, financial transactions, and *data protection*.

Android Pay A *mobile wallet* originally launched by Google and was subsequently replaced by *Google Pay* and *Google Wallet*.

Anti-Money Laundering (AML) The collection of laws, processes, and regulations that prevent illegally obtained money from entering the financial system. Increasingly, AML frameworks go beyond just *financial crime* to include Counter-Terrorism Financing (CTF) provisions, as well as tax-related offences. Also referred to as AML/CFT or AML/CTF.

API See *Application Programming Interface*.

API aggregator A *Third-Party PSP (TPP)* which enables businesses to operate across payment *ecosystem* participants and regions by taking the interfacing work unto themselves and offering their client one set of APIs to operate across standards (e.g. geographies and jurisdictions). They essentially aggregate multiple APIs into one API or a reduced set of APIs. Also see *Open Banking*.

APM See *Alternative Payment Method*.

APP scam See *Authorised Push Payment fraud*.

APP fraud See *Authorised Push Payment fraud*.

Apple Pay[12] A *mobile wallet* provided by Apple Inc. A *pass-through digital wallet*.

application fraud See *new account fraud*.

Application Programming Interface (API) A software interface allowing parties to communicate with each other through an agreed set of definitions and protocols. The document or standard that describes how to build or use such an interface is called an "API specification". See also *Open Banking*.

Application Specific Integrated Circuit (ASIC) A custom-designed integrated circuit chip optimised for a specific purpose or application, rather than for general-purpose use. In *blockchain* contexts, ASICs are often used for *cryptocurrency mining* due to their high efficiency in performing the repetitive calculations required for *Proof-of-Work consensus mechanisms*.

approval In the cards world, a positive reply from the *issuer* following a *transaction authorisation request*. An *authorisation decision*.

approval code See *authorisation decision*.

approval rate See *authorisation rate*.

arbitrage The practice of buying an asset in one market where the price is low and simultaneously selling it in another market where the price is higher, thereby profiting from the price difference without taking on significant risk. In the context of *crypto assets*, arbitrage involves purchasing a crypto asset on one exchange where its price is lower and selling it on another exchange where its price is higher. This process takes advantage of price discrepancies across different cryptocurrency exchanges, allowing traders to earn a profit from the differences in market prices. See also *flash loan* and *automated market maker*.

arbitrageur A market participant who exploits price discrepancies between identical or similar assets across different markets or exchanges to generate profit with minimal risk. These traders capitalise on temporary inefficiencies by simultaneously buying an asset at a lower price in one market and selling it at a higher price in another. Arbitrageurs play a crucial role in financial markets by helping to align prices, increase *liquidity*, and improve market efficiency. Their activities typically involve rapid execution and often use advanced technologies (e.g. algorithmic trading systems, smart order routing systems, and low-latency networks) to identify and act on fleeting opportunities. See also *automated market maker*.

arbitration A method of resolving disputes outside of traditional court systems, where an impartial third party (the arbitrator) reviews evidence, hears arguments, and makes a binding decision to settle the disagreement between two or more parties. This process is often faster, less formal, and more cost-effective than litigation. In the context of payment processes, arbitration refers to the resolution of disputes between parties involved in financial transactions, such as merchants, customers, or payment service providers. When conflicts arise over charges, refunds, or service quality, arbitration can be used to reach a fair settlement without resorting to legal action. Many payment platforms and financial institutions include arbitration clauses in their terms of service to manage disputes efficiently and maintain trust in their systems. For example, on the *card rails*, arbitration is a process that can be invoked by *card scheme* members to resolve a *chargeback*-related *dispute* between two members.

archival full node A type of blockchain *node* that stores the complete history of the *blockchain* from its *genesis block*, including all transactions and state changes. This node type provides full verifiability and allows querying of historical data but requires significant storage capacity. See *full node*.

ARN See *Acquirer Reference Number.*

AR payments See *augmented reality payments.*

artificial intelligence (AI) A branch of computer science concerned with building smart machines capable of performing tasks that typically require human intelligence. See also *machine learning*, *deep learning*, and *large language model.*

ASIC See *Application Specific Integrated Circuit.*

ASPSP See *Account Servicing PSP.*

assessment fee A fee that may be levied by a *card scheme* on their members. See *card scheme fee.*

asset-backed security token A digital representation of ownership in a *real-world asset*, such as real estate, art, or commodities, issued on a *blockchain*. These tokens allow for *fractional ownership*, increased *liquidity* of traditionally illiquid assets, and automated management through *smart contracts*. They are subject to securities regulations and typically traded on specialised platforms. See also *security token exchange.*

asset tokenisation See *tokenisation.*

asymmetric cryptography See *public key cryptography.*

asymmetric encryption See *public key cryptography.*

ASV See *Accredited Scanning Vendor.*

ASV scan See *network vulnerability scan.*

ATM See *Automated Teller Machine.*

ATM card See *cash card.*

ATM interchange fee See *interchange.*

ATO See *account takeover fraud.*

atomic settlement A type of *settlement* which aims to mitigate *settlement risk* of traditional settlement systems, where the trade and settlement processes are separate and may occur on different days. To address the risk, the *Delivery-versus-Payment (DvP)* (for financial markets) and *Payment-versus-Payment (PvP)* (for FX markets) settlement arrangements were developed, whereby one leg of a transaction only settles if the other leg also settles on an "all-or-nothing" basis. A type of settlement that may also be facilitated by *blockchain* infrastructures on the basis of *smart contracts*. Transactions usually happen on a single ledger, although cross-ledger transactions may be possible. See also *atomic swap.*

atomic swap An emerging type of simultaneous *settlement* that aims to facilitate the exchange of crypto assets within a *blockchain* or more commonly across separate blockchains (and, therefore, separate ledgers) without the need for an intermediary such as a *crypto exchange*. Most atomic swap-enabled *crypto wallets* and blockchains use *smart contracts*, where the parties agree the price between themselves. Atomic swaps are useful if you only have one *cryptocurrency* but need to use another in a transaction. See also *atomic settlement*.

ATV See *Average Transaction Value*.

augmented reality payments (AR payments) Financial transactions conducted within an AR environment, where digital information is overlaid onto the real world. This technology allows users to make purchases, transfer funds, or manage accounts by interacting with virtual elements superimposed on their physical surroundings, typically through a smartphone, tablet, or AR glasses. AR payments can enhance the shopping experience by providing real-time product information, virtual try-ons, or seamless checkout processes in both physical and online retail environments. This integration of AR with payment systems aims to create more intuitive, engaging, and convenient financial interactions for consumers.

authentication The method used to verify the origin of a message or to verify the identity of a participant on a given *payment scheme*. This is the method by which a *cardholder* or bank account holder is authenticated. *Authentication* factors may take many forms, such as a password, an account number, a PIN, a signature, and *biometrics*. See also *two-factor authentication*, *multi-factor authentication*, *delegated authentication*, *decoupled authentication*, *knowledge-based authentication*, *biometric authentication*, and *risk-based authentication*.

authorisation A process by which an *Account Servicing PSP (ASPSP)* is asked to verify that a payer is genuine and allowed to make a payment transaction (e.g. sufficient funds) after the payer has given their consent (*payment instruction*) for the transaction. The process is different for *card rails* and bank rails, but generally involves an authorisation request made to the *ASPSP*, which will return their *authorisation decision*. See also *authentication*.

authorisation amount The card transaction amount submitted to the *issuer* for approval during the *authorisation request*.

authorisation code A code that an *issuer* provides to indicate their *authorisation decision*. For approved transactions, the approval code is returned in the authorisation decision message and is usually recorded on the transaction receipt as proof of authorisation.

authorisation decision The second step of the payment account holder *authorisation* process. Sometimes referred to as authorisation response.

authorisation fee A type of *card scheme fee* levied for each transaction *authorisation*.

authorisation only A process by which a *merchant* accepts a card transaction and requests authorisation without also capturing the funds, resulting in a pending charge on the cardholder's account. Depending on the *Merchant Category Code* (MCC), *card scheme*, and *issuer*, these holds may expire after a period of time (usually 5–30 days).

authorisation request The first step of the payment account holder *authorisation* process.

authorisation rate The percentage of transactions that successfully pass through the *authorisation* process and result in an approved transaction. Also called "approval rate".

authorisation retry A sales optimisation strategy that may be used by merchants. Authorisation retries can be automated by the *merchant's PSP*, or they can be planned to increase the chances of successful authorisation. Some authorisation retry methods include updating the *Merchant Category Code*, using an automation service, or getting more accurate customer data.

authorised fraud A term used to describe a type of fraud where the payment transaction has been authorised by the *payer* who has typically been duped into sending funds to a *payee's* account that is controlled by a fraudster. See also *authorised push payment fraud*.

authorised push payment A *push payment* that has been authorised by the payment account holder.

Authorised Push Payment fraud (APP fraud) A type of *authorised fraud* that happens on the *bank rails* where a fraudster impersonates a known or trusted entity and tricks a payer into sending funds to a bank account controlled by a fraudster. This type of attack generally starts through *phishing* via an attack called *Business Email Compromise* (BEC). Also referred to as "APP scam". See also *social engineering*.

authority node A node in a *permissioned blockchain* network that has been granted special privileges to validate transactions and add new blocks to the chain. These nodes are typically operated by known and trusted entities within the network. See also *consensus node* and *validator node*.

Automated Banking Machine (ABM) See *Automated Teller Machine*.

Automated Clearing House (ACH) Used to describe legacy bank *payment schemes* with longer settlement cycles (i.e. a few days) when compared to more modern *real-time payment systems*, which settle in real-time or near real-time. The first ACH system in the world, BACS, was launched in the UK in 1968. The first ACH system in the US, FedACH, was launched in 1972 and was operated by the Federal Reserve Bank of San Francisco.

Automated Market Maker (AMM) A decentralised protocol that uses *smart contracts* and *liquidity pools* to facilitate *cryptocurrency* trading without relying on traditional order books. AMMs allow users to become liquidity providers by depositing assets into pools in exchange for rewards, with algorithms determining asset prices based on the ratio of tokens in the pool. AMMs use algorithmic pricing mechanisms to determine asset prices, which can sometimes deviate from prices on external markets. This deviation creates *arbitrage* opportunities, for traders can profit by buying assets at lower prices and selling them at higher prices across different platforms. Through this arbitrage activity, prices on AMMs tend to align with those on external markets, ensuring that AMM prices reflect broader market conditions. See also *arbitrageur*.

Automated Teller Machine (ATM) A self-service card terminal that allows cardholders to withdraw or deposit money, check their balances, transfer funds between accounts, pay bills, etc. Whilst all ATMs will allow cardholders to withdraw cash, not all ATMs will offer additional functionality. Sometimes referred to as an Automated Banking Machine (ABM), and historically, cash dispenser.

autonomous purchasing The process by which machines or *artificial intelligence* systems independently identify needs, evaluate options, make decisions, and execute transactions for goods or services without direct human intervention. This technology leverages advanced algorithms, *machine learning*, and data analytics to automate the entire purchasing cycle, from demand forecasting and supplier selection to order placement and payment processing. Autonomous purchasing systems can adapt to changing market conditions, optimise for cost and efficiency, and even negotiate terms within predefined parameters. This capability is increasingly important in various sectors, including manufacturing, retail, and supply chain management, where it can significantly reduce operational costs, minimise human error, and enable more responsive and efficient procurement processes. As part of the broader trend towards automation and AI-driven decision-making, autonomous purchasing represents a significant evolution in how businesses and machines interact with the commercial ecosystem. See also *machine-to-machine payments* and machine customer.

auto-representment The process by which information to defend a *chargeback* is sent automatically to the *card scheme* on behalf of a *merchant* without the merchant's intervention.

Avalanche[13] A blockchain using the *Proof of Stake consensus protocol.*

average block creation time The average duration it takes to mine or validate a block in a *blockchain* network, influenced by factors such as network *hashrate* and *difficulty target* in *Proof of Work* systems, or validator selection process in *Proof of Stake* systems. High values may indicate network congestion and scalability issues.

average block size The average amount of data, measured in bytes, stored in each block of a *blockchain.* It reflects the typical size of blocks over a given period and can indicate network congestion if values approach the *block size limit.*

Average Transaction Value (ATV) A measure of the average amount that customers spend on each purchase over a period of time (e.g. a month). The ATV is a valuable metric that can help merchants inform their product and pricing strategy. For example, if a merchant generates £20,000 over 100 transactions in a month, the ATV for that month will be £200. Sometimes referred to as "average ticket".

average validator uptime The percentage of time validators are online and actively participating in the consensus process over a specific period in a *Proof of Stake blockchain.* High uptime indicates a more secure, stable, and attack-resistant network.

AVS See *Address Verification Service.*

Notes

1 EMVCo, 3D Secure. https://www.emvco.com/emv-technologies/3-d-secure/ (Accessed 21 November 2023)

2 Unique Identification Authority of India. https://uidai.gov.in/en/ (Accessed 21 November 2023)

3 Unique Identification Authority of India. https://uidai.gov.in/en/ (Accessed 11 December 2023)

4 PCI SSC (ASVs). https://listings.pcisecuritystandards.org/assessors_and_solutions/approved_scanning_vendors (Accessed 14 December 2023)

5 Affirm. https://www.affirm.com/ (Accessed 21 November 2023)

6 Airtel Money Nigeria. https://www.airtel.com.ng/support/airtel_money (Accessed 21 November 2023)

7 Algorand. https://algorandtechnologies.com/ (Accessed 1 December 2023)

8 Alipay. https://global.alipay.com/platform/site/ihome (Accessed 21 November 2023)

9 Amazon One. https://one.amazon.com/ (Accessed 21 November 2023)

10 Amazon Pay. https://pay.amazon.com/ (Accessed 21 November 2023)

11 American Express. https://www.americanexpress.com (Accessed 21 November 2023)

12 Apple Pay. https://www.apple.com/uk/apple-pay/ (Accessed 21 November 2023)

13 Avalanche. https://www.avax.network/ (Accessed 1 December 2023)

B

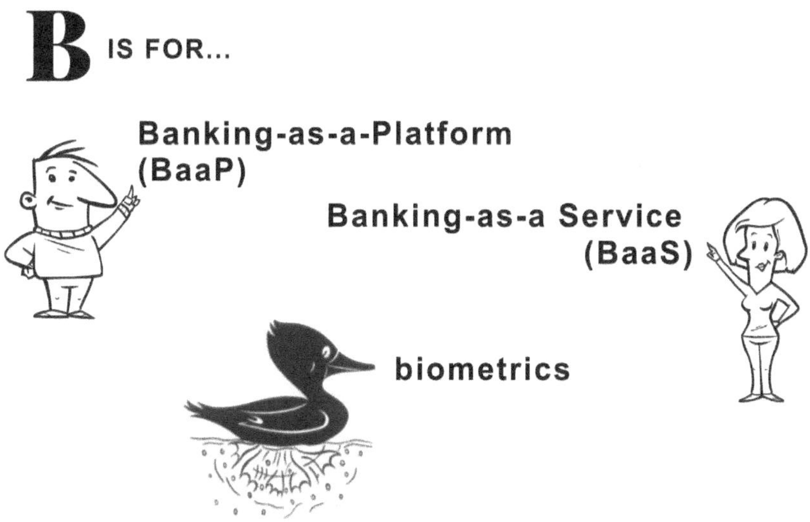

B2B See *Business-to-Business.*

B2C See *Business-to-Consumer.*

B2G See *Business-to-Government.*

BaaP See *Banking-as-a-Platform.*

BaaS See *Banking-as-a-Service, Blockchain-as-a-Service.*

BACS See *Bankers Automated Clearing Services.*

DOI: 10.4324/9781003571131-3

Baidu[1] a Chinese multinational technology company founded in 2000, specialising in Internet services and *artificial intelligence*. It is the leading search engine in China, often referred to as the "Chinese Google", and offers a wide range of services including online advertising, cloud computing, autonomous driving technology, and various digital products such as Baidu Maps and Baidu Baike (an online encyclopaedia). With a significant market share in China's search engine market, Baidu plays a crucial role in the country's digital landscape and has invested heavily in AI development.

Bancomat[2] An Italian *domestic card scheme*.

Bancontact[3] A Belgian *domestic card scheme*.

bank A financial services institution that is authorised to accept deposits from customers, as well as lend money to customers and offer other financial services. In a payment context, a bank can be an *Account Servicing PSP (ASPSP)* on the bank rails or an *issuer* on the *card rails*. Banks are defined as "credit institutions" in Europe and as "depository institutions" in the United States.

Bank Identification Number (BIN) The first six or first eight digits of a card number. The modern term is Issuer Identification Number (IIN), which was supposed to replace the original term of BIN to reflect the fact that issuers don't have to be banks (e.g. eMoney institutions). But the term BIN is so well established that the industry still sticks with it. The BIN identifies a number of elements, including the *card scheme* (e.g. Visa), the *issuer* (e.g. Santander), the type of card (e.g. credit, debit, and purchasing), and the country (e.g. UK). Both six- and eight-digit BINs exist. See also *Primary Account Number*.

bank rails A term used to describe the bank payment *ecosystem*, its operating procedures, and infrastructure.

bank rate See *Merchant Service Charge*.

bank run An event where the customers of a bank or other financial institutions withdraw their deposits at the same time over fears about the bank's solvency, potentially leading the bank to fail. Silicon Valley Bank[4] and Credit Suisse[5] are recent examples.

bank transfer A *payment method* by which the funding mechanism is a bank account.

Bankaxept[6] A Norwegian *domestic card scheme*.

BANKART[7] A Slovenian payment processor.

Bankers Automated Clearing Services (BACS) A domestic UK *ACH Scheme* used for regular bulk *credit transfers* and *direct debits*. BACS is managed by Pay.UK and was the first ACH Scheme in the world when it was launched in 1968.

BankID A *digital identity* framework in Sweden[8] and Norway.[9] Whilst the name is the same in both countries, they are separate frameworks.

Banking-as-a-Platform (BaaP) Where banks integrate within their infrastructure technology provided by *fintech* firms, allowing the banks to provide innovative services to their customers. This can kick-start digital transformation for banks.

Banking-as-a-Service (BaaS) Technology provided by regulated institutions (e.g. banks) to *non-bank Payment Service Providers* (*PSPs*) to enable the latter to provide financial services to their customers. Also see *embedded finance*.

Banknet The *Mastercard* network. See also *card scheme*.

Bank Secrecy Act (BSA)[10] A US law requiring financial institutions to help government agencies in detecting and preventing *money laundering*.

Barter Dollar The *closed-loop* medium of exchange used in the Bartercard[11] *barter system*.

barter system An alternative method of trading without using traditional monetary systems. The main difference between a barter system and a traditional monetary system (such as *bank rails* or *card rails*) is that barter systems involved exchanging value, goods, or services directly between parties through bartering. Many informal barter systems emerged during the COVID-19 pandemic and also as a result of the cost of living crisis. Barter systems may be legal or illegal depending on the jurisdiction. For example, in the US, the IRS considers bartering to be a form of income that incurs taxes. In addition, as technology constantly evolves, *blockchain*-based barter systems are emerging. Also referred to as Informal Value Transfer System (IVTS) or alternative remittance.

base fee The minimum transaction fee required for inclusion in a block on certain *blockchain* networks, particularly Ethereum after the London upgrade. This fee is algorithmically determined based on network congestion and is burned (removed from circulation) upon transaction completion, helping to manage network demand and reduce fee *volatility*.

basis point (bps) A unit of measurement used in finance to express percentage changes or differences. One basis point is equal to 0.01% or

1/100th of a percentage point. For example, a change from 5.00% to 5.25% is an increase of 25 basis points. Basis points are commonly used to describe changes in interest rates, *yields*, and other financial metrics where small variations can have significant impacts. This precise measurement allows for clear communication of small changes in financial values.

batch processing In a payment context, the transmission or processing of a group of related *payment instructions*.

BATX An acronym for Baidu,[12] Alibaba,[13] Tencent,[14] and Xiaomi,[15] the four biggest tech firms in China. These platforms are increasingly involved in payments and financial services. See also *Big Tech*, *GAFA*, *FANG*, *MAMAA*, and *FAANG*.

BCI technology Brain–Computer Interface technology. A direct communication system between the brain and an external device that allows for the translation of neural signals into commands without the use of normal neuromuscular pathways. BCIs capture brain activity through methods such as electroencephalography (EEG), electrocorticography (ECoG), or implanted electrodes and use signal processing algorithms to interpret the user's intentions. These interpreted signals are then used to control external devices or software applications, enabling individuals to interact with their environment through thought alone. BCIs have applications in assistive technology, rehabilitation, and human augmentation, ranging from non-invasive wearable devices to surgically implanted neural interfaces.

Beacon Chain The core component of *Ethereum's* transition to *Proof of Stake*, introduced in December 2020. It coordinated the network of *validators*, randomly assigning validators to verify transactions, and managed the *consensus protocol*. The Beacon Chain merged with Ethereum's original chain in September 2022, marking the network's full transition from *Proof of Work* to Proof of Stake.

bearer wallet A type of *Central Bank Digital Currency* (CBDC) wallet where funds are stored directly on a secure physical device (e.g. smartcard and smartphone) and ownership is determined by possession of the device. It can operate offline and typically synchronises with the ledger when reconnected. See also *hardware wallet*.

BEC See *Business Email Compromise*.

behavioural biometrics An *authentication* method that analyses unique patterns in a user's digital behaviour and interactions to verify their identity. It continuously monitors measurable characteristics such as keystroke dynamics, mouse movements, touchscreen interactions, and cognitive behaviours to distinguish between legitimate users and potential fraudsters. Unlike physical *biometrics*, behavioural biometrics operates passively in the background, providing ongoing authentication without requiring explicit user actions.

beneficial ownership A concept describing the relationship between a business signatory and any underlying beneficial owners, especially if they have significant control over the business. Beneficial owners are entitled to receive some or all the benefits in an asset or business. In payments, this term is used in the context of *Anti-Money Laundering* regulations. See also *shell company* and *legal ownership*.

Berlin Group[16] The German *Open Banking* standard.

BI-FAST[17] A *real-time payment system* (*RTP system*), *retail payment system* (RPS) in Indonesia, operated by Bank Indonesia.

BIC See *Business Identifier Code*.

Big Data analytics The process of examining large and complex datasets to uncover hidden patterns, correlations, trends, and other valuable insights. It involves collecting, processing, and analysing vast amounts of structured, semi-structured, and unstructured data from various sources using advanced analytical techniques, statistical algorithms, and *machine learning* tools. Big Data analytics enables organisations to make data-driven decisions, improve operational efficiency, enhance customer experiences, and gain competitive advantages by extracting actionable intelligence from diverse data sources that traditional data processing methods cannot handle effectively. This approach typically uses specialised technologies and frameworks designed to manage and analyse data at scale, such as distributed computing systems, data lakes, and real-time processing engines.

Big Tech A collective term used to describe large technology companies and platforms. These platforms are increasingly involved in payments and financial services. See also *GAFA*, *BATX*, *FANG*, *MAMAA*, and *FAANG*.

billing descriptor A short description of a transaction that appears on a *cardholder* statement. Usually contains the name of the business where the transaction was made. Sometimes called transaction descriptor.

BIN See *Bank Identification Number*.

BIN rental See *BIN sponsorship*.

BIN sponsorship The process by which BIN sponsors, which can be *acquirers* or *issuers*, enable other eligible organisations to issue cards by allowing them to use BIN ranges that they control (this is sometimes described as "BIN rental"). Working with a *principal* scheme member allows these eligible organisations to issue cards and adhere to the *card scheme* rules and regulatory requirements, giving them quick time to market. This is traditionally associated with the prepaid and *eMoney* markets. Also see *scheme membership*.

Binance[18] A centralised *crypto exchange*.

biometric authentication The use of *biometrics* for *authentication* purposes.

biometric payment card A credit or debit card that incorporates *biometric authentication* technology, typically a fingerprint sensor, directly on the card itself. This allows cardholders to verify their identity and authorise transactions by simply placing their finger on the sensor, eliminating the need for a *PIN* or signature. The cardholder's biometric data is securely stored and processed within the card, enhancing security by ensuring that only the authorised user can make payments. This technology aims to provide a more convenient, secure, and hygienic payment experience whilst reducing the risk of fraud associated with lost, stolen, or compromised cards

biometrics A term used to describe the biological measurements or physical characteristics of individuals. Common examples are fingerprint mapping, facial recognition, palm vein recognition, and retina scans. *Behavioural biometrics* is a subset of biometrics that analyses a user's digital physical and cognitive behaviour, such as phone movement, keyboard behaviour, touchscreen behaviour, mouse behaviour, phone pressure, gait, gesture, and voice pattern. In payments, biometrics may be used during the *authentication* of *Payment Service Users (PSU)*.

BiR[19] A *real-time payment system (RTP system)*, *retail payment system* (RPS) in Sweden (also referred to as "Payments in Real-Time"), operated by Bankgirot.[20]

BIS[21] Bank for International Settlements. A bank whose mission is to support *central banks*' pursuit of monetary and financial stability through international cooperation and to act as a bank for central banks.

Bitcoin (BTC)[22] A *cryptocurrency*, also a *coin*. Bitcoin also refers to the *layer 1 blockchain* infrastructure on which BTC operates (i.e. the Bitcoin blockchain). A *permissionless blockchain*. See also *Satoshi*.

Bitfinex[23] A centralised *crypto exchange*.

black list[24] A list of high-risk countries defined by the *Financial Action Task Force* as those with serious strategic deficiencies to counter *money laundering*, *terrorist financing*, and financing of proliferation. See also *grey list*.

Black Market PESO Exchange (BMPE) A *barter system* in Colombia and Mexico associated with drug trafficking and *money laundering*.

blended pricing A pricing model by which a *merchant* only sees one rate on their *Merchant Service Charge* (MSC), and this rate has no contractual link to *interchange*. This is the least transparent pricing model and will be typically used for small- to medium-sized merchants. *Independent Sales Organisations* (ISOs) and *Payment Service Providers* (PSPs) may favour this model, although *acquirers* will generally try to use it for smaller merchants if applicable regulations don't prevent them from doing so.

Blik[25] An *account-to-account payment* service in Poland.

block A data structure in a *blockchain* that contains a list of transactions and associated metadata, such as a timestamp, a reference to the previous block (*hash*), and a *nonce*. Blocks are linked together in chronological order to form the blockchain, ensuring the integrity and immutability of the transaction history.

block 0 See *genesis block*.

blockchain A type of *Distributed Ledger Technology* (DLT) that uses *public key cryptography* to create and share transactions (the data blocks) across participants for validation. Time-stamped "blocks" of data are strung together (chain), and these blocks are intermittently validated (*consensus protocol*) by users of the network (i.e. *miners* or *validators*). These blocks of data are characterised as being *on-chain*. Blockchains can't access real-world data (*off-chain*) directly and need special services or data feeds for access to real-world information, such as *oracles*.

Blockchain-as-a-Service (BaaS) Cloud-based services offering a complete package for *blockchain* development, offering a pre-built blockchain infrastructure consisting of a managed network of *nodes*, the implementation of a specific *consensus protocol*, development tools (e.g. programming languages, *APIs*, and *SDKs*), and various security features (e.g. *encryption*, access management, and intrusion detection). Some BaaS providers may choose to support established *blockchain development frameworks*.

blockchain development framework A development environment specific to *permissionless blockchain* infrastructures. They offer a) pre-built functionality in the form of pre-built modules and tools for common blockchain development tasks such as *consensus protocol* interaction, *smart contract* development, and identity management; b) an abstraction layer to hide the complexities of the underlying blockchain protocol, allowing developers to focus on application logic; and c) security features as they will often prioritise security due to the nature of blockchain applications.

blockchain explorer A web-based tool that allows users to view and analyse transactions, blocks, addresses, and other data on a *blockchain* network in real-time. It provides a user-friendly interface to search and track the movement of cryptocurrencies, examine smart contracts, and verify transaction details, enhancing transparency and accessibility of blockchain data.

blockchain fork See *fork*.

blockchain oracle See *oracle*.

blockchain protocol The entire set of rules and specifications that govern the operation of a *blockchain*. It includes data structures, *cryptography algorithms*, and *consensus protocol*; how nodes communicate; and generally how the whole network operates.

blockchain settlement A *blockchain* mechanism by which transactions are settled (i.e. become final). This mechanism is decentralised and relies on a *consensus protocol* as a trust framework. Once a transaction has been confirmed and added to a block in a blockchain network, the transaction is considered "recorded". However, the transaction will generally be considered "final" (i.e. immutable) only after the *confirmation time* has passed. See also *block finality, immutability, and settlement*.

blockchain trilemma A concept coined by Ethereum's co-founder, Vitalik Buterin, describing the challenge faced by *blockchain* developers stating that optimal levels of decentralisation, security, and scalability are hard to achieve, as one of the three elements must be sacrificed in favour of the other two. Modern blockchains try to address this issue by using *scaling solutions*.

blockchain utility The practical usefulness and real-world applicability of a *blockchain* network or application beyond its underlying *cryptocurrency*. It refers to the ability of a blockchain to solve specific problems or improve existing processes in areas including supply chain management, digital identity, voting systems, or *decentralised finance (DeFi)*.

block finality The point at which a block of transactions in a *blockchain* is considered permanently added to the chain and cannot be reversed or altered. Once a block reaches finality, all transactions within it are confirmed and irreversible. The time to reach finality varies between blockchain protocols and consensus mechanisms. See also *blockchain settlement*.

block formation The process of creating a new *block* in a *blockchain* by collecting and validating a set of transactions, computing the block *hash*, and adding relevant metadata. This process is typically performed by *miners* or *validators* and includes steps such as transaction selection, ordering, and applying the *consensus protocol* rules.

block header In a *blockchain* context, a data construct used to ensure the integrity of a *block*. As such, the block header will typically include a version number (referring to the validation rules used), the *hash* of the previous block, a *Merkle root* (for all transactions, including the *coinbase transaction*), a timestamp, the digital signature of the block creator, and additional fields specific to the protocol.

block interval The time it takes for a new block is added to a *blockchain*. For example, the Bitcoin blockchain has a block interval of about 10 minutes, and the Ethereum blockchain claims 12–20 seconds (at the time of writing). See also *blockchain settlement* and *settlement cycle*.

block reward A term commonly used to describe the economic incentives that validating nodes receive for their participation in maintaining the *blockchain* network's security and integrity. In some blockchains, it is a combination of newly minted coins and transaction fees, such as in the Bitcoin blockchain. In other blockchains, such as Ethereum, the block reward consists only of the newly minted coins, and transaction fees are a distinct component treated as additional incentives.

block size The actual amount of data contained in a single *block* on a *blockchain*. This includes all the transactions and associated metadata within that block.

block size limit The maximum amount of data that can be included in a single *block* on a *blockchain*. It determines the upper limit for the number of transactions that can be processed per block and affects the network's throughput and scalability.

block validation The process of verifying that a new *block* and all transactions within it conform to the network's consensus rules before adding it to the *blockchain*. This includes checking the block's format, timestamps, size, and that all transactions are valid and properly signed. Block validation is typically performed by *full nodes* in the blockchain network.

BMPE See *Black Market Peso Exchange*.

BNPL See *Buy-Now-Pay-Later*.

Boleto Bancário[26] A *post pay* service provided by PagBrasil popular in Brazil, regulated by the Bank of Brazil.

BOPIS See *Buy Online Pick Up in Store*.

BOPUS See *Buy Online Pick Up in Store*.

bot Short for "robot". A software application designed to automate tasks and interact with users or systems over the internet. Bots can perform a variety of functions, including answering queries, processing transactions, and executing repetitive tasks, often using *artificial intelligence* and *machine learning* to enhance their capabilities. Common types of bots include *chatbots* for customer service, web crawlers for indexing web content, and trading bots for executing financial trades. By automating processes, bots improve efficiency and can operate 24/7, making them valuable tools in various industries, including finance, *e-commerce*, and customer support.

botnet A network of compromised computers or devices, known as "bots" or "zombies", that are controlled remotely by a malicious actor, often without the knowledge of the device owners. Botnets are typically created by infecting devices with malware, allowing the attacker to issue commands to the entire network. They are commonly used to conduct various cybercriminal activities, including *DDoS attacks*, spam distribution, data theft, and the propagation of additional malware. The scale and coordination of botnets can significantly amplify the impact of cyber threats.

BouncyCastle A *Java*-based *cryptography* library providing a similar *API* to *OpenSSL*, making it easier to port code between languages.

bps See *basis point*.

Brain–computer interface payment (BCI payment) An emerging technology that enables users to initiate and authorise financial transactions directly through neural signals, without the need for traditional physical interfaces. This system uses *BCI technology* to interpret brain activity related to payment intentions, translating these signals into commands that can execute transactions. BCI payments could potentially allow users to make purchases, transfer funds, or manage financial accounts using thought processes alone, offering a hands-free and potentially more secure alternative to conventional payment methods. Whilst still largely experimental, this technology aims to provide enhanced accessibility for individuals with physical disabilities and could revolutionise the way we interact with financial systems in the future.

breakage A term used to describe revenue gained by retailers through unredeemed or unspent funds on *gift cards* or other prepaid *payment instruments*. In such cases, the retailer keeps the money paid without providing the service or item for which the customer initially paid.

Bretton Woods agreement Agreement struck in July 1944 across 44 countries under which a new international monetary system was established aiming to promote economic growth after World War II, stabilise exchange rates, and prevent competitive currency devaluations. At that point, the US dollar was pegged to gold at $35 per ounce, and other currencies were pegged to the US dollar, essentially creating an indirect gold standard system (dubbed the Bretton Woods system) and leading to the creation of the International Monetary Fund and the World Bank. Whilst agreed upon in 1944, the Bretton Woods system didn't become fully operational until 1958 and came under pressure in the 1960s due to increased circulation of the US dollar and economic growth in other countries. In 1971, President Richard Nixon announced the suspension of the US dollar convertibility into gold, effectively ending the Bretton Woods system, in a move commonly dubbed as the "Nixon Shock". Since then, the US dollar has been a *fiat currency*.

brick and mortar A term used to describe a *merchant* that accepts payments at a physical location.

BRICS An intergovernmental organisation comprising Brazil, Russia, India, China, South Africa, Egypt, Ethiopia, Iran, Saudi Arabia, and the United Arab Emirates. In 2006, Brazil, Russia, India, and China created the "BRIC" group, and South Africa was added in 2010, making it "BRICS". Ethiopia, Iran, Saudi Arabia, and the United Arab Emirates joined in January 2024. These countries aim to act as a counterbalance to Western influence and aim to reduce their dependence on the US dollar, a process known as *de-dollarisation*.

bridge A mechanism in *blockchain* technology that facilitates the transfer of assets, data, or functionality between different blockchain networks or between a blockchain and traditional systems. Bridges can operate within the same blockchain ecosystem (e.g. connecting a main chain to its *layer 2 scaling solutions*) or between entirely separate blockchains. They typically work by locking assets on the source chain and *minting* equivalent representations on the destination chain, often using *smart contracts* to ensure secure and verifiable transfers. Bridges are crucial for enhancing interoperability in the blockchain space, enabling users to leverage the strengths of multiple networks. See also *cross-chain bridge*.

BSA See *Bank Secrecy Act*.

burning In *blockchain*, burning refers to the permanent removal of *cryptocurrency* tokens or crypto assets from circulation by sending them to an unspendable address. This process effectively destroys the tokens, reducing the total supply. Burning is often used as a deflationary mechanism, to increase scarcity, maintain price stability, or as part of governance processes in *decentralised finance (DeFi)* protocols. See also *minting*, *seigniorage*, and *tokenomics*. This term specifically applies to blockchain assets, but in traditional financial markets, stock buybacks, debt retirement, and currency *demonetisation* are analogous, although not similar in terms of reversibility, frequency, and transparency.

business card See *commercial card*.

Business Email Compromise (BEC) A type of *phishing* attack where a fraudster compromises the email environment of a business so they can impersonate that business and trick victims into, for example, sending funds to accounts they own. See also *authorised push payment fraud*, *cybercrime*, and *social engineering*.

Business-to-Business (B2B) A term used to describe a business model where one business makes a commercial transaction with another business.

Business-to-Consumer (B2C) A term used to describe the business model of selling products directly to customers without needed an intermediary (e.g. wholesalers, distributors, and intermediaries).

Business-to-Government (B2G) A term used to describe the trade between the business sector as a supplier and a government body as a customer.

Business Identifier Code (BIC) The ISO 9362 international standard for the identification of financial services institutions. SWIFT is the designated registration authority to issue BICs.

Buy-Now-Pay-Later (BNPL) A *payment method* where consumers can pay for goods by instalments after delivery, interest-free. It is a form of *credit* that is rapidly gaining popularity and increasingly attracting regulatory scrutiny. BNPL is a value-added service that can be offered to *merchants* for integration into their payment facilities. Sometimes called "e-invoices". A form of *deferred payment*. See also *split payment*, *alternative payment method*.

Buy Online Pick Up in Store (BOPUS, BOPIS) A sales method that allows customers to make a purchase online and pick it up later at a nearby location rather than having it shipped to them.

bytecode An intermediate, platform-independent code generated by compiling the source code, which is then interpreted or further compiled by a *Virtual Machine* for execution on various hardware platforms. In the context of *blockchains*, bytecode is a machine-readable instruction set designed for efficient execution by a *virtual machine (VM)*. It acts as an intermediate representation derived from the original high-level smart contract code (e.g. Solidity for Ethereum). Unlike the traditional compiled code specific to a particular hardware architecture, bytecode offers portability across different systems. The VM interprets the bytecode instructions and executes them within a secure sandbox environment, promoting security and isolation on the blockchain network. This standardised approach enables developers to write *smart contracts* in various languages and deploy them on compatible blockchain platforms.

Byzantine General's Problem A conceptual problem in distributed systems where components may fail and there is insufficient information on whether a component has failed, rendering decision-making difficult. The allegory stems from an example where a group of generals, each commanding a portion of an army, must coordinate an attack or retreat on a city. However, some generals may be traitors and might provide false or conflicting information to other generals, making coordination of the attack or retreat difficult. The challenge is for the loyal generals to reach a consensus despite the presence of traitors and potentially unreliable communication mechanisms in order to ensure that they either all attack or all retreat to avoid defeat. In the context of blockchains, the problem describes the challenge of achieving consensus among nodes in the presence of faulty or malicious actors. This is particularly relevant to *permissioned blockchains*, where participants are known and trusted entities and may abuse their influence through *Byzantine faults*. The consensus mechanism must therefore be resilient to malicious or compromised nodes who may send conflicting information, become unresponsive, or deliberately attempt to disrupt the network's operation. There are various mitigating features that a *blockchain protocol* may implement to resist Byzantine faults, such as thresholds on the number of nodes required to validate, node reputation systems, redundant communication channels, message replication, audits, network monitoring and intrusion detection, and *cryptography*. See also *distribution* and *decentralisation*.

Byzantine faults A type of malicious network attack. Byzantine faults include *Sybil attacks*, *DDoS attacks*, *eclipse attacks*, packet tampering, time synchronisation attacks, *double-spending*, and collusion.

Byzantine Fault Tolerance (BFT) A *blockchain consensus protocol* popular in *permissioned blockchains*. Unlike *Proof of Work (PoW)* or *Proof of Stake (PoS)* blockchains who have a specific mechanism for achieving consensus (i.e. *mining* and *staking*), consensus protocols based on BFT rely on voting, quorum systems, and messaging within a (smaller) network of known entities and are designed to ensure that the blockchain can still achieve consensus and maintain its integrity and security even in the presence of *Byzantine faults*.

Notes

1 Baidu. https://www.baidu.com/ (Accessed 29 September 2024)
2 Bancomat. https://bancomat.it/ (Accessed 21 November 2023)
3 Bancontact. https://www.bancontact.com/ (Accessed 21 November 2023)
4 'The First Twitter-Fuelled Bank Run': How Social Media Compounded SVB's Collapse. *The Guardian*, 16 March 2023. https://www.theguardian.com/business/2023/mar/16/the-first-twitter-fuelled-bank-run-how-socialmedia-compounded-svbs-collapse (Accessed 11 December 2023)
5 £55bn Withdrawn from Credit Suisse Before Rescue. *BBC News*, 24 April 2023. https://www.bbc.co.uk/news/business-65370751 (Accessed 11 December 2023)

6 Bankaxept. https://bankaxept.no/ (Accessed 21 November 2023)
7 Bankart. https://www.bankart.si/ (Accessed 21 November 2023)
8 BankID Sweden. https://www.bankid.com/en/privat/skaffabankid (Accessed 21 November 2023)
9 BankID Norway. https://bankid.no/ (Accessed 21 November 2023)
10 Office of the Comptroller of the Currency (Bank Secrecy Acts). https://www.occ.treas.gov/topics/supervision-and-examination/bsa/index-bsa.html (Accessed 21 November 2023)
11 Bartercard. https://bartercard.com/ (Accessed 30 November 2023)
12 Baidu. https://ir.baidu.com/ (Accessed 11 December 2023)
13 Alibaba. https://www.alibaba.com/ (Accessed 11 December 2023)
14 Tencent. https://www.tencent.com/en-us/ (Accessed 11 December 2023)
15 Xiaomi. https://www.mi.com/ (Accessed 11 December 2023)
16 Berlin Group. https://www.berlin-group.org/ (Accessed 21 November 2023)
17 Bank Indonesia. https://www.bi.go.id/en/fungsi-utama/sistem-pembayaran/ritel/infrastruktur/default.aspx (Accessed 21 November 2023)
18 Binance. https://www.binance.com (Accessed 21 November 2023)
19 Bankgirot. https://www.bankgirot.se/en/services/clearing-andsettlement/clearing-and-settlement/ (Accessed 21 November 2023)
20 Bangirot. https://www.bankgirot.se/en/ (Accessed 18 January 2024)
21 Bank for International Settlements. https://www.bis.org/ (Accessed 21 November 2023)
22 Bitcoin. https://bitcoin.org/en/ (Accessed 21 November 2023)
23 Bitfinex. https://www.bitfinex.com/ (Accessed 21 November 2023)
24 FATF Black and Grey Lists. https://www.fatf-gafi.org/en/countries/black-and-grey-lists.html (Accessed 15 December 2023)
25 Blik. https://www.blik.com (Accessed 21 November 2023)
26 PagBrasil Boleto Bancário. https://www.pagbrasil.com/paymentmethods/boleto-bancario/ (Accessed 21 November 2023)

C

C IS FOR...

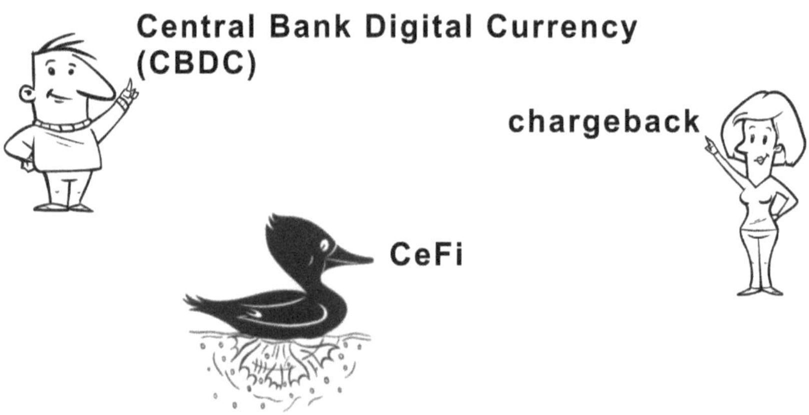

C A general-purpose, procedural programming language developed by Dennis Ritchie at Bell Labs in 1972. It is known for its efficiency, portability, and low-level control over computer hardware. C provides a structured approach to programming with features like functions, arrays, and pointers. It is widely used for system programming,

DOI: 10.4324/9781003571131-4

embedded systems, and developing operating systems. C's syntax has influenced many subsequent programming languages, and it remains a fundamental language in computer science education and software development. Its ability to directly manipulate memory and produce an efficient machine code makes it suitable for applications requiring high performance and close hardware interaction.

C++ A high-level, general-purpose programming language developed by Bjarne Stroustrup in 1979 as an extension of C. It is an object-oriented language that supports features such as classes, inheritance, and polymorphism, whilst also maintaining the efficiency and low-level control of C. C++ is widely used for developing system software, application software, device drivers, embedded software, and video games due to its performance, efficiency, and flexibility. The language is standardised by the *International Organization for Standardization (ISO).*

C# Pronounced "C-sharp". A modern, object-oriented programming language developed by Microsoft as part of its NET framework. First released in 2002, C# combines the power and efficiency of C++ with the simplicity of Visual Basic, featuring a syntax similar to that of C-family languages. It supports multiple programming paradigms, including imperative, declarative, functional, and generic programming. C# is designed for building a wide range of applications, from Windows desktop applications and web services to mobile apps and games, particularly within the Microsoft ecosystem. It offers features such as strong typing, lexical scoping, garbage collection, and native support for component-oriented programming.

CA See *Certificate Authority.*

Call Center Apart from being the US spelling of "call centre", in the cards world, this term refers to an *authorisation decision* from the *issuer* (or through *Stand In-Processing*) where the *merchant* must "call" for *voice authorisation.* If an approval is given, the merchant must manually enter the *approval code* for the transaction to proceed.

cancellation code A code issued by a *merchant* to confirm a *cardholder's* cancellation of a hotel booking or car rental reservation. This code can be used later in case the cardholder is charged in error for the cancelled transaction.

CApp Centralised Application. A broad term encompassing any application that interacts with a *blockchain* in some way and is controlled by a single entity. A CApp primarily operates on blockchain technology – leveraging one or more blockchains – but will have some elements built on traditional databases. A CApp may lack features like trustless transactions or native governance mechanisms, and the level of centralised control can vary depending on the implementation. An example could be a loyalty programme managed by a company that uses blockchain to store points but has centralised control over how they are issued and redeemed.

capture A term sometimes used to describe the submission of a card transaction for subsequent *clearing* and *settlement* process on the *card rails*.

capture only A request to capture funds for a card transaction where the transaction was previously authorised by the *issuer* outside of the payment gateway. Merchants will typically submit these requests through the phone using a previously assigned *authorisation code*.

card A *payment instrument* used on the *card rails*. Cards can be physical or virtual.

Card Absent An attempt from Visa to rename *Card Not Present* (CNP). This has not caught on.

card acceptance The process by which merchants take payments by card. Also referred to as payment acceptance.

card acceptor ID In the cards world, a numeric string that identifies a store location or transaction point.

Cardano (ADA)[1] A *layer 1 blockchain* using the *Proof-of-Stake* (PoS) consensus protocol. ADA is the native cryptocurrency for the Cardano blockchain.

card association See *card scheme*.

Card Authorisation Value (CAV) What JCB calls the *Card Verification Value* (*CVV*).

Card-Based Payment Instrument Issuer (CBPII) A *Third-Party PSP* (*TPP*) that issues card-based payment instruments (physical or virtual) that can be used to initiate a payment transaction from a payment account (e.g. a bank account) held with *an Account Servicing Payment Service Provider* (*ASPSP*) other than the issuer. Essentially, a CBPII is a combination of an *Account Information Service Provider* (*AISP*), *Payment Initiation Service Provider* (*PISP*), *issuer*, and *money remittance*. This is a form of *decoupled debit*. CBPIIs come in two forms: closed loop (don't involve a *card scheme*) and open loop (involve a card scheme). See also *closed loop* and *closed loop card*.

card brand A *card scheme*.

card code See *Card Verification Value (CVV)*.

card code status A value returned to the merchant following an *Address Verification Service (AVS)* check for a card transaction.

card factoring See *card laundering*.

Card Identification Number (CID) What American Express calls the *Card Verification Value (CVV)*.

card imprinting machine A manual card reader that takes the paper imprint of a physical card. The card must have *embossed elements* to be processed with a card imprinting machine, which has metal plates for taking the imprint. Also known as a "zip zap machine", "card imprinter", "imprinter", or "knuckle buster" (for obvious reasons).

card issuing See *issuing*.

card laundering When a *merchant* engages in the processing of card transactions on behalf of another merchant not directly affiliated with them. This is a breach of the *merchant agreement* and can lead to *money laundering*. Also referred to as "card factoring".

card network A term generally used to describe a *card scheme*, but it sometimes may only refer to the infrastructure provided by a card scheme, such as VisaNet for Visa or Banknet for Mastercard. See *card scheme*.

Card Not Present (CNP) The terminology used to describe remote card payment transactions. This falls into two categories: *e-commerce* and MOTO (*Mail Order Telephone Order*). Sometimes referred to as Customer Not Present (CNP).

card number See *Primary Account Number*.

Card on File (CoF) A type of transaction where a cardholder authorises a merchant to store their card information securely and bill the cardholder's account for future purchases without the cardholder's intervention. A form of a *Merchant Initiated Transaction* (MIT).

Card on File transaction See *recurring transaction*.

card optimisation See *payment optimisation*.

card payment channel A card payment channel describes the cardholder mode of interaction with the merchant. It can be *Card Present* (face-to-face) or *Card Not Present* (e-commerce, telephone, mail order, etc.).

card payments value chain The card payments *value chain* is the set of activities performed by its stakeholders to deliver valuable products and services to the card payment market. See also *acquirer*, *issuer*, *merchant*, *PSP*, *four-party model*, and *three-party model*.

Card Present (CP) The terminology used to describe physical face-to-face card payment transactions. Also referred to as Customer Present.

card rails A term used to describe the card payment *ecosystem*, its *operating regulations*, and its infrastructure.

card scheme A *payment scheme* (or payment system) that provides an *ecosystem* for card payments. See *card network*.

card scheme fee Any fee that that is paid to a *card scheme* for their contribution to the *value chain* (e.g. authorisation fee, chargeback fee, and retrieval fee).

card scheme rails See *card rails*.

card security code See *Card Verification Value*.

card skimmer See *skimmer*.

card skimming A way to collect data fraudulently from the *magnetic stripe* of a *card*. A counterfeit reader is placed in an *Automated Teller Machine (ATM)* or *Point-of-Sale* (POS) terminal, where it reads the information off the card at the same time as the genuine terminal. See *skimmer*.

card swipe A term used to describe a card transaction using the *magnetic stripe* (aka magstripe).

card terminal manufacturer A type of *payee's PSP* (aka merchant's PSP) on the *card rails*. They supply card payment terminals to *merchants* (directly or indirectly) to enable them to accept physical card payments.

card testing fraud A type of fraud that happens when a fraudster in possession of multiple stolen cards attempts small value card transactions to determine which cards are still valid.

Card Verification Code (CVC) What Mastercard calls the *Card Verification Value (CVV)*.

Card Verification Value (CVV) Whilst Card Verification Value (CVV) is a generic term to describe all card verification values, in common language, it refers to the *CVV2*. The CVV2 is a three-digit code found on the signature panel for most cards (e.g. Visa and Mastercard), but for American Express, it has four digits and is printed on the front of the card. The CVV2 is used to authenticate remote transactions (e.g. e-commerce or telephone) to verify that the cardholder has the card in their possession. Sometimes called "card code". See also *CVV1*, *iCVV*, and *Dynamic CVV (dCVV)*.

cardholder A consumer or business that has a card account. A type of *payer* or *Payment Service User (PSU)*.

cardholder account number The part of the *Primary Account Number (PAN)* that identifies the *cardholder* and is the next nine digits after the *BIN* for six-digit BINs or the next seven digits after the *BIN* for eight-digit BINs.

cardholder data In PCI DSS terms, cardholder data consist of the Primary Account Number (PAN), cardholder name, expiry date, and service code.

Cardholder Data Environment (CDE) Consists of the people, processes, and technologies that store, process, or transmit *cardholder data* or *sensitive cardholder data*. The *PCI DSS* security requirements apply to all system components that are included in or connected to the CDE.

Cardholder Preferred Currency (CPC) See *Dynamic Currency Conversion (DCC)*.

cardholder settlement Cardholder settlement is part of the commercial arrangement between the *cardholder* and the *issuer*. With debit cards, this is usually a "banking" arrangement. With credit cards, it is a "lending" arrangement.

Cardholder Verification Method (CVM) The verification method used to confirm that a *payment instrument* used for a payment transaction is in the possession of the cardholder.

Cardholder Verification Method limit (CVM limit) Usually refers to the *contactless payment* limit. This can be either for a single transaction (e.g. £100 in the UK) or for consecutive transactions (e.g. £300 in the UK). If this threshold is reached, the cardholder has to be authenticated to reset the counter (e.g. use a PIN).

cart abandonment Refers to the situation when an online shopper places one or more items in their shopping cart and subsequently leaves the website without completing the checkout process.

Cartes Bancaires[2] A French *domestic card scheme*. See also *payment scheme*.

cash Banknotes and coins. Cash is a direct claim on a *central bank*.

cash advance See *merchant financing*.

Cash App[3] A *peer-to-peer payment app* provided by Block Inc.

cash card A card used only in *ATMs* to withdraw cash and therefore has limited usage (although, in some geographies, they can be used at approved retailers (i.e. those that are able to accept cards for a specific ATM network). Other multifunction cards (i.e. those issued on *card schemes* such as Visa or Mastercard) also enable cardholders to withdraw cash. Also called ATM card.

cashback A payment facility which can be either:

A payment incentive offered by *issuers* to cardholders by which a percentage of purchases is offered back in various forms to credit card holders.

Or

A facility by which a physical merchant can give a *cardholder* cash back as part of a card transaction, within agreed limits. The amount of the cash given back to the cardholder is added to the transaction amount. This is useful to maintain access to cash where *ATMs* are not available.

cashflow The movement of money into and out of a business or individual's accounts over a specific period. It encompasses all cash transactions, including income from sales, investments, and financing activities, as well as expenses such as operating costs, loan repayments, and capital expenditures. Positive cashflow indicates that more money is coming in than going out, which is essential for maintaining *liquidity* and supporting ongoing operations. Conversely, negative cashflow can signal financial difficulties and may require corrective actions to ensure stability. Cashflow is a critical metric for assessing financial health and performance in both personal finance and business management. Also spelled "cash flow".

cashflow underwriting A method of assessing creditworthiness that focuses on an applicant's income and spending patterns rather than traditional *credit scores*. It involves analysing bank transaction data, including revenue trends, operating cashflow, and gross profit, to evaluate a borrower's ability to repay a loan. This approach allows lenders to consider applicants with limited credit history or unconventional financial profiles, potentially expanding access to credit for small businesses and individuals. Whilst not entirely new, cashflow underwriting has gained prominence in recent years due to advancements in financial technology and data analytics, enabling more efficient and accurate assessments of financial health and repayment capacity. See also *Open Banking*.

cashless society An economic state where financial transactions are conducted exclusively through digital means, eliminating the need for physical *currency*. In this model, payments are made using electronic methods such as credit and debit cards, mobile wallets, digital currencies, and other forms of *electronic fund transfers*. The concept encompasses a shift towards digital financial infrastructure, widespread adoption of digital payment technologies, and changes in consumer behaviour and business practices. Proponents argue that a cashless society can increase transaction efficiency, reduce costs associated with cash handling, and potentially decrease certain types of *financial crime*. However, it also raises concerns about *privacy*, *financial inclusion*, and the digital divide. The term is often used to describe both the ongoing trend towards reduced cash usage and a potential future state of complete cash elimination.

Cash-on-Delivery (CoD) A transaction in which a payment for goods is made at the time of delivery. Specific to countries and suppliers. Very popular in some regions, such as Central Europe. A form of *delayed payment*. Sometimes referred to as "Collect-on-Delivery" (CoD) since delivery may allow for cash, cheque, or electronic payments to be used.

CAV See *Card Authorisation Value*.

CBDC See *Central Bank Digital Currency*.

CBPII See *Card-Based Payment Instrument Issuer*.

CD/ATM[4] A *real-time payment system* (RTP system), *retail payment system* (RPS) in South Korea, operated by KFTC.

CDD See *Customer Due Diligence*.

CDE See *Cardholder Data Environment*.

CEC[5] Belgium's domestic *ACH scheme*.

CEC-IP A *real-time payment system* (RTP system), *retail payment system* (RPS) in Belgium, operated by CEC.

CeDeFi A contraction of *CeFi* and *DeFi*. A combination of centralised and decentralised finance in the crypto world. See also *TradFi*.

CeFi An abbreviation of "Centralised Finance". Used to describe centralised crypto businesses, such as centralised *crypto exchanges* or custodian *crypto wallets*. The CeFi platform serves as the custodian of the digital assets, and as such the service user relinquishes control of their *cryptocurrency* to the CeFi platform. The CeFi platform provides services and secures the assets for a fee. If the platform is compromised, the assets could be at risk. Ironically, one of the fundamental characteristics of *Distributed Ledger Technology (DLT)* is decentralisation, and CeFi introduces some degree of centralisation. Examples of CeFi platforms are *Binance* and *Coinbase*. Also see *custody*, *DeFi*, *CeDeFi*, and *TradFi*.

CEFTS[6] An *account-to-account payment* service in Sri Lanka, operated by LankaPay.

central bank An institution which has been given, through a legal act, the responsibility to conduct the *monetary policy* for a specific area. Examples are the Bank of England, the Monetary Authority of Singapore, the Federal Reserve banks in the US, etc.

Central Bank Digital Currency (CBDC) A type of *virtual asset*. It is different from a *cryptocurrency* or *virtual currency*, as it is issued by a *central bank* and has *legal tender* status. CBDC implementations may use *Distributed Ledger Technology (DLT)*, but they don't have to as they may use conventional centralised mechanisms, or a combination of both (hybrid infrastructure). Essentially the digital equivalent of notes and coins. See also *retail CBDC* and *wholesale CBDC*.

centralised exchange (CEX) See *crypto exchange*.

centralised ledger A database that is managed and controlled by a single trusted entity, or set thereof, such as a business, government body, or financial institution. In a centralised ledger system, such as traditional card or bank rails, all data are stored in one location, and access to that data is managed by trusted individuals or institutions. See also *distributed ledger* and *Distributed Ledger Technology*.

CENTROLink[7] Lithuania's domestic bank *payment scheme*.

Certificate Authority (CA) A trusted organisation that issues and manages *digital certificates*. CAs validate the identity of entities (such as websites, individuals, or organisations) and bind their *public keys* to their identities by issuing digitally signed certificates. These certificates are used to establish secure communications and authenticate entities in various online transactions. CAs play a crucial role in *public key infrastructure (PKI)* by serving as trusted third parties that help maintain the security and integrity of digital communications.

CEX Centralised Exchange. See *crypto exchange*.

chain analysis Also called *blockchain* analysis. A service that offers the ability to link *blockchain* addresses to real-world identities, which is particularly relevant in an *Anti-Money Laundering* context for *Virtual Asset Services Providers (VASPs)*. Not to be confused with *on-chain analysis*.

chaincode A *smart contract* implementation specific to the *Hyperledger Fabric* blockchain platform. It encapsulates business logic and rules for modifying the ledger state, typically written in Go, Node.js, or Java.

Chaincode is executed in a *Trusted Execution Environment* (TEE), which is a secure and isolated area within a processor that ensures the confidentiality and integrity of the code and data processed within it.

chainwork A cumulative measure of the total computational effort expended to create a *blockchain* up to a specific block. It represents the sum of the expected number of hash operations required to mine all blocks from the *genesis block* to the current one. Chainwork is used to determine the most valid chain in case of *forks* and to assess the overall security of a *Proof-of-Work* blockchain network. It increases with each new block and is typically expressed as a large hexadecimal number.

CHAPS See *Clearing House Automated Payment System*.

charge card A card granting the *cardholder* a line of *credit* for a specified period. These cards don't offer extended credit (unlike credit cards) as the full amount of the debt must be settled at the end of the specified period (usually monthly). The cardholder is usually charged an annual fee. Sometimes referred to as "travel and entertainment cards" and "delayed debit cards". American Express's charge card is probably the most famous one.

chargeback A reversal of a payment made by a card *issuer* or payment processor at the request of a *cardholder*, typically initiated due to disputes over unauthorised transactions, fraud, or dissatisfaction with goods or services. Chargebacks are designed to protect consumers from fraudulent activity and ensure fair treatment in transactions, but they can also pose challenges for merchants, including financial losses and potential penalties from payment processors. A *cardholder* can invoke the chargeback process through their issuer to get the transaction amount back from the merchant for a disputed purchase, or it can be invoked directly by the card issuer when they suspect fraud. For merchants, chargebacks are most painful.

chargeback activism A type of *first-party fraud* where activists raise *chargebacks* to punish a company for ideological differences or disagreements.

chargeback category *Chargeback reason codes* are classified into categories, and although these will differ in their description depending on the *card scheme*, the industry broadly agrees on four categories: authorisation, fraud, consumer disputes, and processing errors.

chargeback defence The process by which a merchant defends a *chargeback*. If a *merchant* fails to defend a chargeback within the period specified by the *card scheme*, their account will be automatically debited for the amount of the disputed transaction. Also called "chargeback representment."

chargeback period The number of calendar days within which the *issuer* has the right to charge the transaction back to the *acquirer*. Time limits vary per *card scheme* and are specified in their *operating regulations*.

chargeback process outsourcing Chargeback process outsourcing services providers are *Independent Software Vendors (ISVs)*, which manage the whole *chargeback* process on behalf of merchants and other card *ecosystem* stakeholders. Some providers have evolved into full-blown *fraud prevention* service providers.

chargeback ratio This represents the number of *chargebacks* filed against a merchant in a given month against their total number of transactions in a month. And because each *card scheme* has their own *operating regulations*, there is a different chargeback ratio for each scheme. Also called "chargeback rate".

chargeback reason code A code associated with a description that must be presented as part of the *chargeback* request to allow the merchant to provide the correct information in defence. These codes are specified by each *card scheme* in their *operating regulations*. See also *chargeback defence*.

chargeback representment See *chargeback defence*.

chatbot An application of *artificial intelligence (AI)* used in a customer service context allowing humans to interact with the facility as if they were interacting with a real person. Also called "virtual assistant".

ChatGPT[8] A *generative AI* service provided by Open AI.

Check 21[9] Check Clearing for the 21st Century Act. A US federal law that gives banks and other financial institutions the ability to create digital images of cheques, which are then sent to the relevant financial institutions to be processed.

checksum The last digit in a *Primary Account Number (PAN)*. It is calculated by applying a mathematical formula called the *Luhn Algorithm* (aka Modulus 10) to the BIN and Cardholder Account Number. The checksum is not part of the account number itself but is essential for the validation of card numbers (e.g. typos and missed digits).

cheque A paper-based written *payment instruction* from a *payer* to a *payee*, requiring the payer to pay a specified amount to the payee on presentment of the cheque. In markets with modern payment infrastructures, this payment instrument is slowly getting abandoned. Referred to as "check" in the US.

cheque guarantee card A card issued as part of a cheque guarantee system used to guarantee cheques, typically up to a specified amount. Validated cheques will be guaranteed up to that amount by the *issuer*, the payer's bank, or the operator.

cheque imaging See *electronic check acceptance*.

Chime[10] A *neo-bank*.

Chip and PIN A deployment of the *EMV Chip* standard where a *Personal Identification Number* (PIN) – a four-digit code selected and managed by the cardholder – is used to authenticate face-to-face transactions at the physical *Point-of-Sale* (POS) (e.g. UK and Europe).

Chip and Signature A deployment of the *EMV Chip* standard where a signature is used to authenticate face-to-face transactions at the physical *Point-of-Sale* (POS) (e.g. United States).

chip card A *credit card* or *debit card* that follows the *EMV Chip* standard. Also called an "EMV card" and historically a "smart card". Sometimes called *Integrated Circuit Card* (ICC).

CHIPS See Clearing House Interbank Payment System.

CID See *Card Identification Number*.

ciphertext Data that has been encrypted from its original state (plain text) using a *cryptography algorithm*. When using *public key cryptography* or *symmetric cryptography*, ciphertext can't be read until it has been decrypted (i.e. converted back to its original state or plain text) with a key. The decryption cipher is an algorithm that transforms the ciphertext back into plain text. Also spelled "ciphertext". See also *public key*, *private key*, *cryptography*, and *hash*.

circulating supply The total number of *coins* or *tokens* that are actively available and circulating in the market. This includes all tokens held by the public, including those staked or locked in *smart contracts*, but excludes tokens held by the project team, in company treasuries, or those that have been permanently removed from circulation (e.g. burned). It's a dynamic figure that can change over time due to factors like new token issuance, token *burning*, or the release of locked tokens. Circulating supply is an important metric for assessing a *cryptocurrency*'s market dynamics and potential value.

clearing The non-monetary exchange of transaction information. On the *card rails*, clearing is the process by which *merchant* transactions are reconciled with *cardholder* transactions. Merchant transactions are managed by the *acquirer*, and cardholder transactions are managed by the *issuer*, and the clearing process is orchestrated by the *card scheme*. On the bank rails, clearing is the process by which banking transactions are reconciled between banks. The banking transactions are managed by the sender's and receiver's banks, and the clearing process is orchestrated by the bank *payment scheme* for transaction reconciliation. Sometimes, this term is used improperly to also include *settlement* (which is wrong since there is no actual fund movement at the clearing stage). In *blockchain* infrastructures, the concept of clearing differs across blockchain implementation and depends on the *consensus protocol* and may include validation of transactions and blocks. See also *settlement*.

clearing account A deposit account held by a financial services institution at a *central bank*. Unlike *reserve accounts*, which institutions are required to maintain, clearing accounts are held by the financial services institution if their required reserve balances are not large enough to cover the total value of their clearing activities and other transfers of funds through the central bank.

clearing cycle In theory, this describes how long it takes for the *clearing* of funds to complete. In practice, the term "clearing cycle" is often associated with cheques (as it takes a few days for cheques to clear). For digital payments (card or bank accounts), the term "settlement cycle" is also used, meaning both *clearing* and *settlement*. The clearing cycle is more difficult to determine in *blockchain* infrastructures as it will be dependent on how the *mempool* is used, the *consensus protocol*, the *block interval*, etc.

clearing file A file produced by a payment scheme *direct participant* for submission to the *payment scheme* so that they can perform the *clearing* process.

clearing house A financial institution or intermediary that facilitates the exchange, *clearing*, and *settlement* of financial transactions between multiple parties. It acts as a middleman between buyers and sellers, ensuring that transactions are completed smoothly and that both parties fulfil their contractual obligations. Clearing houses reduce *settlement risk* by assuming the role of *counterparty* to each side of a transaction, guaranteeing the settlement even if one party defaults. They also streamline the process by netting transactions, reducing the number of payments and securities transfers required. Clearing houses play a crucial role in various financial markets, including securities, derivatives, and commodities trading, as well as in payment systems.

Clearing House Automated Payment System (CHAPS)[11] A UK bank *payment scheme* that launched in 1984 and is used for same-day high-value *wholesale payments* as well as time-critical high-value *retail payments*. CHAPS uses the *SWIFT* messaging network for *cross-border* payments. CHAPS is a *large-value payment system (LVPS)*, *real-time payment system (RTP system)* managed and operated by the Bank of England and operates on a *Real-Time Gross Settlement* basis. See also *settlement cycle*.

Clearing House Interbank Payment System (CHIPS)[12] A US *large-value payment system (LVPS)* privately operated by *The Clearing House*.

closed loop Any system that is limited in its scope.

closed loop card A payment card that is limited in its scope. Examples are gift cards, fuel cards, and some store cards. These are not generally run on *card scheme* networks.

closed wallet See *stored value digital wallet*.

cloud computing The on-demand delivery of computing resources – including servers, storage, databases, networking, software, analytics, and intelligence – over the internet ("the cloud") with pay-as-you-go pricing. Instead of owning and maintaining physical data centres and servers, users can access technology services from a cloud provider on an as-needed basis. This model offers benefits such as increased flexibility, scalability, and cost-efficiency compared to the traditional on-premises IT infrastructure. Cloud computing enables organisations to quickly provision resources, innovate faster, and focus on their core business rather than managing IT infrastructure.

cloud mining See *Mining-as-a-Service (MaaS)*.

CNP See *Card Not Present*.

COBOL Launched in 1959, COmmon Business-Oriented Language is a high-level programming language designed for business applications known for its English-like syntax, making it easier to read and maintain compared to more complex languages. COBOL remains widely used in enterprise systems for many tasks, including financial transaction processing (e.g. bank statements, managing accounts, and handling payments), inventory management (e.g. tracking stock levels, orders, and logistics), payroll processing (e.g. calculating salaries, deductions, and tax withholdings), and data reporting (e.g. sales reports, expenses, and business metrics). COBOL's strength lies in its stability and ability to handle large datasets efficiently. Whilst newer languages are emerging, COBOL persists due to the vast amount of legacy code powering critical business operations.

co-branded card A type of card where a *merchant* partners with a *card scheme* for a card product. These are typically *open loop* store cards, airline cards, etc.

CoD See *Cash-on-Delivery*.

Code 10 authorisation A phone call merchants can make to the *issuer* to alert them of suspected fraud without tipping off the *cardholder*. The issuer representative will then ask a series of yes or no questions in order to understand the situation and then instruct the merchants on how to proceed.

codebase fork A copy of an existing software project's source code that is used to start a new, independent development effort. Unlike other types of forks, a codebase fork creates an entirely separate project with its own distinct history, often with different goals or features from the original. It typically does not share any ongoing development or transaction history with the original project after the point of forking. Commonly used term in *blockchain* ecosystems. See also *fork*.

coin In traditional payments, a coin is physical *legal tender* and represents a claim on the issuing *central bank*. In decentralised systems, such as *blockchain* infrastructures, a coin is a *crypto asset* native to its blockchain such as Bitcoin (BTC) on the Bitcoin blockchain, or Ethereum (ETH) on the Ethereum blockchain. In practice, for blockchain infrastructures, the terms "coin" and "*token*" are often used interchangeably, although there is a technical difference.

Coinbase[13] A centralised *crypto exchange*.

coinbase transaction In a *blockchain* context, this is the first transaction in the block. It specifies the rewards that the block creator will get. It may include newly minted coins/tokens and transaction fees. The term is usually associated with *Proof-of-Work (PoW)* blockchains, as *Proof-of-Stake* blockchains tend to use the terms "staking reward transaction", "validator reward transaction", or "block reward transaction", although the term coinbase transaction may also be used. See also *genesis block*.

coin design The process of creating and defining the characteristics of a native *coin* within a *blockchain* ecosystem. This includes determining its purpose (such as transaction fees or rewards), supply limits, distribution mechanisms, and economic incentives to encourage participation and secure the network. Effective coin design is crucial for the sustainability and functionality of blockchain projects. See also *tokenomics*.

Coinomize[14] A *coin mixer*.

coin mixer Also known as "crypto currency tumbler" or "crypto mixer" or "crypto mixing service". A service that enables users to mix potentially traceable coins (for example, stolen coins) with other, clean coins in an effort to make it harder to trace them. Can be used for *money laundering* and increasingly attracting regulatory scrutiny. Also see *privacy coin* and *traceability*.

coin voting A governance mechanism in *blockchain* networks where participants' voting power is proportional to the amount of cryptocurrency they hold or stake, allowing those with larger holdings to have greater influence in decision-making processes. This method aligns the decision-making influence with economic stake in the network, whilst alternatives include one-person-one-vote systems, *quadratic voting*, reputation-based voting, delegated voting, and *futarchy*, which uses prediction markets for governance.

cold wallet A type of *crypto wallet* that keeps the *private keys* offline, typically on a hardware device or paper, providing enhanced security against online threats. Cold wallets are not connected to the internet, making them less vulnerable to hacking attempts but also less convenient for frequent transactions. They are often used for long-term storage of significant cryptocurrency holdings. Also referred to as "cold storage". See also *hot wallet*.

collateralisation The practice of securing a loan or financial obligation with an asset that can be seized if the borrower defaults. In crypto assets, it refers to backing a *token's* value with reserves of other assets (e.g. fiat currencies, cryptocurrencies, or commodities) to maintain stability and reduce risk. The collateralisation ratio and type of collateral used vary depending on the specific crypto asset and its design. See also *peg*.

Collect-on-Delivery See *Cash-on-Delivery*.

collusion A secret agreement or cooperation between two or more parties to deceive or defraud others, often for mutual benefit. In various contexts, such as business, politics, or cybersecurity, collusion can involve conspiring to manipulate outcomes, share sensitive information, or engage in anti-competitive practices. In decentralised systems, collusion among participants can undermine trust and fairness, leading to compromised integrity in processes like voting, *consensus protocols*, or resource allocation. Detecting and preventing collusion is crucial for maintaining transparency and accountability in any collaborative environment.

commercial card A generic term used to refer to payment cards issued to business for use by their employees. They include corporate cards, purchasing cards, and travel and entertainment cards. Sometimes referred to as "company card" or "business card".

commodity A basic good or raw material that is interchangeable with other goods of the same type, typically used as inputs in the production of other goods or services. Commodities are often standardised and traded on exchanges, and they can be classified into two main categories: hard commodities (natural resources like oil, gold, and metals) and soft commodities (agricultural products like wheat, coffee, and livestock). The value of a commodity is primarily determined by supply and demand dynamics in the market.

commodity-backed stablecoin A type of *stablecoin* that is backed by reserves of tangible assets, such as precious metals like gold or silver. These stablecoins aim to provide a store of value independent of government-issued currencies by using physical commodities as collateral. The valuation of the commodities can fluctuate, and the physical storage and management of these assets introduce operational complexities. Commodity-backed stablecoins often exhibit a degree of centralisation due to the need for secure storage and management of the underlying commodities. Also referred to as "commodity-collateralised stablecoin". See also *collateralisation*.

company card See *commercial card*.

compile-to-chain A *blockchain* development approach where *smart contracts* are compiled directly into machine code and executed on each network node without an intermediary *virtual machine* (*VM*). This contrasts with virtual machine-based approaches like the *Ethereum Virtual Machine* (*EVM*). Examples include Cardano's Plutus and Tezos' Michelson languages. Whilst potentially offering enhanced security through formal verification and improved performance, compile-to-chain approaches may have steeper learning curves and limited interoperability compared to VM-based alternatives.

Computer Misuse Act[15] A regulation in the UK which aims to protect the integrity and security of computer systems and data through criminalising systems or data access that is unauthorised by the owners of these systems or data.

confirmation depth Usually expressed in minutes; this is the time taken for a specified number of blocks that must be added to the *blockchain* after the block containing the recorded transaction has been added. The value depends on the *blockchain* and its approach to security. This is a security measure rather than a technical one and is used to mitigate risk and fraud (e.g. the rough equivalent of managing *settlement risk* on traditional financial infrastructures). Sometimes called "confirmation number". See also *confirmation time*.

Confirmation of Payee (CoP) An *overlay service* implemented on top of a bank *payment scheme*. CoP enables payers to check the name and *sort code* / bank account number before they complete a bank payment. CoP is intended to help with reducing *authorised push payment fraud*.

confirmation time The time taken from the point at which a transaction is recorded (i.e. its containing block has been added to the blockchain) to the point when the required number of new blocks have been successfully added (i.e. the *confirmation depth*). This value is dependent on the *average block creation time*. This is a dynamic metric, and blockchain explorers usually track it. On some blockchains, confirmation times can be several hours or even days. See also *blockchain settlement*, *block finality*.

consensus node A type of *full node* in a *blockchain* network that actively participates in the consensus process to validate and agree on the state of the blockchain. These nodes are responsible for proposing, validating, and adding new blocks to the chain according to the network's *consensus protocol*. Types of consensus nodes include *validator nodes*, *authority nodes*, and *masternodes*.

consensus protocol The *blockchain* trust framework by which transactions are validated. *Nodes* "listen" to the network and gather valid transactions (i.e. legal and not *double-spending*) to fit in a block. These nodes may be called *miners* or *validators*, and they add valid transactions to their blocks. The consensus protocol (e.g. *Proof of Work (PoW)* and *Proof of Stake (PoS)*) determines which valid blocks gets added to the chain, the ordering of validated blocks, and enables the blockchain network to be trustless. When the validated winning block is added to the chain, the transaction becomes irreversible. This is the equivalent of the *settlement* process on centralised payment systems. Also known as "consensus mechanism" and "consensus algorithm". See also *immutability* and *blockchain settlement*.

consent Consent in financial services and data privacy refers to a customer's freely given, specific, informed, and unambiguous agreement that allows a financial institution to collect, use, or share their personal data for clearly defined purposes. This agreement must be explicitly obtained, typically through a clear affirmative action, and customers have the right to withdraw their consent at any time. Financial institutions are required to clearly communicate what data is being collected, why it's needed, how it will be used, and with whom it may be shared, ensuring transparency and building trust with customers. Proper consent management is crucial for regulatory compliance, risk mitigation, and maintaining customer trust in an increasingly data-driven financial landscape.

consortium blockchain A type of *permissioned blockchain* controlled by a group.

consumer alerts A communication service that may be offered by *issuers* to cardholders to notify them of unusual activity (e.g. potential fraud) or other events (e.g. nearing limit and used by other family member) affecting their accounts.

contact card A card that requires physical contact with a card reader or *payment terminal*. See also *Card Present*.

contactless Technology or methods that allow for transactions or interactions without physical contact, typically using wireless communication.

contactless card A card that doesn't require physical contact with a card reader or card terminal. See also *contactless payment* and *Card Present*.

contactless payment A method of payment where a cardholder pays for something by tapping or waiving their *contactless card* or contactless-enabled device (e.g. smart phone, card, key fob, and other *wearables*) over a card terminal.

contactless payment limit See *Cardholder Verification Method limit*.

contagion risk A type of risk where the failure of one financial services institution (not necessarily a bank) may spill over to a large number of other financial services institutions, and possibly the financial system as a whole. Also referred to as systemic risk. Recent examples are the collapse of Wirecard,[16] Terra/Luna,[17] and FTX.[18] Also called "systemic risk".

contentious hard fork A significant, non-backwards compatible update to a *blockchain's* protocol that results in a split of the network due to disagreement among participants. This leads to two separate chains with different rules, potentially creating two distinct cryptocurrencies and communities. Unlike planned hard forks, contentious forks are characterised by lack of consensus and can lead to rivalries between the resulting chains. See also *fork*.

contextual commerce A retail strategy that seamlessly integrates purchasing opportunities into consumers' everyday activities and environments. It allows customers to make purchases at the moment of discovery or inspiration, without disrupting their current experience or requiring them to visit a separate store or website. This approach leverages technologies like social media integrations, chatbots, and *IoT* devices to enable frictionless transactions within the context of a user's immediate surroundings or digital interactions. By reducing barriers between product discovery and purchase, contextual commerce aims to enhance customer convenience, increase conversion rates, and create more personalised shopping experiences. See also *universal commerce*, *unified commerce*.

contingent liability A potential debt that may become an actual financial obligation if certain conditions materialise or fail to materialise. On the *card rails*, the *liability shift* is a type of contingent liability.

contingent reimbursement A reimbursement model used in the context of *authorised fraud* by which victims of scams may be reimbursed subject to certain conditions and standards of care being met by both the customer and the payment service providers involved.

Continuous Payment Authority (CPA) See *recurring transaction*.

control number A unique numerical identifier that is assigned to a *chargeback* or *retrieval* request.

conversational AI Technologies that enable machines to understand, process, and respond to human language in a natural and contextually appropriate manner. It combines *natural language processing (NLP)*, *machine learning*, and other *artificial intelligence (AI)* techniques to facilitate human-like interactions through text or voice interfaces. In the payments industry, conversational AI is applied to enhance customer experiences and streamline financial transactions. It powers intelligent *chatbots* and virtual assistants that can handle tasks such as balance inquiries, fund transfers, bill payments, and transaction history reviews. Conversational AI in payments also enables voice-activated banking, personalised financial advice, and *fraud detection* through natural language interactions, making financial services more accessible and user-friendly, whilst maintaining security and compliance standards.

CoP See *Confirmation of Payee.*

correspondent bank A *bank* authorised to provide services on behalf of another bank.

correspondent banking An arrangement under which one bank holds funds owned by another bank (the respondent bank) and provides payment and other services to that respondent bank. A "vostro account" is the term used by a correspondent to describe an account held on behalf of a foreign bank; the foreign bank would in turn regard this account as its "nostro account".

Cosmos SDK An *open-source* framework for building application-specific *blockchains*. It provides a modular architecture that allows developers to easily compose blockchain applications using pre-built modules or custom ones. The *Software Development Kit (SDK)* includes tools for creating, testing, and deploying blockchain networks, and it's designed to work with the Tendermint *consensus protocol*. It features inter-blockchain communication (IBC) capabilities, enabling interoperability between different blockchains. The Cosmos SDK emphasises security, scalability, and customisability, making it suitable for a wide range of use cases from *decentralised finance (DeFi)* to supply chain management.

counterfeit card A payment card that has been fraudulently printed, embossed, or encoded to appear as a genuine payment card. This can also refer to cards that were originally legitimately issued but subsequently altered without the *issuer's* knowledge or consent (sometimes referred to as altered card).

counterfeiting The illegal production, distribution, or use of fake *currency*, documents, or goods that are designed to closely resemble genuine items. In financial contexts, it primarily refers to the unauthorised manufacture of false banknotes or coins that mimic *legal tender.*

Counterfeiters aim to deceive recipients into accepting these forgeries as authentic, thereby profiting from the face value of the fake currency, whilst undermining the integrity of the monetary system. This criminal activity can have severe economic consequences, including *inflation*, loss of confidence in the currency, and financial losses for individuals and businesses. Governments and central banks employ various anti-counterfeiting measures, such as complex designs, special inks, and security features, to protect the authenticity of their currencies.

counterparty An entity or individual involved in a financial transaction or contract, representing the opposite side of the deal. For example, in a loan agreement, the lender and borrower are counterparties. The reliability and creditworthiness of a counterparty are crucial as counterparty risk refers to the potential for one party to default on their obligations, which could lead to financial loss for the other party. See also *settlement risk*.

counterparty risk See *settlement risk*.

Counter-Terrorist Financing (CTF) The collection of laws, processes, and regulations that prevent the financing of terrorism. Also referred to as CFT (Combatting the Financing of Terrorism).

CP See *Card Present*.

CPA See *Continuous Payment Authority* and *recurring transaction*.

CPC Cardholder Preferred Currency. See *Dynamic Currency Conversion*.

CR An abbreviation for the word *credit*. Generally seen on financial statements and reports.

credential stuffing A type of *cybercrime*. A brute force attack that automates large amounts of login attempts to targeted websites using stolen credentials (available for sale widely on the dark web) on the off-chance that the same credentials have been re-used by their owners across multiple websites and platforms (which is bad practice).

credit The ability of one party to obtain funds, goods, or services from another party where the first party doesn't reimburse the first party immediately, based on the trust that payment will be made in the future to settle the debt. Often associated with fees (e.g. interest and membership). Also see *credit card*, *credit risk*, and *credit score*.

credit bureau A financial services company that collects, researches, and maintains *credit* information and sells that data to lenders, creditors, and consumers as credit reports, including a *credit score*. Notable examples are Equifax, Experian, and TransUnion.

credit card A card granting the user a line of *credit*, usually over an extended period. The *cardholder* may make purchases and/or withdraw cash up to a specified limit. The debt may be settled at the end of a specified period or, in part, with the balance taken as extended credit, for which interest is charged. Cardholders may also be charged an annual fee.

credit card company See *card scheme*.

credit institution In the EU, this is the definition given to a *bank*.

credit risk The possibility of a financial loss happening due to a borrower's failure to repay a loan or to satisfy contractual obligations.

credit score Traditionally, a three-digit number assigned to an individual or entity by a *credit bureau* based on their *credit* history, which includes information like the number credit accounts, total levels of debt, repayment history, and new account openings. Lenders use credit scores to evaluate credit worthiness (see *credit risk*) or the likelihood that credit will be repaid in a timely manner. The credit score model was created by the Fair Isaac Corp. (FICO) and is used by financial institutions. Whilst other *credit scoring* systems exist, the FICO Score is the most commonly used. With the advent of *Open Banking*, a new credit rating system has emerged, involving access to bank account data to determine good and bad behaviour in an attempt to foster the *financial inclusion* of those without access to traditional credit products.

credit scoring The process of evaluating an individual's creditworthiness by analysing their credit history and financial behaviour. This process involves the use of statistical models to generate a *credit score* that predicts the likelihood of timely repayment on loans or credit obligations, helping lenders make informed decisions about extending credit and determining interest rates. See also cashflow underwriting.

credit transfer A *payment instruction* from the bank account holder (the *payer*) to their bank to transfer funds to a *payee*. The *payee* can be the same person as the instructing bank account holder (e.g. a bank account holder moving funds between their own accounts), and this includes single *ad hoc* payments or different (e.g. a bank account holder moving funds to another person's account). For *retail payments*, these generally have lower-value thresholds than credit transfers on *large-value payment systems (LVPS)* and are mostly associated with consumer transactions. Credit transfers can also be submitted through *batch processing* by the account holder's bank to the bank payment scheme (e.g. salaries and pension contributions), but in this case, each fund transfer in the batch counts as a single transaction. This latter type of payment usually has high-value minimum thresholds (not necessarily by the scheme rules, but mostly due to economics) and is not supported by all bank *payment schemes*. Also referred to as direct deposit or *push payment*.

CRM Customer Relationship Management. A CRM platform is a technology solution that enables a business to manage their interactions with customers and prospects. Typically involves the use of data to derive actionable insights and inform sales and marketing strategies. Salesforce[19] is a well-known example.

cross-border International. In payments terms, a cross-border payment or transaction is one where the *payer*'s account and the *payee*'s account are managed by entities in different jurisdictions. Sometimes spelled "x-border".

cross-border settlement A *settlement* that takes place in a country other than where one or both counterparties to a transaction are located.

cross-chain bridge A specific type of *bridge* designed to enable interoperability between two or more distinct blockchain networks. Cross-chain bridges allow for the transfer of assets, data, or functionality across otherwise incompatible blockchain ecosystems. They typically employ complex cryptographic mechanisms, such as *atomic swaps* or relay chains, to ensure the secure and verifiable movement of assets or information between chains. This technology is fundamental in creating a more interconnected and fluid blockchain ecosystem, allowing users to leverage the unique advantages of different networks, whilst maintaining asset *liquidity* and functionality across platforms.

cross-chain staking In a *Proof of Stake* (*PoS*) context, this is where validators may participate in cross-chain *staking* protocols that enable them to stake their *coins/tokens* across multiple blockchains in order to maximise their stake and reduce their risk exposure to a single *blockchain*.

crowdfunding A method of raising capital through the collective efforts of a large number of individuals, typically via online platforms. It allows entrepreneurs, startups, and projects to solicit small contributions from a diverse pool of backers, often in exchange for rewards, equity, or other incentives. Crowdfunding democratises access to funding, enabling creators to finance their ideas, whilst engaging with potential supporters and building a community around their projects.

crowdfunding platform A website or an application or other software that is used to raise funds or *cryptocurrency* through donations.

crypto airdrop See *airdrop*.

crypto asset At a high level, a crypto asset is a type of *virtual asset* that lives on a *blockchain*, is secured by *cryptography*, and comes in five types: *cryptocurrency*, *Non-Fungible Token* (NFT), *utility token*, *stablecoin*, and *security token*. (Author's note: there is no formally accepted definition or classification of crypto assets).

crypto ATM A crypto ATM (*Automated Teller Machine*) is a kiosk that allows users to buy and sometimes sell cryptocurrencies with cash or debit cards. These machines connect to digital wallets and use *QR codes* to process transactions, offering a familiar ATM-like experience for buying and selling cryptocurrencies.

crypto-backed stablecoin A type of *stablecoin* designed to maintain a stable value relative to a target asset (usually the US dollar) by using other cryptocurrencies as collateral. These stablecoins are typically over-collateralised, meaning the value of the crypto collateral exceeds the value of stablecoins issued, to account for potential price volatility. Smart contracts manage the *collateralisation*, *minting*, and *burning* processes to maintain a *soft peg* to the target asset. Unlike *fiat-backed stablecoins* that aim for a hard 1:1 *peg*, crypto-backed stablecoins typically maintain a soft peg, allowing for slight fluctuations around the target value, whilst using their mechanisms to continually adjust towards the desired price point. Also called "crypto-collateralised stablecoin". Examples include wBTC and LUSD. See also *peg*.

crypto credit card A type of *credit card* that enables cardholders to earn *cryptocurrency* rewards on purchases instead of *cashback* or other rewards (e.g. points and travel rewards). The rewards earned are automatically used to purchase cryptocurrencies that are then deposited into the cardholder's connected cryptocurrency account (e.g. a *crypto wallet*). The type of cryptocurrency earned depends on the card *issuer* who will usually co-brand the card with a major *card scheme* (e.g. Visa, Mastercard, and American Express). They are called crypto credit cards because they earn cryptocurrency rewards, not because they use cryptocurrencies to make purchases. As cryptocurrencies are volatile, the cryptocurrency rewards earned could lose significant value from one day to the next (unlike standard credit card *cashback*) and may also be subject to tax in some jurisdictions. See also *crypto debit card* and *volatility*.

cryptocurrency A type of digital or virtual currency that uses *cryptography* for security. Cryptocurrencies are typically decentralised and operate on *blockchain* technology, ensuring transparency and security by recording all transactions on a public ledger maintained by a network of computers (*nodes*). A type of *crypto asset* intended to be used as a medium of exchange. This was the original purpose of *Bitcoin* (BTC), but over the years, BTC has morphed into a store of value used for speculative purposes. Some even refer to *Bitcoin* as "digital gold", which is a misnomer since gold is a stable asset and cryptocurrencies are highly volatile. To this day, no cryptocurrency can claim to be a true medium of exchange. Also spelled "crypto currency". See also *volatility* and *stablecoin*.

cryptocurrency tumbler See *coin mixer*.

crypto debit card A type of *prepaid card* that can be loaded with *cryptocurrency* to make payments online or face-to-face to entities that don't accept cryptocurrencies. This allows cryptocurrency holders to spend it without first having to convert it into *fiat currency* (i.e. without having to use another crypto *off-ramp* service). As with standard prepaid cards, cardholders will need to have cryptocurrency funds already available (this is referred to as *staking* and issuers may require cardholders to "stake" a particular *coin* or *token*) in their funding *crypto wallet* or investment account before they can use it to make payments. Crypto debit cards may also offer rewards on purchases (e.g. points and travel rewards), and issuers may co-brand the card with a major *card scheme* (e.g. Visa, Mastercard, and American Express). See also *crypto credit card*.

crypto ETF See *Exchange Traded Fund (ETF)*.

crypto exchange A service that allows customers to trade cryptocurrencies for other assets, such as *fiat money* or *cryptocurrency*. There are two types of crypto exchanges: centralised exchanges (CEX), where the exchange is in control of the user's private keys and therefore their crypto assets, and decentralised exchanges (DEX), where the user has full control of their keys, and therefore their assets. A CEX, such as *Binance* or *Coinbase*, is also referred to as a "custodial exchange" because a third party has custody of the keys (not the user). A DEX, such as Uniswap and PancakeSwap, is also referred to as a "non-custodial exchange" as the user has custody of their keys. Users can connect their *crypto wallet* to a crypto exchange, and some crypto exchanges also provide crypto wallet services. Also called cryptocurrency exchange. There are also some specialised crypto exchanges called security exchanges which specifically deal with assets that are classified as securities (e.g. *security tokens* and tokenised real-world assets). Also see *CeFi*, *DeFi*, *crypto wallet*, *off-ramp*, and *on-ramp*.

cryptography The science of concealing messages between two parties with a secret code so that third parties are unable to read the message in its concealed form (the *ciphertext*). Although the term "cryptography" refers to the science, and the term *encryption* describes the process by which the science is applied, nowadays, both terms are used interchangeably. Also see *cryptography algorithm*, *symmetric cryptography*, *public key cryptography*, *hash*, and *quantum cryptography*.

cryptography algorithm A mathematical function used to scramble plain text and make it unreadable (*ciphertext*). There are three types of cryptography algorithms: *public key cryptography*, *symmetric cryptography*, and hashing algorithms. Also referred to as "cryptographic algorithm". When referring to public key or symmetric cryptography, the algorithms are sometimes referred to as the "encryption algorithm". Also see *public key*, *private key*, *cryptography*, *encryption*, *hash*, and *quantum cryptography*.

crypto mixer See *coin mixer*.

crypto mixing service See *coin mixer*.

crypto off-ramp See *off-ramp*.

crypto wallet A type of *digital wallet* used to store the user's *public keys* and *private keys* which act as a certificate of ownership for *crypto assets* that are stored on *Distributed Ledger Technology (DLT)*, usually a *blockchain*. There are two types of crypto wallets: custodial wallets, where the third party is in control of the user's private keys and therefore their crypto assets, and non-custodial wallets (also referred to as "self-custodial wallets"), where the user has full control of their keys, and therefore their assets. Also see *public key*, *private key*, *CeFi*, *DeFi*, and *crypto exchange*.

CSS Cascading Style Sheets. A stylesheet language used to describe the presentation and layout of web pages written in HTML or XML. It allows developers to separate content from design, enabling control over various visual aspects such as colours, fonts, spacing, and positioning of elements. By defining styles in CSS files, developers can maintain a consistent look across multiple web pages and easily update the design by modifying a single stylesheet. CSS supports responsive design, allowing web pages to adapt to different screen sizes and devices, thus enhancing user experience on the web.

CTF See *Counter-Terrorist Financing*.

currency A medium of exchange that is widely accepted for goods and services, facilitating trade by eliminating the complexities of barter systems. It has evolved from physical forms like coins and paper notes to include digital representations. In the context of modern finance, currency encompasses various types, including *fiat currency*, which is government-issued and not backed by any physical *commodity*, as well as digital currencies such as *cryptocurrency* and *e-money*.

currency pair A quotation of two different currencies, where one *currency* is quoted against another, indicating how much of the second currency is needed to purchase one unit of the first.

custodial exchange See *crypto exchange*.

custodial wallet See *crypto wallet*.

custody A term used to refer to the safekeeping and management of assets on behalf of others. In the traditional financial services world, assets can be securities, financial instruments, etc. In the *blockchain* world, custody refers to the safeguarding of users' public and private keys. See also *crypto exchange* and *crypto wallet*.

Customer Due Diligence (CDD) The process by which businesses verify that their customers are who they say they are and is usually conducted at the *underwriting* stage or when creating a new business relationship. CDD allows businesses to assess *money-laundering* and terrorism-financing risks to which customers may potentially expose them. A form of *due diligence*. See also *Enhanced Due Diligence (EDD)*.

Customer Not Present See *Card Not Present*.

Customer Present See *Card Present*.

Custom Virtual Machine (CVM) A software layer designed to execute the code specifically for a particular platform or application. Unlike a standard *Virtual Machine (VM)*, a CVM isn't as common and requires dedicated development for its functionality.

CVC See *Card Verification Code*.

CVM See *Cardholder Verification Method* or *Custom Virtual Machine*.

CVV See *Card Verification Value*.

CVV1 A static *Card Verification Value (CVV)* stored on *Track 1* and *Track 2* of the *magnetic stripe* (magstripe) of a physical payment card. The CVV1 is used to authenticate magstripe card transactions (this process takes place between the magstripe, the physical card payment terminal, and the *issuer* during the *authorisation* process).

CVV2 The static *Card Verification Value (CVV)* printed on a card.

CVV3 See *iCVV*.

CX An abbreviation of "customer experience". Also a programming language developed specifically for the Skycoin *blockchain*.

cyber Literally meaning "relating to computers or computer networks". An abused term that has become mostly associated with computer security and cybercrime.

cybercrime A type of crime involving computers or computer networks. Common types of cybercrime include *phishing, malware, hacking, ransomware, identity theft, Business Email Compromise (BEC)*, data breaches, and online fraud.

cybersecurity The practice of protecting computers, networks, and data from unauthorised access, attacks, damage, or theft. It encompasses various technologies, processes, and practices designed to safeguard digital information and systems from cyber threats. In the context of digital assets and cryptocurrencies, cybersecurity is crucial for ensuring the integrity and confidentiality of transactions, protecting user wallets and exchanges from hacking attempts, and maintaining trust in the digital financial ecosystem.

Notes

1 Cardano. https://cardano.org/ (Accessed 1 December 2023)
2 Carte Bancaire. https://www.cartes-bancaires.com/ (Accessed 21 November 2023)
3 Cash App. https://cash.app/ (Accessed 21 November 2023)
4 Bank of Korea. https://www.bok.or.kr/eng/main/contents.do?menuNo=400045 (Accessed 21 November 2023)
5 CEC. https://www.cecbelgium.be/en (Accessed 21 November 2023)
6 Lankapay. https://www.lankapay.net/products-and-services/cefts/ (Accessed 21 November 2023)
7 CENTROlink. https://www.lb.lt/en/centrolink (Accessed 21 November 2023)

8 ChatGPT. https://chat.openai.com/ (Accessed 21 November 2023)
9 Federal Reserve (Check 21). https://www.frbservices.org/education/products-services-education/check21-act.html (Accessed 21 November 2023)
10 Chime. https://www.chime.com/ (Accessed 21 November 2023)
11 CHAPS. https://www.bankofengland.co.uk/payment-and-settlement/chaps (Accessed 21 November 2023)
12 The Clearing House, CHIPS. https://www.theclearinghouse.org/payment-systems/CHIPS (Accessed 21 November 2023)
13 Coinbase. https://www.coinbase.com/ (Accessed 21 November 2023)
14 Coinomize. https://coinomize.biz/ (Accessed 16 December 2023)
15 Legislation.gov.uk (Computer Misuse Act 1990). https://www.legislation.gov.uk/ukpga/1990/18/contents (Accessed 21 November 2023)
16 How the Biggest Fraud in German History Unravelled. *The New Yorker*, 27 February 2023. https://www.newyorker.com/magazine/2023/03/06/how-the-biggest-fraud-in-german-history-unravelled (Accessed 6 December 2023)
17 Anatomy of a Run: The Terra Luna Crash. National Bureau of Economic Research, April 2023. https://www.nber.org/papers/w31160 (Accessed 6 December 2023)
18 Why Did FTX Collapse? Here's What to Know. *The New York Times*, 10 November 2022. https://www.nytimes.com/2022/11/10/technology/ftx-binance-crypto-explained.html (Accessed 6 December 2023)
19 Salesforce. https://www.salesforce.com/ (Accessed 18 January 2024)

D

D IS FOR...

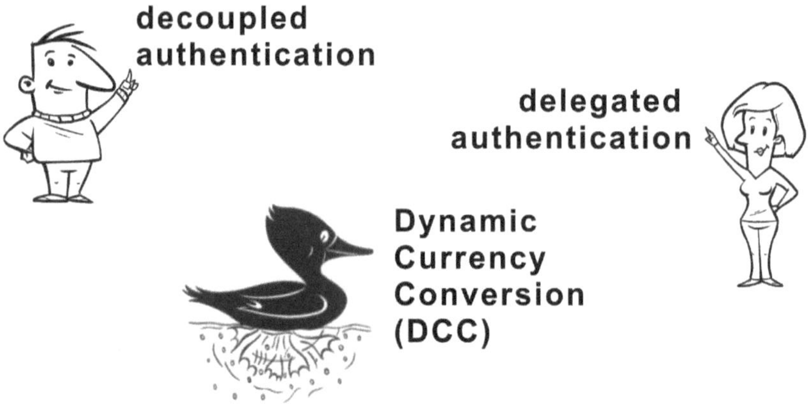

DAG See *Directed Acyclic Graph*.

Dankort[1] A Danish *domestic card scheme*.

DAO See *Decentralised Autonomous Organisation*.

dApp Decentralised Application. A software application built on *Distributed Ledger Technology (DLT)* (e.g. a *blockchain*) consisting of a *smart contract* at the backend and a front-end user interface. The user interface is just like

DOI: 10.4324/9781003571131-5

any app and is usually built using traditional web technology. Since smart contracts are typically public on the blockchain, anyone can inspect the code and transactions associated with the dApp.

Dapper Network A scalable, user-friendly *blockchain* platform developed by Dapper Labs to support high-performance *decentralised applications (dApps)* and digital collectibles, featuring a *Proof-of-Stake* consensus and tools for developers to build and deploy *dApps* with a focus on accessibility and energy efficiency.

dark web A segment of the internet that is not indexed by traditional search engines and requires specific software, such as the Tor browser, to access. It operates on overlay networks that use *encryption* to provide *anonymity* for users and website operators, allowing them to communicate and conduct activities without revealing their identities or locations. Whilst the dark web is often associated with illegal activities, such as drug trafficking and the sale of stolen data, it also serves legitimate purposes, including protecting *privacy* for political dissidents and journalists in oppressive regimes.

data breach A security violation where sensitive, protected, or confidential data is copied, transmitted, viewed, stolen, modified, or used by a fraudster or cybercriminal. Also described as unintentional information disclosure, data leak, information leakage, and data spill. See also *data protection* and *data privacy*.

data privacy A subset of *data protection*. The process by which access to personal data is controlled (e.g. through policies and technology). Personal data should be protected from those who should not have access to it, and individuals should have the ability to control who can access their personal information. Nowadays, as the amount of data being created and stored is continuously increasing, data privacy has become a crucial part of any business strategy, especially in the payments world. Data privacy is recognised as a universal human right in the Universal Declaration of Human Rights (Article 12), the European Convention of Human Rights (Article 8), and the European Charter of Fundamental Rights (Article 7). See also *data protection*.

data protection The process of protecting sensitive information from damage, loss, unauthorised access, or corruption through processes, policies, and technology. Nowadays, as the amount of data being created and stored is continuously increasing, data protection has become a crucial part of any business strategy, especially in the payments world. Used interchangeably with "data security". See also *data privacy*.

Data Subject Access Request (DSAR) A request that can be made by an individual to a business, whereby the business must provide all of the information they hold about that individual within a specified time frame. These requests are usually associated with *data protection* regulations, especially in Europe.

DCB See *Direct Carrier Billing*.

DCC See *Dynamic Currency Conversion*.

dCVV See *Dynamic CVV*.

DD See *direct debit*.

DDoS attack A Distributed Denial of Service (DDoS) attack is a malicious attempt to disrupt the normal functioning of a targeted server, service, or network by overwhelming it with a flood of internet traffic from multiple sources. This coordinated attack uses numerous compromised computer systems as sources of attack traffic, often leveraging a *botnet*. The goal is to exhaust the target's resources, such as bandwidth, system memory, or processing capacity, rendering the service unavailable to legitimate users. DDoS attacks can cause significant downtime, financial losses, and reputational damage to organisations and networks.

de-banking A relatively recent phenomenon in the financial services sector by which banks either close customer accounts or refuse to open accounts. This practice applies to both retail and business customers and has been brought about by the recent geo-political climate which has seen an increase in *sanctions*. In the payments space, this may particularly affect new companies and startups, such as crypto companies or *non-bank PSPs*, whose business is deemed too risky by larger banks as it would increase their compliance burden. Also spelled "debanking". See also a *de-risking* and *Politically Exposed Person (PEP)*.

debit A sum charged as due or owing. Usually, a debit is a record of the money taken from a bank account, for example, when an account holder writes a cheque or uses a *debit card*.

debit card A card enabling the cardholder to make payment transactions that are charged directly to a bank account. A debit card is usually directly linked to a bank account, but new models have emerged, such as provided by a *Card-Based Payment Instrument Issuer (CBPII)*. See also *credit card*.

debt security token A digital representation of a debt instrument, such as a bond or loan, created through *tokenisation* on a *blockchain*. These tokens represent the holder's right to receive repayment of principal and interest according to specified terms. Tokenisation allows for *fractional ownership*, potentially increasing *liquidity* and accessibility of debt securities. Debt security tokens typically use *smart contracts* to automate interest payments and enforce terms, whilst providing transparency through the blockchain technology. They bridge traditional debt markets with blockchain innovation, enabling new models for issuance, trading, and management of debt instruments.

decentralisation the distribution of power, control, or functions away from a central authority or location to multiple independent entities. Unlike mere *distribution*, which simply spreads resources or data across multiple points, decentralisation involves granting decision-making authority and autonomy to these dispersed entities. In technology and governance, decentralisation aims to reduce single points of failure, enhance resilience, and promote more democratic or collaborative systems. Whilst distribution focuses on the spread of resources, decentralisation emphasises the spread of control and authority.

decentralised application See *dApp*.

Decentralised Autonomous Organisation (DAO) A group of people without a central leader or company dictating any of the decisions. Its structure and governance processes are built on a *blockchain* using *smart contracts* to enforce the rules. DAOs intend to give every member a voice, vote, and opportunity to propose initiatives, and DAO members often buy their way in by purchasing *governance tokens* specifically for the DAO.

decentralised exchange See *crypto exchange*.

decentralised finance See *DeFi*.

decentralised identity A digital identity management approach where identity data is distributed across multiple nodes or entities, often using *blockchain* technology, rather than controlled by a single centralised authority. It aims to give individuals more control over their personal information. *Self-sovereign identity* (SSI) is a specific implementation of decentralised identity that focuses on giving users full control over their identity credentials, typically stored in a *digital wallet* and shared selectively as needed.

decline A card *authorisation decision* when the card *issuer* denies the transaction. Possible reasons are insufficient funds, expired card, or incorrect PIN.

decoupled authentication A form of *authentication* different from the standard authentication process. Here, *cardholder* authentication happens outside of their payment interaction with the merchant, at a different time, even if the cardholder is offline. Merchants can set a time limit (e.g. one minute or one week) for the cardholder to complete the authentication process, and this can take place on a device different to that used by the cardholder during the transaction.

decoupled debit A concept by which non-bank *issuers* could issue debit cards that are not tied to a specific bank account. Early examples are associated with retailers (e.g. Target REDcard™ Debit[2]) and can only be used at that retailer (*closed loop*). Newer examples include cards provided by *Card-Based Payment Instrument Issuers (CBPIIs)*.

decryption The process of converting encoded or encrypted data back into its original, readable format. This is achieved using a specific algorithm and a key, which is required to reverse the *encryption* process. Decryption is essential for accessing secure information that has been protected to ensure confidentiality and prevent unauthorised access.

de-dollarisation A term referring to the attempt at shrinking the US dollar influence on the economies of countries other than the US, specifically those belonging to the *BRICS* block. Even as some BRICS countries have called for the creation of a common currency across the block for trade and investment,[3] the dollar is still by far the most widely held reserve currency and remains essential for conducting international business.

deep learning A subset of *machine learning* which uses neural networks, designed to mimic the human brain, which can ingest and process vast amounts of data to extract meaning. These networks consist of layers of interconnected *nodes* that process information. The more layers, the deeper the network, allowing it to learn more complex features and perform more complex tasks. See also *artificial intelligence*.

deferred net settlement A settlement method where payment transactions are grouped and settled at specific times throughout the day, rather than immediately. This means the final exchange of funds between parties happens later, even though the sender's account might show a decrease initially. This allows for streamlined processing and reduced costs, but it can also introduce some temporary risk before the final settlement. See *settlement cycle* and *settlement risk.*

deferred payment A type of payment where an agreement between a *payer* and a *payee* is made for the purchase of goods or services and there is an agreed delay for the payment, in part or in full, from the time of purchase. This allows the person or business making the payment more time to meet their financial obligations. In this construct, the merchant usually supplies the goods or services to the customer when the transaction is authorised, and the transaction is not fully settled until the final *due date*. See also *BNPL*, *split payment*, and *group payment*.

deferred settlement See *settlement cycle.*

DeFi Decentralised Finance. A generic term for decentralised applications (*dApps*) providing financial services on a *blockchain* settlement layer. Examples of DeFi services include investments, insurance, asset management, payments, lending, and trading. DeFi services rely on *smart contracts* and are accessible through dApps, allowing users to buy, sell, store, and trade their funds without the need for a central authority and don't usually require a *KYC* process (although these may be implemented depending on features and regulatory requirements). DeFi emphasises user control and self-*custody*. See also *CeFi*, *CeDeFi*, and *TradFi*.

deflationary mechanism A process or policy designed to reduce the overall supply of a *currency* or asset, potentially increasing its scarcity and value over time. In *blockchain* ecosystems, deflationary mechanisms are features built into some *blockchain protocols* that systematically reduce the total supply of coins or tokens. Examples include token *burning* (permanently removing a portion of tokens from circulation), *halving* events (periodic reductions in *block rewards* for miners), and transaction fee *burning* (destroying a portion of transaction fees instead of distributing them to validators). These mechanisms aim to counter inflationary pressures and potentially increase the long-term value of the remaining tokens.

delayed payment See *deferred payment.*

delegated authentication This is where *issuers* delegate the *authentication* process to a third party (e.g. *merchant*, *acquirer*, and *digital wallet* provider). For example, if a merchant can perform the cardholder authentication through a card-scheme-approved method, information can be passed on to the issuer to confirm the cardholder's identity, and there will be no need for the issuer to authenticate the transaction. This means a lot less friction for cardholders. Also see *one click payment*. See also *Stand-In Processing*.

delegated governance A governance model in *blockchain* networks where the decision-making authority is assigned to elected representatives or *nodes*, rather than being exercised directly by all participants. This model allows token holders to delegate their voting power to trusted individuals or entities who make decisions on their behalf. It aims to balance efficiency and inclusivity by enabling knowledgeable representatives to participate in governance, whilst still allowing token holders to retain ultimate control over their voting power.

delegated Proof of Stake (DPoS) A blockchain *consensus protocol* where token holders vote for a limited number of delegates (also called witnesses or block producers) to validate transactions and create new blocks on their behalf. This system aims to improve the scalability and transaction speed compared to traditional *Proof of Stake* by reducing the number of active validators whilst maintaining a degree of decentralisation through the voting process.

Delivery-versus-Payment (DvP) A common form of *settlement* used in the securities industry, which guarantees the transfer of securities only happens after payment has been made, alleviating *settlement risk*. DvP specifies that the buyer's cash payment for securities must be made prior to or at the same time as the delivery of the security. See also *Payment-versus-Payment (PvP)*, *atomic settlement*, and *atomic swap*.

delta-hedging A risk management strategy in option trading that aims to neutralise directional risk by continuously adjusting a portfolio to maintain a delta-neutral position. Delta measures the sensitivity of an option's price to changes in the underlying asset's price. In the context of *crypto assets*, delta-hedging is particularly valuable due to the high volatility of *cryptocurrencies*, allowing traders to manage risk and capitalise on price fluctuations without taking on significant directional exposure. See also *synthetic stablecoin*.

demonetisation A *monetary policy* action where a government or *central bank* withdraws the *legal tender* status of a specific *currency* unit or series of banknotes from circulation. This process typically involves replacing old currency notes with new ones or introducing entirely new denominations. Demonetisation aims to address issues such as *counterfeiting*, tax evasion, or the *shadow economy* by forcing the conversion of undeclared cash holdings. It can also be implemented to modernise a country's currency system or to combat *inflation*. Whilst potentially effective in achieving certain economic goals, demonetisation can cause significant short-term disruptions to the economy and daily financial transactions.

depository institution In the US, this is the definition given to a *bank*.

de-risking A process where banks or other financial services institutions either terminate some or all services or restrict access to services from customers, sectors, or regions they determine to present unacceptable risk. This is a risk avoidance practice rather than a risk management one. Also spelled "derisking". See also a *de-banking*, *Politically Exposed Person (PEP)*, and *sanction*.

device fingerprinting The process of collecting data that can be used to identify a particular device through a combination of information about the software and hardware of the device (e.g. OS version, browser version, region and language settings, screen resolution, and *geo-location*). The information is usually assimilated into a unique identifier using a fingerprinting algorithm. With enough information, device fingerprinting can achieve high levels of accuracy. See also *authentication*.

DEX Decentralised Exchange. See *crypto exchange*.

DIAS[4] Greece's domestic *ACH scheme*.

difficulty target In *Proof-of-Work (PoW)* blockchains, a value representing the mining difficulty level set by the *blockchain protocol* that miners have to achieve when mining the block (i.e. find a *hash* that is below the difficulty target).

Diffie–Hellman key exchange A *public key cryptography* algorithm. Also known as "Diffie-Hellman key agreement protocol".

digital asset See *virtual asset*.

digital bond A debt security issued, recorded, and traded using *blockchain* or *distributed ledger technology (DLT)*. Digital bonds use *smart contracts* to automate interest payments, enforce terms, and manage ownership. They can offer increased efficiency, transparency, and *fractional ownership* compared to traditional bonds. Digital bonds may be issued by corporations, governments, or other entities and can represent various types of debt instruments. See also *debt security token*.

digital certificate An electronic document that uses *cryptography* to verify the authenticity and identity of an entity (such as a website, organisation, or individual) in digital communications. It contains information about the entity's *public key*, identity details, and a *digital signature* from a trusted *Certificate Authority* (*CA*). Digital certificates are crucial components of *public key infrastructure* (*PKI*), enabling secure, encrypted communications and *authentication* over networks like the internet.

digital currency A broad term used to describe any *currency*, *money*, or money-like asset that exists purely in a digital form. There are several types of digital currencies and many ways of defining the subsets, sometimes conflicting. They can be regulated or unregulated, and some can be secured by *cryptography*. See also *cryptocurrency*, *Central Bank Digital Currency*, *crypto asset*, *eMoney*, *virtual asset*, and *virtual currency*.

digital divide The gap between individuals, households, businesses, or geographic areas with regard to their access to and use of information and communication technologies. This divide encompasses disparities in physical access to devices and internet connectivity, as well as differences in the skills, knowledge, and ability to effectively use digital technologies. Factors contributing to the digital divide include socioeconomic status, education level, age, geography, and infrastructure availability. The concept highlights inequalities in access to digital resources and the resulting disparities in opportunities for education, employment, healthcare, civic participation, and economic advancement in an increasingly digital world.

digital euro A proposed *Central Bank Digital Currency* (CBDC) issued by the European Central Bank, designed to be a digital form of the euro for use by households and businesses across the Eurozone, complementing cash and existing electronic payment methods.

digital identity Information used digitally to represent real-world identities, including individuals, organisations, applications, and devices. Digital identity can be used for a range of purposes and may offer benefits, ranging from *authentication* and *authorisation* of users for access to information and resources, to facilitating e-commerce and personalised digital experiences. Also see *eID*.

digital invoicing The electronic creation, transmission, and processing of invoices between suppliers and buyers, streamlining the payment process. These invoices are structured for automatic processing, reducing manual data entry and errors. Businesses can send digital invoices through various channels, including email, SMS, WhatsApp, or specialised payment platforms that offer "Pay by Link" functionality. Customers can receive and view these invoices on multiple devices and pay using various digital methods such as credit cards, bank transfers, or mobile wallets. This approach enhances efficiency, accelerates cash flow, improves customer experience, and supports regulatory compliance in the *fintech* ecosystem.

digital-only bank See *neo-bank*.

digital signature A cryptographic mechanism used to verify the authenticity, integrity, and non-repudiation of digital messages or documents. It is the electronic equivalent of a handwritten signature or seal, but with added security features. Using *public key cryptography*, a digital signature is created by encrypting a *hash* of the message with the sender's *private key*. Recipients can then use the sender's *public key* to decrypt the signature and verify that the message hasn't been altered and truly comes from the claimed sender. Digital signatures are widely used in various applications, including secure email, software distribution, and financial transactions, to ensure trust and security in digital communications.

digital twin A virtual representation of a real-world entity, system, or process that uses real-time data and advanced modelling techniques to simulate, analyse, and optimise its physical counterpart. In financial services and payments, digital twins can be applied to create virtual models of financial systems, payment networks, or customer behaviours. These models can be used to simulate market conditions, test new financial products, optimise payment processing, enhance *fraud detection*, and improve risk management. By leveraging digital twins, financial institutions can gain deeper insights into their operations, predict outcomes, and make data-driven decisions to enhance efficiency, security, and customer experience in areas such as transaction processing, *credit scoring*, and regulatory compliance. See also *machine customer*.

digital wallet A broad term used to describe a digital payment facility that enables digital transactions. See also *e-wallet*, *mobile wallet*, *pass-through digital wallet*, *stored value digital wallet*, *staged digital wallet*, and *crypto wallet*.

Direct Carrier Billing (DCB) An online *payment method* by which users can make purchases by charging the payment to their mobile phone bill for single or recurring payments. DCB is usually confined to digital goods, and spending limits may apply, but this will depend on the geography, mobile carrier, and applicable regulations. Two options are technically feasible: postpaid (purchase amount added to the mobile carrier's monthly bill) and prepaid (purchase amount deducted from the current load balance). Sometimes called Direct Mobile Billing (DMB).

direct CDBC A CBDC architecture model by which a CBDC is issued by a *central bank* which also maintains the ledger of all retail transactions, performs *retail settlement*, and offers accounts and services directly. *Onboarding*, *KYC*, and *authentication* may be performed by intermediaries. This model places significant operational and technical burden on the central bank and distracts from its main role of formulating *monetary policy*, acting as "bank to banks", being the "lender of last resort" and regulating the domestic banking system. There is no known deployment of this model, although Iceland explored this option. See also *intermediated CBDC (sCBDC)* and *multi-CBDC (mCBDC)*.

direct debit (DD) A type of payment on the *bank rails* that is used to make regular payments without needing to re-authorise once the direct debit is set up (e.g. utility bills and subscriptions). This is a type of *recurring transaction* and a type of *pull payment*.

direct deposit See *credit transfer*.

Directed Acyclic Graph (DAG) An implementation of *Distributed Ledger Technology (DLT)* designed as a mathematical construct offering a conceptual representation of the ordering of a series of activities that are represented by circles, some of which connected by lines representing the flow from one activity to another. Examples of implementations are NANO,[5] Obyte,[6] and IOTA.[7] See also *blockchain*, *Hashgraph*, and *Holochain*.

Direct Mobile Billing (DMB) Direct Mobile Billing. See *Direct Carrier Billing*.

direct participant A term used to describe bank payment scheme participants who are directly connected to the bank payment scheme. See also *directly connected settling participant*, *directly connected non-settling participant*, *principal*, and *indirect participant*.

direct payment instruction See *payment instruction*.

directly connected non-settling participant A bank *payment scheme* participant who can connect to the *payment scheme* but cannot settle funds directly with the payment scheme. These participants will settle funds through *directly connected settling participants*. These participants may offer payment scheme access services to *indirect participants*.

directly connected settling participant A bank *payment scheme* participant directly connected to the scheme and able to settle directly through the *settlement agent* for that scheme (a *central bank*) through their settlement account. These participants may offer payment scheme access and settlement services to *indirect participants* and *directly connected non-settling participants*. See also *RTGS account*.

Directory Server In the cards world, the Directory Server is the element within the interoperability domain (*card scheme*) that enables communication between the *3DS Server (3DSS)* (*acquiring* domain) and the *Access Control Server (ACS)* (*issuing* domain). It validates and routes *3D Secure* messages to authenticate the *cardholder* during the transaction process. Both the ACS and the 3DSS need to be enrolled by the Directory Server.

Discover[8] A *card scheme* operating according to the *three-party model*.

discretionary data Data on a payment card representing the balance of digits available on *Track 1* (79 digits), *Track 2* (40 digits), and the *EMV chip* (40 digits) after the *Primary Account Number (PAN)*, cardholder name, and *service code*. It is used by *issuers* pretty much as they see fit. For example, they may use the discretionary data to create new card products with specific characteristics (e.g. a student card) or for security. On Tracks 1 and 2 of the *magnetic stripe*, it may include *PIN* verification elements like the *CVV1*. On the chip, it will contain the *iCVV*.

distributed ledger A database that is shared, replicated, and synchronised across multiple locations or entities. Unlike traditional centralised databases, a distributed ledger allows all participants to have access to the same data in real-time, enhancing transparency and security. This technology underpins *cryptocurrencies* and various *blockchain* applications, enabling secure and tamper-proof record-keeping without the need for a central authority. See also *Distributed Ledger Technology*.

Distributed Ledger Technology (DLT) A type of distributed database enabling the storage, recording, and sharing of digital information between consenting parties where the data is spread across multiple sites, regions, or participants. Each of the data stores, the ledgers, has the same data records and is maintained and controlled through a distributed network of computer servers referred to as *nodes*. DLT is based on *peer-to-peer networking*, where peers communicate with each other without the need for a central authority or intermediary. The integrity and security of the ledger, as well as the validation of updates to the ledger, are governed by the *consensus protocol* of the system. *Blockchain* is a form of DLT, but there are others, such as Hashgraph, Directed Acyclic Graph (DAG), Holochain, and Tempo (Radix). See also *centralised ledger.*

distribution The process of spreading or allocating resources, products, or information across different locations, entities, or individuals. Unlike *decentralisation,* which focuses on dispersing control and decision-making authority, distribution primarily concerns the physical or logical arrangement of elements. Distribution can occur within centralised or decentralised systems and often involves the organised dissemination of goods, services, or data from a source to multiple recipients. In various contexts, distribution can refer to

The delivery of products to consumers or businesses

The allocation of resources or wealth across a population

The geographical spread of natural phenomena or populations

The arrangement of data points in statistical analysis

Whilst *decentralisation* aims to redistribute power and control, distribution focusses on the efficient and effective spread of tangible or intangible assets without necessarily altering the underlying power structure.

DLT See *Distributed Ledger Technology.*

DMB See *Direct Carrier Billing.*

Doge The smallest subdivision of a *DOGE* where 100,000,000 Doge represent one DOGE. The unit of measurement for *Dogecoin* transaction costs. See also *Dogecoin* and *gas price.*

Dogecoin (DOGE) A *layer 1 blockchain* using the *Proof-of-work consensus protocol.* A *permissionless blockchain.* Also refers to the native Dogecoin *cryptocurrency* (*coin*), abbreviated as DOGE. See also *Doge, cryptocurrency, meme coin,* and *altcoin.*

double-spending A term referring to the attempted spending of the same funds twice, which creates a discrepancy between the actual amount of funds available and how it is recorded on a ledger. Double-spending is extremely improbable in centralised payment systems because they have mature processes, established regulations, robust security, and trusted intermediaries who oversee all transactions, from *payment instruction* to *settlement.* Double-spending is an issue for *blockchain* infrastructures as they don't rely on trusted intermediaries and operate a distributed trust model where participating *nodes* ensure the integrity of the system. In order to prevent double-spending, blockchains use various mechanisms including the *consensus protocol*, the validation of transactions by nodes before they are added to the blockchain ledger, and timestamping of transactions. See also *replay attack*.

domestic card scheme A *card scheme* which operates only in one geography. Also referred to as "local card scheme". *Issuers* can also issue cards that are cobranded between a domestic card scheme and an *open-loop* scheme (see *cobranded card*), in which case, these cards can be used domestically (through the domestic card scheme) and internationally (through the *open loop card* scheme, such as Visa or Mastercard).

domestic settlement A *settlement* that takes place in the country where both counterparties to a transaction are located.

domestic transaction A transaction where the *payer's* and *payee's* payment accounts are managed by entities located in the same jurisdiction.

DPoS See *Delegated Proof of Stake*.

DSA Digital Signature Algorithm. A *public key cryptography* algorithm.

DSAR See *Data Subject Access Request*.

DTMF masking See *Dual Tone Multi-Frequency (DTMF) masking*.

Dual Tone Multi-Frequency (DTMF) masking A technology deployed in telephone operations where the consumer enters their *Primary Account Number (PAN)*, expiry date, and *Card Verification Value (CVV)* using their telephone keypad during a telephone payment transaction, rather than speaking their payment card data. The telephone agent will not hear the phone tones (as these could be used to derive digits and therefore card numbers), helping with security and *Payment Card Industry Data Security Standard (PCI DSS)* compliance.

due date The date by which a payment is due to take place. For *payment instruments* involving interest-bearing *credit* (such as a credit card), this is the date the payment is due after which interest, or penalties, may apply. For forward-date payments, this is the scheduled date when the payment will be made.

due diligence The process of conducting the relevant checks that a business or person should perform before entering into an agreement or contract with another party. See also *Customer Due Diligence* and *Enhanced Due Diligence*.

DuitNow[9] An *account-to-account payment* service in Malaysia.

Durbin Amendment[10] A US regulation that caps *interchange* fees on debit cards. This was an amendment to the Dodd–Frank Act in 2010.

DvP See *Delivery-versus-Payment*.

Dynamic Currency Conversion (DCC) A value-added service that can be sold to merchants by *Payment Service Providers (PSPs)* or *Independent Software Vendors (ISVs)*. It enables cardholders to see the amount of their transaction displayed in either their home currency or the local currency when using their card abroad. This service relies on a pricing structure involving exchange rates, conversion fees, and transaction fees. Sometimes called Cardholder Preferred Currency (CPC).

dynamic CVV An enhancement to the card verification process whereby an *issuer* supplies the cardholder with a little device as well as a card. The little device calculates a dynamic CVV (dCVV) each time a remote transaction is initiated by the cardholder, and this is the three-digit number that the cardholder would use on an e-commerce website or over the telephone. This can also be achieved through the card itself, where a small electronic screen is embedded directly onto the back of the card to perform the same function. It is meant to replace the static *CVV2* that is printed on payment cards. The cost of production of these cards/devices is such that deployments are somewhat rare. See also *Card Verification Value*.

dynamic gas fee A "base fee" set by some *blockchain protocols* which validating nodes must use to calculate the transaction fee (the base fee can be changed at any time through blockchain governance according to a number of factors, including network congestion). This is a governance method to manage blockchain operations. In this model, users don't set the *gas price*.

dynamic pricing A strategy where businesses adjust prices in real-time based on current market demand, supply conditions, competitor pricing, and other relevant factors. This flexible pricing model uses algorithms and data analysis to optimise prices, aiming to maximise revenue or profit. It's commonly used in industries with perishable inventory or fluctuating demand, such as *e-commerce*, hospitality, and transportation. Dynamic pricing allows companies to respond quickly to market changes, capitalise on peak demand periods, and stimulate sales during slower times.

dynamic routing The process and technology used to simplify and optimise *payment acceptance* for businesses by routing payment transactions in real time to the most suitable *acquirer* or PSP (e.g. *payment gateway*), with the objective of enhancing *authorisation* success rates, reducing failed transactions, reducing downtime impact, distributing payment load, and lowering transaction processing costs. See also *payment orchestration*.

Notes

1 Dankort. https://dankort.dk/ (Accessed 21 November 2023)
2 Target REDcard Debit. https://www.target.com/redcard/debit-card-application (Accessed 18 January 2024)
3 What Is a BRICS Currency and Is the U.S. Dollar in Trouble? *Reuters*, 24 August 2023. https://www.reuters.com/markets/currencies/what-is-brics-currency-could-one-be-adopted-2023-08-23/ (Accessed 9 January 2024)
4 DIAS. https://www.dias.com.gr/en/about-us/ (Accessed 21 November 2023)
5 NANO. https://nano.org/en (Accessed 12 January 2024)
6 Obyte. https://obyte.org/ (Accessed 12 January 2024)
7 IOTA. https://www.iota.org/ (Accessed 12 January 2024)
8 Discover. https://www.discover.com/ (Accessed 21 November 2023)
9 DuitNow. https://www.duitnow.my/ (Accessed 21 November 2023)
10 Legal Information Institute. (Durbin Amendment). https://www.law.cornell.edu/uscode/text/15/16930-2 (Accessed 21 November 2023)

E

E IS FOR...

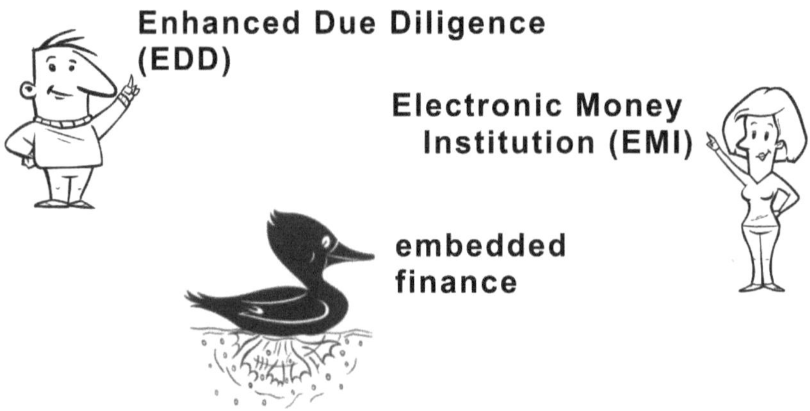

early termination fee A fee that may be charged to merchants by the provider of their card payment facility, such as an *acquirer*, in the event that a merchant should terminate their agreement before the end of the specified period of time therein.

EBA See *European Banking Authority*.

DOI: 10.4324/9781003571131-6

EBA clearing (STEP2 & RT1)[1] A bank *payment scheme* provided by EBA clearing and used in *SEPA* countries such as Germany, which doesn't have its own domestic bank payment scheme.

EBS[2] A real-time payment system (RTP system), retail payment system (RPS) in South Korea, operated by KFTC.

ECA See *Electronic Cheque Acceptance.*

ECB See *European Central Bank.*

ECDSA Elliptic Curve Digital Signature Algorithm. A *public key cryptography* algorithm.

ECI See *Electronic Commerce Indicator.*

eCheck Electronic Check. In the US, where cheques are still widely used, this is a digital representation of a paper cheque where money is electronically withdrawn from the *payer's* bank (checking) account and transferred over an *ACH* network and eventually credited to the payer's account. A type of *ACH payment.*

eclipse attack A type of network-level threat in *peer-to-peer* systems where a malicious actor isolates a target node from the rest of the network by monopolising all of its connections. The attacker floods the target with connections to nodes under their control, effectively "eclipsing" the victim from legitimate network activity. This isolation allows the attacker to manipulate the target's view of the network, potentially enabling *double-spending*, disrupting *mining* operations, or compromising the node's ability to verify transactions accurately. Eclipse attacks exploit limitations in peer discovery and connection protocols, posing risks to *blockchain* networks' security and *decentralisation.*

eCNY The Chinese *Central Bank Digital Currency* (CBDC).

e-commerce The sale of purchase of goods and services through electronic transactions conducted online over the internet or other digital networks. Also spelled "ecommerce".

economic crime The illegal acts committed to obtain financial or economic gain, encompassing a wide range of offenses such as financial fraud (e.g. wire transfer scams and credit card fraud), *money laundering*, bribery, corruption, embezzlement, identity theft, tax fraud, investment fraud, insurance fraud, *cybercrime*, and intellectual property theft.

economic node A generic term used to describe a participant in a *blockchain* network that engages in the network's economic activities, such as *staking* cryptocurrency or providing *liquidity*, without necessarily contributing to block validation or consensus. These nodes help secure the network through financial incentives rather than computational power, and they typically earn rewards for their participation, which may include transaction fees or newly minted tokens. Economic nodes can include staking nodes in *Proof-of-Stake* systems, liquidity providers in *decentralised finance* (*DeFi*) platforms, and other participants that support the network's financial ecosystem whilst maintaining lower technical requirements compared to *full nodes* or *validators*.

ecosystem A business ecosystem is an arrangement by which participants will create value for a common set of customers and share the benefits of value creation. Every business ecosystem has participants, and at least one member acts as the orchestrator of the participants. The most famous ecosystem is Amazon. A notable difference between an ecosystem and a *value chain* is that an ecosystem is not necessarily built around a fixed chain of processes and is all about seizing opportunities and innovating. The payments industry is at various stages of transitioning between value chains and ecosystems.

ECP See *Excessive Chargebacks Program*.

EDD See *Enhanced Due Diligence*.

edge AI The deployment of *artificial intelligence* algorithms and models directly on edge devices or local edge servers, rather than in centralised cloud data centres. This approach enables real-time data processing, analysis, and decision-making at or near the source of data generation, reducing latency and bandwidth requirements, whilst enhancing privacy and security. In the payments industry, edge AI can be applied to enable faster and more secure transaction processing, real-time *fraud detection*, personalised customer experiences, and improved point-of-sale systems. By processing sensitive financial data locally, edge AI helps maintain data privacy and compliance with regulations, whilst allowing for quick, intelligent decision-making in payment scenarios, even in environments with limited connectivity.

edge computing A distributed computing paradigm that brings data processing and storage closer to the sources of data generation, such as *Internet of Things* (*IoT*) devices, sensors, or local servers, rather than relying on a centralised cloud or data centre. This approach reduces latency, conserves network bandwidth, enhances real-time capabilities, and improves data privacy and security. By processing data near its origin, edge computing enables faster response times, more efficient use of network resources, and the ability to operate in environments with limited connectivity. It is particularly useful for applications requiring rapid decision-making, such as autonomous vehicles, industrial automation, and smart cities.

EDI See *Electronic Data Interchange.*

EFT See *Electronic Funds Transfer.*

EFTPOS Electronic Funds Transfer at the Point of Sale. See *electronic Point of Sale.*

eID A generic term to describe electronic identification to ensure secure access to government services, other online services, or carry out payment transactions.

eIDAS[3] Electronic Identification and trust services. A European regulatory framework aiming to ensure that people and businesses can use their own national electronic identification schemes (eIDs) to access public services available online in other EU countries.

EKS[4] Elektroniskā Klīringa Sistēma. Latvia's domestic bank *payment scheme.*

Elavon[5] An *acquirer.*

Electronic Check Acceptance (ECA) A term mostly used in the US. A system that captures banking information from a paper cheque and converts it into data that can be processed through the *ACH* network. The clearing cycle is usually shorter than for paper cheques. Also called "cheque imaging" in other countries, including the UK. To users, the image capture is usually done through the mobile banking app. See also *eCheck.*

Electronic Commerce Indicator (ECI) A number that is returned by the *Directory Server* and *Access Control Server (ACS)* indicating the outcome of *authentication* requested on transactions for *3D Secure.* Merchants can use ECI values to determine whether to proceed to authorisation or not. For example, an ECI value of 05 or 02 means that the authentication was successful, whilst a value of 07 or 00 means that the authentication failed.

Electronic Data Interchange (EDI) A mature electronic data exchange format which has been around since the 1960s, used between organisations across industries, typically used to format and exchange business documents electronically (e.g. purchase orders, invoices, and shipping notices). EDI represents a set of standards that are used in different industries, including manufacturing, healthcare, logistics, retail, and finance. The most well-known formats are ANSI X12 and EDIFACT. Whilst EDI is still used in financial services, there are other standards that are specifically focused on the financial services sector, such as *ISO 8583* and *ISO 20022*. See also XML.

Electronic Funds Transfer (EFT) A catch-all term used to describe electronic transfer of funds between financial institutions.

electronic money See *eMoney*.

Electronic Money Institution (EMI) A regulated payment business allowed to manage *eMoney* on behalf of its users. In Europe, there are two types of eMoney institutions, the *Small eMoney Institution* (SEMI) and the *authorised eMoney Institution* (EMI). In some geographies, these may be referred to as a Money Service Business (MSB). Electronic money institutions may be called Payments Banks in India or Fintech Banks in the US.

Electronic Payments Network (EPN)[6] A US *ACH retail payment system* (RPS) operated by *The Clearing House* (TCH) and governed by *NACHA*.

Electronic Point-of-Sale (EPOS) An EPOS system is a combination of hardware and software designed to help merchants accept card payments and run their business more effectively. Some providers specialise in specific industries and provide turnkey solutions (e.g. hospitality and retail). Their functionality may include features such as sales management, accounting, data collection, product, and stock management, as well as the capability to accept payments. Modern EPOS systems may include technologies such as touchscreen and apps. A type of *Point-of-Sale* (POS) system.

Electrum[7] A *crypto wallet*.

Embark A development framework for building and deploying *decentralised applications (dApps)* on *blockchain* platforms, primarily *Ethereum*. It provides a comprehensive suite of tools that streamline the development process, including *smart contract* management, front-end integration, and testing capabilities. Embark supports multiple blockchain protocols and allows developers to easily create, manage, and deploy their dApps whilst facilitating seamless interaction with decentralised storage and communication systems. Its modular architecture and built-in features enhance productivity and simplify the complexities of dApp development, making it accessible for both beginners and experienced developers.

embedded finance Describes services that integrate financial services including lending, payment processing, or insurance into non-financial business infrastructures, processes, or customer journeys. See also *Banking-as-a-Service* and *merchant financing*.

embedded payments The integration of payment processing functionality directly within a software platform or application, allowing users to make transactions seamlessly without being redirected to external payment systems. This approach enables businesses to offer a unified user experience, streamline the payment process, and maintain control over the entire customer journey. Embedded payments typically leverage *Application Programming Interfaces (APIs)* to connect with payment processors, handling tasks such as *authentication*, *authorisation*, and *settlement* behind the scenes. By incorporating payments natively into their software, companies can enhance user convenience, reduce friction in transactions, and potentially generate additional revenue through payment processing fees.

embossed elements Data elements contained in a card that are slightly raised from the surface of the physical card. Data elements may include the *Primary Account Number (PAN)*, the start date, the expiry date, the cardholder name, and the *sort code* and *bank account number* (where present on some *debit cards*). The embossed elements are present so the card can be used in a *card imprinting machine*.

EMD agent In Europe, a small business that acts as an *agent* of an *Authorised eMoney Institution (EMI)*, the latter being referred to as the *principal*.

EMI See *Electronic Money Institution*.

eMoney A type of *virtual asset* functioning as an electronic store of value that acts as a cash substitute and is issued by regulated entities (e.g. an e-money Institution in the EU, an entity operating under the US Special Purpose National Bank Charter, or a "Payments Bank" in India, or banks in general). E-money may be used for making payments to entities other than the issuer (unlike a virtual currency). Types of e-money include prepaid cards, electronic prepaid accounts, and virtual payment accounts for use online. Also spelled "eMoney", "eMoney", "e-money", and "emoney". A notable example is PayPal.

eMoney Institution See *Electronic Money Institution*.

EMV The set of standards for cards, managed by *EMVCo*.

EMV card A credit or debit card that follows the *EMV Chip* standard. Also called a "chip card" and historically a "smart card".

EMV Chip An *EMV* standard for *chip cards*. The EMV chip itself is an integrated circuit consisting of a microprocessor and a memory constructed according to ISO/IEC 7816 (contact) and ISO/IEC 14443 (contactless). The chip contains the data required for EMV transactions at the *Point-of-Sale (POS)*.

EMVCo[8] A consortium controlled equally by Visa, Mastercard, American Express, UnionPay, and Discover. EMVCo is responsible for developing and maintaining EMV card standards. EMV takes its initials from Eurocard, Mastercard, and Visa, the original founders in 1999. In 2002, Mastercard merged with Europay International SA, the owners of the Eurocard brand. Whilst the Europay name disappeared, the EMV name remains.

eNaira The Nigerian *Central Bank Digital Currency (CBDC)*.

encryption The process by which data is encrypted and decrypted. See also *cryptography* and *Secure Element*.

Enhanced Due Diligence (EDD) The process by which businesses perform more stringent *Customer Due Diligence (CDD)* on customers at the underwriting stage or during the course of a business relationship. EDD is usually performed where the customer is not present when KYC is performed, when *Politically Exposed Persons (PEPs)* are involved, where the nature of the customer's business changes, where there is a high risk of *money laundering* or terrorism financing, or where the customer is in a high-risk country. See also *sanction*.

EOSIO An *open-source* blockchain platform designed for building and deploying high-performance *dApps*. Developed by Block.one, it uses a Delegated Proof-of-Stake (DPoS) *consensus protocol* and features a WebAssembly (WASM) C++ development environment. EOSIO aims to provide scalability, flexibility, and user-friendly experiences by offering fast transaction speeds, low latency, and fee-less transactions for users. The platform includes tools for *smart contract* development, account management, and resource allocation, making it suitable for a wide range of *blockchain* applications from *decentralised finance (DeFi)* to supply chain management.

EPC payment scheme[9] The European Payments Council (EPC) payment schemes are used by thousands of *Payment Service Providers (PSPs)* across Europe. To the EPC, a payment scheme represents the set of rules which PSPs have agreed upon to execute transactions through a specific *payment instrument* (e.g. credit transfer and direct debit) and doesn't include the infrastructure to deliver them. Elsewhere, what is generally referred to as a "payment scheme" (i.e. *card scheme* and bank payment scheme) is the set of governing rules as well as the technical infrastructure that processes transactions (the EPC refers to these as "*payment systems*").

EPI See *European Payments Initiative.*

epoch length The duration of an operational cycle in a *PoS* blockchain, typically expressed in time intervals (seconds and days) or number of blocks. It defines the period between the creation of epoch boundary blocks, during which *validators* actively participate in block validation and consensus. Epoch length influences network security, transaction confirmation speed, and overall efficiency. Shorter epochs may lead to faster *block finality* but potential instability, whilst longer epochs can enhance security at the cost of slower confirmations. Blockchain designers use this metric to balance scalability, security, and efficiency in the network's operation.

EPOS See *Electronic Point-of-Sale.*

EPN See *Electronic Payments Network.*

Equens Worldline[10] A payment *clearing* and *settlement* infrastructure provider in Europe and other geographies. The Netherlands' domestic bank payment scheme is an example.

Equifax[11] A *credit bureau.*

equity token A type of *security token* created through *tokenisation* that represents ownership in an asset, typically shares in a company. Equity tokens function similarly to traditional stocks, providing holders with rights such as voting and profit-sharing, but are issued and traded on a *blockchain.* Tokenisation allows for *fractional ownership,* increased *liquidity,* and automated dividend distribution through *smart contracts.* Equity tokens are subject to security regulations in most jurisdictions. See also *security.*

escrow A legal arrangement where a third party (the escrow agent/holder) holds assets, such as money or property, temporarily until specific conditions of a transaction are met, ensuring all parties fulfil their obligations before the assets are released.

ESG An acronym for Environmental, Social, and Governance. This term is often used interchangeably with "sustainability" and represents a set of standards measuring the impact a business has on the environment, society, and how transparent and accountable the business is. In recent years, investors increasingly consider ESG factors when making business investment decisions. Depending on the jurisdiction, businesses, especially large ones, may have regulatory obligations to report on some ESG factors (e.g. carbon footprint, diversity, and inclusion). See also *greenwashing.*

ETF See *Exchange Traded Fund.*

Ethereum (ETH)[12] A *layer 1 blockchain* using the *Proof-of-stake consensus protocol*. Prior to "The Merge" in September 2022, the Ethereum *blockchain* used the PoW *consensus protocol*. Also refers to the native Ethereum *cryptocurrency* (*coin*), abbreviated as ETH. See also *Gwei*.

Ethereum Virtual Machine See *EVM*.

eToro[13] A social trading and multi-asset investment company that is also a *crypto exchange*.

European Banking Authority (EBA)[14] An independent EU authority which works to ensure effective and consistent prudential regulation and supervision across the European banking sector.

European *Central Bank* (ECB)[15] Together with the national *central banks* of the EU Member States whose currency is the euro, the ECB defines and implements the *monetary policy* for the euro area.

European Payments Initiative (EPI)[16] In February 2021, 31 major European banks created a joint venture with *acquirers* Worldline and Nets (now owned by Nexi), aiming to build a pan-European network to rival Visa and Mastercard. In March 2022, the EPI seemingly disbanded, but in April 2023, at the time P27 collapsed, in a surprising move, the EPI acquired Dutch payment scheme iDeal and Belgian mobile payments App Payconiq, progress which was welcomed by the European *Central Bank*. In September 2024, rolled out the *Wero* wallet across much of Europe.[17] Watch this space, as this may very well become the EU equivalent of the American *Zelle*.

Europe Zone 1 A geographical zone determined by *EMVCo* that includes the following countries: Andorra, Austria, Belgium, Bulgaria, Cyprus, the Czech Republic, Denmark, Estonia, Finland, France, Germany, Gibraltar, Greece, Greenland, Hungary, Iceland, Ireland, Israel, Italy, Liechtenstein, Latvia, Lithuania, Luxembourg, Malta, the Netherlands, New Caledonia, Norway, Poland, Portugal, Romania, Slovak Republic, Slovenia, Spain, Sweden, Switzerland, Turkey, and the UK. The other zones are "Canada, Latin America and the Caribbean", "Asia Pacific", "*Europe Zone 2*", and the United States.

Europe Zone 2 A geographical zone determined by *EMVCo* that includes the following countries: Albania, Armenia, Azerbaijan, Belarus, Bosnia & Herzegovina, Croatia, Georgia, Kazakhstan, Kyrgyzstan, Macedonia, Moldova, Serbia & Montenegro, Tajikistan, Turkmenistan, Russia, Ukraine, and Uzbekistan. The other zones are "Canada, Latin America and the Caribbean", "Asia Pacific", "*Europe Zone 1*", and the United States.

Eurosystem The central banking system of the euro area. It comprises the ECB and the national central banks of those EU Member States whose currency is the euro.

EVM (Ethereum Virtual Machine) A *Virtual Machine (VM)* specific to the *Ethereum blockchain*. The EVM establishes a standard environment for *smart contract* execution, promoting interoperability and simplifying development. Additionally, the isolated execution within the EVM enhances security and fosters decentralisation by distributing smart contract execution across the network. Finally, the EVM offers a developer-friendly approach, allowing programmers to use existing tools and languages to create smart contracts, making blockchain development more accessible. In essence, the EVM acts as a virtual computer within the Ethereum blockchain, executing the code behind *dApps* in a secure, standardised, and developer-friendly manner.

e-wallet A generic term used to describe a web application that can be accessed from any connected device and is used to make payments, usually with several funding options (e.g. cards and bank accounts). PayPal is an example of an e-wallet. Also spelled "ewallet".

eW IP CSM A *real-time payment system (RTP system)*, *retail payment system* (RPS) in The Netherlands, operated by Equens Worldline.

exception A term used to describe what happens when a card transaction is questioned or doesn't go as expected. Exceptions can lead to *cardholder* disputes. Types of exceptions include *retrievals*, *refunds*, and *chargebacks*.

Excessive Chargebacks Program (ECP)[18] A Mastercard *merchant monitoring programme* for *chargeback* control. In general, merchants will be included in a *card scheme* chargeback-monitoring programme if their *chargeback ratio* exceeds the card scheme limit.

exchange token A type of *utility token* which is only used in a specific *crypto exchange*.

Exchange Traded Fund (ETF) A type of investment fund that is traded on stock exchanges, generally tracking a specific index, market, or group of markets. They are offered by funds managers who charge a fee for their services, and investors usually use them for short-term returns and ETFs are taxed for capital gains. They are designed to provide investors with the flexibility to buy and sell a diversified portfolio of assets, such as stocks, bonds, commodities, or other financial instruments in a single security. Increasingly, *cryptocurrency* ETFs have emerged, where they track the performance of the underlying asset (e.g. *Bitcoin*), allowing investors to gain exposure to Bitcoin without actually owning the asset. Cryptocurrency ETFs are increasingly attracting regulatory scrutiny.

exemption In the context of the EU *Second Payment Services Directive* (PSD2), an exemption allows a transaction to take place without adhering to the *Strong Consumer Authentication (SCA)* requirement. Examples include low-value transactions (below €30), whitelisting/trusted beneficiaries, *Transaction Risk Analysis*, and secure corporate payments.

Exemption Threshold Value (ETV) A fraud indicator used in the context of the PSD2 *Transaction Risk Analysis (TRA)* exemption to *Strong Customer Authentication (SCA)*, representing a maximum transaction amount. The ETVs are specified as follows: up to €100, up to €250, and up to €500. A transaction may qualify for the TRA *exemption* if its value is below the relevant ETV for that transaction type and the business complies with the *Reference Fraud Rate* for that transaction type.

Exodus[19] A *crypto wallet*.

Experian[20] A *credit bureau*.

expiry date The date until which a payment card is valid.

explainable AI (XAI) Methods and techniques used to make *artificial intelligence* systems more transparent and interpretable to humans. It aims to provide clear explanations for AI decisions, predictions, and behaviours, allowing users to understand the reasoning behind AI outputs. In the payments industry, XAI is crucial for building trust in AI-powered systems that handle sensitive financial transactions. It helps explain decisions related to *fraud detection*, *credit scoring*, risk assessment, and personalised financial recommendations. XAI enables payment providers to justify automated decisions to customers, regulators, and internal stakeholders, ensuring compliance with financial regulations, detecting potential biases, and improving the overall reliability and accountability of AI-driven payment processes.

Notes

1 EBA Clearing. https://www.ebaclearing.eu/ (Accessed 21 November 2023)

2 Bank of Korea. https://www.bok.or.kr/eng/main/contents.do?menuNo=400045 (Accessed 21 November 2023)

3 European Commission. (eIDAS Regulation). https://digital-strategy.ec.europa.eu/en/policies/eidas-regulation (Accessed 21 November 2023)

4 Latvijas Banka. https://gadaparskats.latvijasbanka.lv/en/2022/operational-areas-of-latvijas-banka/payment-and-settlement-systems (Accessed 21 November 2023)

5 Elavon. https://www.elavon.com/ (Accessed 21 November 2023)

6 The Clearing House, ACH. https://www.theclearinghouse.org/payment-systems/ACH (Accessed 21 November 2023)

7 Electrum. https://electrum.org/ (Accessed 21 November 2023)

8 EMVCo. https://www.emvco.com/ (Accessed 21 November 2023)

9 European Payments Council (Payment Schemes). https://www.europeanpaymentscouncil.eu/what-we-do/sepa-payment-schememanagement/what-payment-scheme (Accessed 21 November 2023)

10 Worldline. https://worldline.com/en/home/top-navigation/mediarelations/press-release/equensworldline-becomes-eurozone%E2%80%99s-largest-processor-of-instant-payments-with-dutch-launch.html (Accessed 21 November 2023)

11 Equifax. https://www.equifax.com/ (Accessed 28 November 2023)

12 Ethereum. https://ethereum.org/en/ (Accessed 21 November 2023)

13 eToro. https://www.etoro.com (Accessed 21 November 2023)

14 European Banking Authority. https://www.eba.europa.eu/(Accessed 21 November 2023)

15 European Central Bank. https://www.ecb.europa.eu/home/html/index.en.html (Accessed 21 November 2023)

16 European Payments Initiative. https://www.epicompany.eu/(Accessed 21 November 2023)

17 EU Banks Launch Wero Payments to Dislodge Visa, Mastercard. Bloomberg, 27 September 2024. https://www.bnnbloomberg.ca/business/2024/09/27/europes-banks-launch-wero-payments-to-dislodge-visamastercard/ (Accessed 28 September 2024)

18 Mastercard. https://www.mastercard.us/en-us/business/overview/support/rules.html (Accessed 21 November 2023)

19 Exodus. https://www.exodus.com/ (Accessed 21 November 2023)

20 Experian. https://www.experian.com/ (Accessed 28 November 2023)

F

F IS FOR...

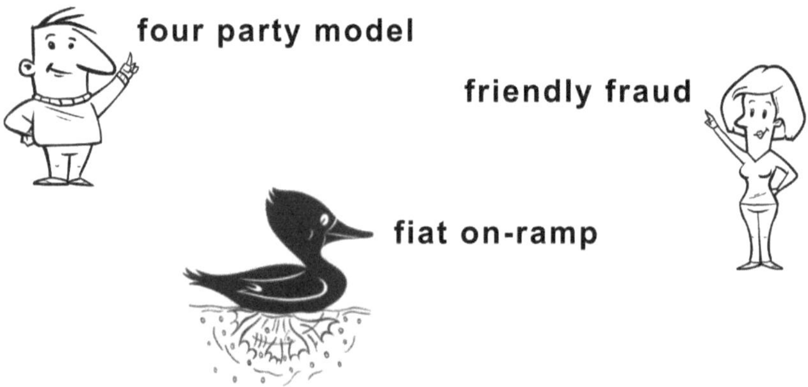

Face ID Apple's implementation of *biometrics* for facial recognition, which can be used as a form of *authentication* for accessing accounts or making payments. See also *delegated authentication.*

Face-to-Face (F2F) payment A payment transaction carried out where the *payer* and the *payee* are both physically present in the same physical location.

DOI: 10.4324/9781003571131-7

factoring See *merchant financing*. (not to be confused with *card factoring*).

FAANG An acronym for Facebook (now Meta), Apple, Amazon, Netflix, and Alphabet (Google's parent company). These platforms are increasingly involved in payments and financial services. See also *Big Tech*, *BATX*, *GAFA*, *MAMAA*, and *FANG*.

failed transaction A transaction that does not settle on the contractual *settlement* date. Such a transaction may be retained and may settle at a later stage. See also *due date*.

fallback A generic term used to describe the mechanisms in place to complete a transaction if the original means are not available. For example, a fallback transaction would occur when a *EMV* chip card presented at a *chip card* reader can't be read, resulting in the transaction "falling back" to reading the *magnetic stripe*. Similarly, when a card terminal is unavailable, card transactions may have to "fall back" to a *card imprinting machine*.

false decline A situation where a valid card transaction is declined either due to the merchant's *fraud prevention* system or the *issuer* mistakenly judging the attempted transaction to be fraudulent. False declines are also referred to as false positives.

false positive See *false decline*.

FANG An acronym for Facebook (now Meta), Amazon, Netflix, and Alphabet (Google's parent company). These platforms are increasingly involved in payments and financial services. See also *Big Tech*, *BATX*, *GAFA*, *MAMAA*, and *FAANG*.

FAST A *real-time payment system* (*RTP system*), *retail payment system* (RPS) in Singapore,[1] operated by BCS. Also a real-time RPS in Turkey,[2] operated by TCMB.

Fast IDentity Online (FIDO)[3] A set of standards for *authentication* protocols ultimately aimed at eliminating passwords. The standards (e.g. WebAuthn) are managed by the FIDO Alliance, an open industry association with members from across the globe, including Amazon, Apple, Bank of America, American Express, Google, Intel, Idemia, Meta, PayPal, and many others.

Faster Payments System (FPS) A bank *payment scheme*. A UK domestic *real-time payment system* (*RTP system*), *retail payment system* (RPS) that operates on a deferred net settlement basis. The FPS[4] was launched in 2008 and is the UK RTP system for payments up to £1 million. It allows customers to make electronic payments almost instantaneously, 7 days/week, 24 hours/day. FPS is managed by Pay.UK. Also an RPS in Hong Kong,[5] operated by HKICL. Also an RPS in Russia,[6] operated by CBR.

FATF See *Financial Action Task Force.*

FATF Travel Rule See *Travel Rule.*

Fawri+[7] An *account-to-account payment* service in Bahrain.

FDP See *forward-dated payment.*

FedACH[8] A US *ACH scheme, retail payment system* (*RPS*) operated by the Federal Reserve Bank and governed by NACHA.

FedNow[9] A US A *real-time payment system* (*RTP system*), *retail payment system* (RPS) operated by the Federal Reserve Bank and governed by NACHA. A bank *payment scheme* that launched in July 2023.

Fedwire[10] A US *Large Value Payment System* (*LVPS*) governed by NACHA and operated by the Federal Reserve Bank. A bank *payment scheme.* See also *wire transfer.*

Fedwire number See *ABA routing number.*

Fei ch'ien A *barter system* in China.

fiat-collateralised stablecoin A type of *stablecoin* designed to maintain a stable value relative to a *fiat currency*, typically the US dollar, through a 1:1 backing of reserves. These stablecoins maintain a *hard peg* to the target fiat currency, aiming for a strict 1:1 exchange rate. The issuer holds reserves of the fiat currency in bank accounts or other financial instruments equal to the number of stablecoins in circulation. Examples include USDT and USDC. Fiat-collateralised stablecoins are typically centralised and subject to regular audits to verify their reserves. Also called "fiat-backed stablecoin".

fiat currency Government-issued currency that is not backed by a physical commodity, such as gold or silver, but rather by the government that issued it. It derives its value from supply and demand and the stability of the issuing government. Fiat currency gives *central banks* greater control over the economy, as they can control how much money is printed. Fiat currency has, therefore, no intrinsic value, and it is often referred to as "paper money". Governments have to make it *legal tender* by setting it as the standard for debt repayment. Most modern currencies are fiat money. Also referred to as fiat money. See also *money.*

fiat on-ramp See *on-ramp*.

FIDO See *Fast IDentity Online*.

finality An irrevocable and unconditional transfer of funds from one party to another, which occurs during *settlement*.

Financial Action Task Force (FATF)[11] An independent intergovernmental body that develops and promotes policies to protect the global financial system against *money laundering*, *terrorist financing*, and the financing of the proliferation of weapons of mass destruction. The FATF is also known as GAFI (Groupe d'Action Financière) and is headquartered in Paris. The FATF identifies countries with weak *anti-money laundering* controls and lists them in two public documents that are published three times a year: the *black list* and the *grey list*.

financial crime A term referring to all crimes committed by an individual or a group of individuals involving unlawfully obtaining *money* or other property that belongs to someone else to obtain a financial or professional gain. In regulatory terms, financial crime may include any offence involving (a) fraud or dishonesty; (b) misconduct in, or misuse of information relating to, a financial market; or (c) handling the proceeds of crime. See also *money laundering*.

financial inclusion Refers to the ability of individuals or businesses to have access to financial services.

fintech A very broad term used to describe any business that uses technology to improve, digitise, automate, or provide enablers to financial services aimed at businesses or consumers.

first party fraud A type of fraud that happens when a payment account holder knowingly commits fraud, for example, when a cardholder tries to get money back on a purchase they made and for which they have received the goods. Also referred to as "friendly fraud", although there is nothing friendly about it, and "cyber-shoplifting".

FIS Group[12] A financial services company. Also an *acquirer*.

Fiserv[13] A financial services company. Also an *acquirer*.

flash loan A type of uncollateralised lending in *DeFi* where a user borrows and repays funds within a single *blockchain* transaction. The loan is facilitated by *smart contracts*, requiring no collateral as the borrowed amount must be returned before the transaction completes, or the entire operation is reversed. Flash loans are often used for *arbitrage*, liquidations, or other complex DeFi strategies.

floor limit On the *card rails*, this is the maximum value the card terminal allows for a transaction when processed offline. Transactions below the floor limit will be automatically authorised. See also *authorisation*.

force majeure chargeback A *chargeback* made using the reason of "force majeure" which releases the cardholder from their obligation to pay the merchant. There have been many force majeure chargebacks linked to the COVID-19 pandemic, especially within the travel and hospitality sectors.

foreign exchange (FX, Forex) The conversion of a country's currency into another country's currency. Foreign exchange also refers to the global trading market, whereby currencies are virtually exchanged around the clock, with the largest centres being based in London, New York, Tokyo, and Singapore.

foreign exchange rate The relative value between two currencies. In particular, it is the quantity of one currency required to buy or sell a unit of the other currency.

forex See *foreign exchange*.

fork A fork is a technical event when a *blockchain* diverges into two separate paths forward. Forks can be accidental, in which case they should be resolved by the blockchain protocol relatively quickly, making the split temporary, or intentional, with the purpose of implementing new rules, reverse the effects of hacking, or resolve disagreements within the community. Forks are classified as either *soft forks* (backward-compatible changes) or *hard forks* (non-backward-compatible changes that may result in two distinct blockchains). How forks are resolved depends on the blockchain implementation and the intent. See also *codebase fork*.

form factor The medium with which a payment is made. It can be a plastic card, a mobile phone, a wearable item (e.g. smartwatch and ring), a *virtual card*, etc.

forward-dated payment A type of payment transaction that is authorised and scheduled by the account holder to occur at a later date (the *due date*). Funds will not be transferred and made available to the *payee* until the due date. Also referred to as a future-dated payment (FDP). Not all *payment schemes* offer this type of payment.

four-party model A two-sided economic model by which there is a separation between *acquirers* and *issuers*. This promotes competition as commercial terms can be set on either side (*merchant* and *cardholder*) to the benefit of merchants and cardholders. This model is also referred to as "open loop". Examples of *card schemes* operating on this model are Visa and Mastercard. The four parties referred to are the cardholder, the merchant, the acquirer, and the issuer.

FPS See *Faster Payments System*.

fractional ownership A method of property ownership where multiple parties share rights to a valuable asset, each holding a percentage of the total. This model allows investors to own a portion of high-value assets they might not be able to afford entirely on their own. Fractional ownership can apply to various assets, including real estate, artwork, luxury goods, or even digital assets like *Non-Fungible Tokens (NFTs)*. It enables broader access to investment opportunities, diversification, and shared costs whilst potentially offering partial usage rights or returns proportional to the owned fraction. See also *tokenisation*.

fraud detection The process of identifying and preventing unauthorised or illegitimate activities within financial transactions or systems. It involves using various techniques, including data analysis, *machine learning* algorithms, and pattern recognition, to monitor transactions in real-time or near real-time. Fraud detection systems examine multiple data points, such as transaction history, user behaviour, and contextual information, to flag suspicious activities that deviate from normal patterns. These systems help financial institutions, merchants, and payment processors minimise financial losses, protect customers, and maintain the integrity of payment ecosystems by quickly identifying and responding to potentially fraudulent activities.

fraud prevention The process of detecting fraudulent transactions or banking/payments interactions and preventing these actions from causing financial and reputational damage to the customer, financial institution, and *ecosystem* at large. Achieved through strategy, policies, processes, and technology.

fraud proof A cryptographic mechanism used in *blockchain* networks, particularly in *optimistic rollups*, to challenge and verify the validity of transactions or state transitions. It allows network participants to contest potentially fraudulent or incorrect data by providing evidence of its invalidity. If a fraud proof is successfully submitted within a specified challenge period, the disputed transactions are reverted, and the network returns to the last known valid state. This system operates on the assumption that all transactions are valid unless proven otherwise, enhancing scalability whilst maintaining security.

fraud-to-sales ratio A key performance indicator used by *merchants* and *payment service providers* to measure the level of fraud in relation to overall sales volume. It is calculated by dividing the total value of fraudulent transactions by the total value of all transactions over a specific period, typically expressed as a percentage. This metric helps businesses assess the effectiveness of their *fraud prevention* measures and compare their fraud rates to industry benchmarks. A lower fraud-to-sales ratio indicates better fraud management, whilst a higher ratio may signal the need for improved *fraud detection* and prevention strategies.

frictionless payment A seamless and effortless transaction process that minimises or eliminates barriers and steps traditionally associated with making a payment. This approach aims to reduce the cognitive load and time required for customers to complete a purchase, often leveraging advanced technologies such as *one-click payment*, *biometric authentication*, or *invisible payments*. By streamlining the payment experience, frictionless payments enhance customer satisfaction, increase conversion rates, and potentially boost sales for merchants whilst maintaining security and compliance with relevant regulations.

friendly fraud See *first-party fraud*.

fuel card A type of *card* that may be used as a *payment instrument* for fuel at gas stations. Most commonly *charge cards*, fuel cards may also be used to pay for vehicle maintenance and expenses at the discretion of the fleet manager. Also referred to as a fleet card.

full node In *blockchain* networks, this is a type of *node* that stores and verifies the complete blockchain history from the *genesis block*. Full nodes validate blocks and transactions to ensure they follow the network rules, providing full verifiability and allowing querying of historical data. They play a crucial role in maintaining the integrity and security of the blockchain network by relaying valid blocks and transactions to other full nodes, thus propagating data across the network. Full nodes require significant storage capacity and computing power due to their comprehensive role. The network's decentralisation and security increase proportionally with the number of full nodes it possesses.

The *Bitcoin* blockchain has in excess of 16,000 full nodes (although this can't be accurately determined as this number is rather dynamic) and has never been hacked (although blockchain-related services, such as a *crypto-exchange*, can be compromised). Types of full nodes include *archival full nodes*, *pruned full nodes*, *light nodes*, and *consensus nodes*. See also *miner* and *validator*.

fungibility A characteristic of assets that are substitutable on account of their being identical. A banknote is fungible, a fine art painting is not.

fungible token A type of *cryptocurrency* or *virtual asset* where each unit is interchangeable and indistinguishable from another unit of the same type. Fungible tokens have equal value and can be divided into smaller units. Examples include cryptocurrencies like Bitcoin and Ethereum, where one unit is equivalent to and can be exchanged for any other unit of the same cryptocurrency. This *fungibility* is a key characteristic that allows these tokens to function as a medium of exchange.

futarchy A proposed system of governance introduced by economist Robin Hanson in 2013.[14] In futarchy, elected officials define measures of national wellbeing, but prediction markets are used to determine which policies will most effectively achieve those goals. Citizens would vote on values and outcomes, whilst betting markets would select the policies most likely to achieve those objectives. This model aims to leverage the wisdom of crowds and market incentives to improve decision-making in government and organisations.

future-dated payment (FDP) See *forward-dated payment*.

FX See *foreign exchange*.

Notes

1 The Association of Banks in Singapore. https://www.abs.org.sg/consumer-banking/fast (Accessed 21 November 2023)

2 TCMB, Electronic Fund Transfer System-Electronic Securities Transfer System-The Instant and Continuous Transfer of Funds (FAST) System. https://www.tcmb.gov.tr/wps/wcm/connect/EN/TCMB+EN/Main+Menu/Core+Functions/Payment+Systems/Payment+Systems+in+Turkey/Electronic+Fund+Transfer+System+and+Electronic+Securities+Transfer+System (Accessed 21 November 2023)

3 FIDO Alliance. https://fidoalliance.org/ (Accessed 21 November 2023)

4 UK Faster Payment System. https://www.wearepay.uk/what-we-do/payment-systems/faster-payment-system/ (Accessed 21 November 2023)

5 Hong Kong Interbank Clearing Limited. https://fps.hkicl.com.hk/eng/fps/index.php (Accessed 21 November 2023)
6 Bank of Russia. https://www.cbr.ru/eng/Psystem/payment_system/ (Accessed 21 November 2023)
7 Central Bank of Bahrain. https://www.cbb.gov.bh/payment-settlement/ (Accessed 21 November 2023)
8 Federal Reserve (ACH). https://www.frbservices.org/financialservices/ach (Accessed 21 November 2023)
9 Federal Reserve (FedNow). https://www.frbservices.org/financialservices/fednow (Accessed 21 November 2023)
10 Federal Reserve (Fedwire) https://www.frbservices.org/financialservices/wires (Accessed 21 November 2023)
11 Financial Action Task Force. https://www.fatf-gafi.org/en/home.html (Accessed 21 November 2023)
12 FIS Group. https://www.fisglobal.com/ (Accessed 21 November 2023)
13 Fiserv. https://www.fiserv.com/en.html (Accessed 21 November 2023)
14 Shall We Vote on Values, But Bet on Beliefs? Economics, George Mason University, Robin Hanson, 2013. https://mason.gmu.edu/~rhanson/futarchy2013.pdf (Accessed 20 September 2024)

G

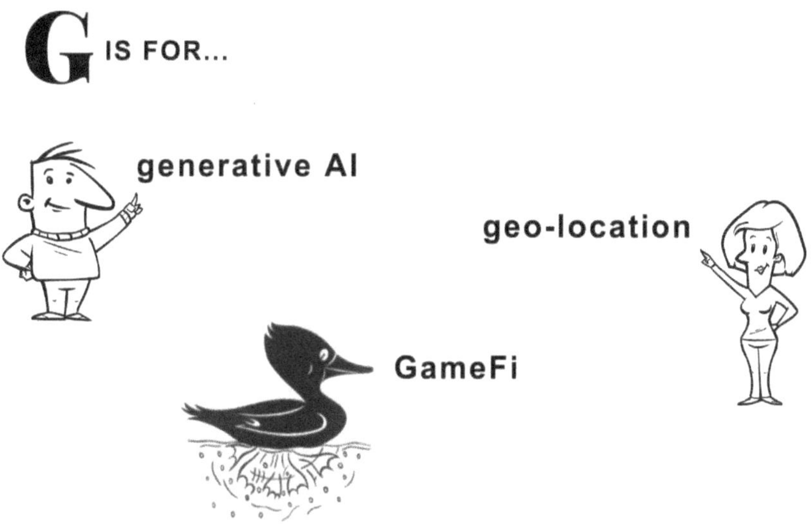

G2C See *Government-to-Consumer.*

GAFA An acronym for Google, Apple, Facebook, and Amazon. These platforms are increasingly involved in payments and financial services. See also *Big Tech, BATX, FANG, MAMAA,* and *FAANG.*

GAFI See *Financial Action Task Force.*

DOI: 10.4324/9781003571131-8

GameFi A combination of gaming and *DeFi* that refers to *blockchain*-based games which allow players to earn cryptocurrencies or tradable digital assets through gameplay. These games typically incorporate *play-to-earn* (P2E) models, *non-fungible tokens* (NFTs), and other DeFi elements to create in-game economies where players can own, trade, and monetise virtual assets.

gamification The application of game design elements and principles in non-game contexts to motivate and engage users. It involves incorporating features like points, badges, leaderboards, challenges, and rewards into activities or processes to make them more engaging and enjoyable. In the payments industry, gamification is used to encourage desired financial behaviours, increase user engagement with payment apps or services, and enhance customer loyalty. For example, credit card companies may offer points for purchases, banks may gamify savings goals, and payment apps may include achievement badges for consistent usage or meeting financial targets. By making payments and financial management more interactive and rewarding, gamification aims to improve user experience, increase adoption of digital payment methods, and promote positive financial habits.

gas fee See *gas price*.

gas limit A term usually associated with *Proof-of-Work (PoW) blockchain* networks where it represents the cost that the sender of a transaction is willing to pay for the transaction to be processed by the network of *miners* or *validators*.

gas price In a *blockchain* context, this is the payment made by crypto traders to compensate *miners* or *validators* for the computing energy and effort required to process and validate transactions on a blockchain. This term is usually associated with *Proof of Work (PoW) blockchain* networks, where it represents the cost of the computing power required by *miners* or *validators* to execute transactions. The gas price is set by the sender of the transaction and is denominated in the native *cryptocurrency* of the blockchain or subdivision thereof (e.g. *Satoshi* on the *Bitcoin* blockchain and *Gwei* on the *Ethereum* blockchain). For other blockchain infrastructures, this may also be referred to as "transaction fee", "gas fee", or "network fee" and may be calculated differently.

gas station service In a *blockchain* context, this is a facility that provides real-time information on current network conditions, number of unspent transactions, and recommended *gas price* for each transaction speed, enabling users to set competitive prices.

GDPR[1] The EU General Data Protection Regulation.

Gemini A centralised *crypto exchange*.[2] Also a *generative AI* service provided by Google.[3]

generative AI A subset of *deep learning*, which itself is a subset of *machine learning*, the latter being an application of *artificial intelligence (AI)*. Generative AI is capable of generating text, images, or other media, using generative data models that learn the patterns and structure of their input training data and then generate new data that has similar characteristics. Abbreviated as GenAI. See also *Large Language Model*.

genesis block Also known as "block 0", this is the very first block added to a *blockchain* after which every subsequent blocks are added. It is essentially the ancestor to which every other block can trace their lineage since every block contains a reference to the block preceding it. The genesis blocks mark the launch of a blockchain and defines the format of all subsequent blocks. It is created differently than all subsequent blocks and, in most blockchains, it will be hardcoded directly into the software, potentially including some initial coin/token supply (initial coinbase reward), and unlike regular blocks, the genesis block has no previous block to reference. In *Proof of Work (PoW)* blockchains, the genesis block may be pre-mined by the blockchain creator or a trusted group of individuals. In *Proof-of-Stake (PoS)* blockchains, the genesis block might be "seeded" by validators typically involving distributing the initial stake to the chosen validators. The genesis block data is usually publicly available for inspection. See also *coinbase transaction*.

geo-location The process of identifying and tracking a user's or user device's geographical location. Geo-location technology is at the core of location-positioning services and location-aware apps. See also *device fingerprinting*.

gift card A physical or *virtual card* entitling the recipient to receive goods or services of a specified value from the *issuer*. Also called a gift voucher. A *closed-loop card*.

gig economy A term referring to a workforce scenario dominated by independent contractors and freelancers, as opposed to traditional full-time employees, where each participant is paid for each short-term job performed ("gig"). Becoming popular through the use of platforms such as Uber, TaskRabbit, and DoorDash.

Gini coefficient A statistical measure of income or wealth inequality within a population. It ranges from 0 to 1, where 0 represents perfect equality (everyone has the same income/wealth) and 1 represents perfect inequality (one person has all the income/wealth, and others have none). The coefficient is based on the Lorenz curve, which plots the cumulative share of income against the cumulative share of the population. A Gini coefficient below 0.3 suggests relatively low inequality, 0.3–0.5 indicates moderate inequality, and above 0.5 signifies high inequality. The Gini coefficient can be adapted to assess the distribution of *cryptocurrency* or *token* ownership within a *blockchain* network. A lower Gini coefficient indicates a more equitable distribution of tokens, contributing to greater decentralisation. Conversely, a higher Gini coefficient suggests a more concentrated ownership, indicating less decentralisation. This metric helps evaluate the fairness and distribution of economic power within blockchain ecosystems.

Girocard[4] A German *domestic card scheme.*

giro payment (Giro) A type of *push payment.* Also see *account-to-account payment* and *credit transfer.*

Global Payments[5] A financial services company. Also an *acquirer.*

Go (Golang) An *open-source*, statically typed, compiled programming language developed by Google in 2007. It emphasises simplicity, efficiency, and built-in support for concurrent programming. Go's concurrency model is based on Communicating Sequential Processes (CSP), which uses goroutines (lightweight threads) and channels for communication between them. This approach allows developers to write highly concurrent programs with ease, making Go well-suited for building scalable network services, distributed systems, and cloud-native applications. The language features fast compilation, garbage collection, and a comprehensive standard library, whilst maintaining a clean and readable syntax.

Goods and Services Tax (GST) See *Value-Added Tax* (*VAT*).

Google Bard The old name of a *generative AI* service provided by Google, now called *Gemini.*

Google Pay A *Digital Wallet* provided by Google. Now incorporated into *Google Wallet* in most markets.

Google Wallet[6] A multipurpose *Digital Wallet* provided by Google. Enables users to store and use payment cards, tickets, passes, keys, and identities. A *staged digital wallet.*

governance node A type of *node* in a *blockchain* network that participates in the decision-making processes related to protocol changes, upgrades, and other governance-related matters. These nodes typically have voting rights and play a crucial role in shaping the network's policies and direction. Governance nodes are integral to decentralised governance structures, allowing stakeholders to influence the development and operation of the blockchain. See also *Decentralised Autonomous Organisation.*

governance token An upgraded version of a *utility token* that gives more rights to their holders (e.g. voting). See also *blockchain* and *Decentralised Autonomous Organisation.*

Government-to-Consumer (G2C) A term used to describe a business model where a government entity provides services directly to consumers (e.g. tax, registration, educational services, and employment help).

green payments Financial transactions and payment solutions designed to promote environmental sustainability and encourage eco-friendly consumer behaviour. These systems integrate environmental considerations into traditional payment processes by providing carbon footprint insights, enabling carbon offsetting, offering rewards for sustainable purchases, and facilitating eco-friendly financing options. Green payments leverage existing payment infrastructure, whilst incorporating features such as sustainability data analytics, support for the sharing economy, and partnerships across the financial ecosystem to create environmentally conscious payment experiences. By combining financial transactions with environmental impact information and incentives, green payments aim to empower consumers and businesses to make more sustainable choices and contribute to environmental conservation through their everyday financial activities. See also *ESG.*

greenwashing A dubious practice by which a business conveys a false impression or provides misleading information about how its products, services, strategy, or policies are environmentally friendly or benefit the environment. See also *ESG.*

grey list[7] A list of countries subject to increased monitoring and defined by the *Financial Action Task Force* as those actively working to address strategic deficiencies in their regimes to counter *money laundering*, *terrorist financing*, and proliferation financing.

group payment A payment transaction where the full transaction amount is divided into multiple parts and distributed among different parties involved in the transaction. See also *split payment* and *deferred payment*.

GST Goods and Services Tax. See *Value-Added Tax (VAT)*.

Gwei The smallest subdivision of one *Ethereum* (ETH) where 100,000,000 Gweis represent one ETH. The unit of measurement for ETH transaction costs. See also *gas price*.

Notes

1 EUR-Lex (General Data Protection Regulation). https://eur-lex.europa.eu/eli/reg/2016/679/oj (Accessed 21 November 2023)
2 Gemini. https://www.gemini.com (Accessed 21 November 2023)
3 Gemini. https://gemini.google.com/app (Accessed 27 September 2024)
4 Girocard. https://www.girocard.eu/ (Accessed 21 November 2023)
5 Global Payments. https://www.globalpayments.com/ (Accessed 21 November 2023)
6 Google Wallet. https://wallet.google/ (Accessed 21 November 2023)
7 FATF Black and Grey Lists. https://www.fatf-gafi.org/en/countries/black-and-grey-lists.html (Accessed 15 December 2023)

H

H IS FOR...

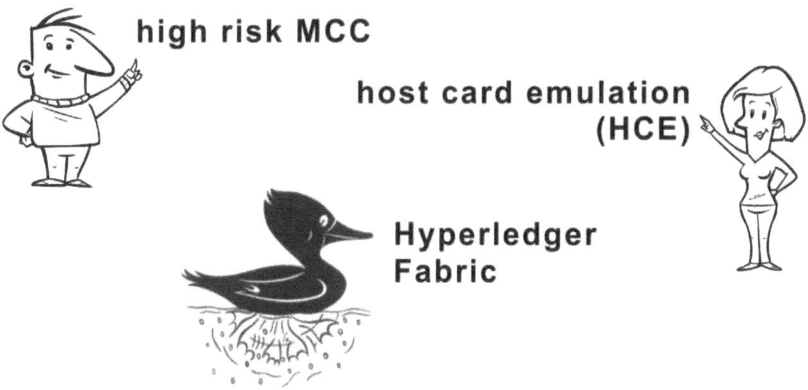

hacking A type of *cybercrime* involving methods and techniques for breaching defences and exploiting vulnerabilities in computer systems, devices, or networks.

hard decline A permanent rejection of a payment transaction by the *issuer* that cannot be resolved through resubmission. Unlike a *soft decline*, which may be temporary, a hard decline indicates a more serious issue,

DOI: 10.4324/9781003571131-9

such as a closed account, stolen card, or insufficient funds. This type of decline typically requires the cardholder to contact their issuer or use a different payment method to complete the transaction. Hard declines are often associated with specific decline codes that help merchants and payment processors understand the reason for the rejection.

hard fork See *fork*.

hard peg See *peg*.

Hardware Security Module (HSM) A hardware device which secures and manages secrets, performs *encryption* and decryption functions used for digital signatures, strong *authentication*, and other functions of *cryptography*.

hardware wallet A physical device designed to securely store crypto asset *private keys* offline. It typically resembles a USB drive and uses advanced cryptographic features to protect digital assets from online threats. Hardware wallets allow users to sign transactions without exposing their private keys to potentially compromised computers, providing an extra layer of security for long-term storage and high-value crypto holdings. See also *crypto wallet* and *bearer wallet*.

hash A mathematical function that converts an input of arbitrary length into an encrypted output of fixed length. This means that regardless of the original size of data used as input, the output is a unique hash that will always have the same size. Hashing is used to secure stored data (data at rest), thus ensuring the integrity and authenticity of the stored data. Hashed data can be checked against the original content to determine that the contents haven't been modified whilst in storage. Hashed data is different from encrypted data inasmuch as there is no decryption key (it is a one-way function). Popular hashing algorithms include MD-5 (one of the earliest, now considered unsafe), RIPEMD-160 (RACE Integrity Primitives Evaluation Message Digest, also an established one, still considered secure), and the SHA family (Secure Hash Algorithm, current version is SHA-3). Commonly used for password security and in *blockchain* infrastructures. See also *cryptography*.

Hashgraph An implementation of *Distributed Ledger Technology (DLT)* claiming to be more scalable than blockchains by virtue of having a validation mechanism (see consensus) based on virtual voting, where participants continuously communicate with each other, sharing information about the transactions they receive. An example of implementation is Hedera.[1] See also *blockchain*, *Holochain*, and *Directed Acyclic Graph (DAG)*.

hashing The process of converting input data of any size into a fixed-size string of characters, typically a sequence of numbers and letters, using a mathematical algorithm known as a *hash* function. This output, called a hash value or hash code, serves as a unique identifier for the original data. Hashing is commonly used in data integrity verification, password storage, and digital signatures as it provides a one-way transformation that is computationally difficult to reverse. See also *encryption*.

hashing power In a *Proof-of-Work (PoW) blockchain* context, the computing resources available for *mining*.

hashrate The measure of computational power used to solve complex mathematical problems in *Proof-of-Work* blockchain networks, typically expressed in hashes per second (H/s). It represents the speed at which a miner or mining network can perform cryptographic hash functions, with higher hashrates indicating greater mining capacity and network security. Hashrate is a key metric for assessing the overall strength and competitiveness of a *blockchain* network's *mining* ecosystem.

halving A predetermined event in some *blockchain* protocols, particularly in *Proof of Work (PoW)* systems like *Bitcoin*, where the *block reward* for *miners* is reduced by half at regular intervals. This mechanism is designed to control the rate of new *coin* issuance and create scarcity over time. Halving events typically occur after a specific number of blocks have been mined or at set time intervals (e.g. approximately every four years for Bitcoin). By reducing the rate of new coin creation, halving events can potentially impact the *cryptocurrency's* supply and demand dynamics, influencing its value and miners' incentives. This *deflationary mechanism* aims to maintain the cryptocurrency's long-term value and mimic the scarcity of precious metals like gold. See also *tokenomics*.

Hawala A type of *barter system* which mimics traditional *money remittance*, where the *Money Transfer Operator* (MTO) is not a financial services institution, but an individual called the hawaladar (or hawala dealer). Hawaladars maintain their own transaction records, and debts between hawaladars can be settled in cash, goods, or services. Payers wanting to transfer money would give money to a hawaladar, as well as the transaction details (e.g. payee's name and payee's address) and a password. The payer would also have given the password to the payee, and this is the equivalent of the "transaction reference" given to the payer in the traditional MTO process. The payer's hawaladar would then contact a hawaladar in the receiving country/city and ask them to give the money to the payee. The hawala system is based on trust and a hawaladar who doesn't discharge their obligations will be considered without honour and ostracised from the community. Hawaladars will charge a fee for their services, just like a traditional MTO, but much cheaper. Hawala can facilitate the flow of money between poor countries where financial services are too difficult to access or expensive and therefore serves the underbanked and helps with *financial inclusion*. As attractive as hawala may be in the previous scenario, it is equally attractive to criminals and money launderers as there are no official transaction records and the source of funds can't be tracked, which is why it is also called "underground banking". This is why hawala has been made illegal in many jurisdictions. Also referred to as *Informal Value Transfer System (IVTS)*. Also see *money laundering*.

HCE See *Host Card Emulation*.

Herfindhal index Also known as Herfindahl–Hirschman Index (HHI). A measure of market concentration used to determine the level of competition within an industry. It is calculated by summing the squares of the market shares of all firms within the market. The index ranges from 0 to 10,000, where a higher value indicates greater market concentration and less competition. An HHI below 1,500 suggests a competitive marketplace, 1,500–2,500 indicates moderate concentration, and above 2,500 signifies high concentration. In a *blockchain* context, the HHI can be adapted to assess the distribution of power or resources across network participants, such as validators, token holders, nodes, and governance contributors. A lower HHI indicates greater decentralisation, whilst a higher HHI suggests more concentration. This helps evaluate the decentralisation of consensus mechanisms, token distribution, node infrastructure, and governance within blockchain networks.

HHI See *Herfindahl index*.

high-risk acquirer An *acquirer* which specialises in *high-risk merchants*. They typically charge higher fees.

high-risk MCC Merchants with a high-risk *Merchant Category Code (MCC)* will usually belong to industries that generate the highest levels of cardholder disputes and represent higher levels of financial risk or create additional brand risk for the *card schemes* (e.g. online pharmaceuticals, online gambling/gaming, and online dating). In addition, card schemes may impose additional requirements for certain *Card Not Present* merchants within MCCs not necessarily classified as high risk (e.g. online tobacco sales vs retail tobacco sales). High-risk MCCs are subject to additional requirements from the card schemes.

high-risk merchant A merchant belonging to a *high-risk sector*.

high-risk sector When an industry or business sector experiences higher levels of chargebacks or fraud, the *card schemes* tend to classify them as "high risk". These will include travel, online pharmaceuticals, adult, dating, gaming, health and wellness, gambling, jewellery, and legal services. They can be subject to additional rules and/or permissions.

HODL In crypto vernacular, an acronym for "Hold On for Dear Life", which means retaining crypto assets that you own for an extended period of time, even during a highly volatile market movement. Another version of the term's origin is as a misspelling of the word "hold". See also *volatility*.

holdback See *merchant reserve*.

Holochain An implementation of *Distributed Ledger Technology* (*DLT*) claiming to be more scalable than blockchains because it doesn't require all participating nodes to store and validate all of the data, which creates a large amount of overhead and doesn't scale easily. The architecture is "agent-centric" rather than "data-centric", meaning that a Holochain application creates its own encrypted peer-to-peer network between users directly with a concept of mutual accountability. Holochain positions itself as a *Web3.0* platform.

hologram A card security feature present on some physical credit or debit cards. Originally designed to prevent fraudsters from cloning cards as it is difficult to reproduce. Each card scheme has a different hologram (e.g. a dove for Visa and interlocking globes for Mastercard), the specifications of which are detailed in their *operating regulations*.

holographic payment interface An advanced *contactless payment* system that uses holographic technology to project a virtual, three-dimensional interface into mid-air. This interface allows users to interact with and complete payment transactions without physically touching any surfaces. It typically employs a combination of holographic displays, motion sensors, and gesture recognition technology to create a floating visual interface that users can manipulate with hand movements. This system offers enhanced hygiene as it eliminates the need for physical contact with payment terminals, whilst providing an intuitive and futuristic user experience for entering *PINs*, selecting payment options, or authorising transactions in a secure, touchless environment.

homomorphic encryption A cryptographic technique that allows computations to be performed directly on encrypted data without decrypting it first, allowing parties to compute functions on private data without revealing the actual data or to search for data without entirely decrypting it.

Host Card Emulation (HCE) The cloud-based technology that allows cardholders to make a payment at a PoS terminal using their mobile phone. The technology allows card details to be stored in a shared secure repository, as opposed to being stored on the phone itself. A form of *Secure Element*.

hotlist A list of credit or debit cards that have been blocked or cancelled by their *issuer* in an attempt to protect cardholders from fraudulent activity and unauthorised transactions (e.g. card lost, stolen, or otherwise compromised). At authorisation stage, the *Merchant PSP* will check the hotlist with the issuer. When a card is hotlisted, it can't be used for any transactions, either online or offline. Once a card is hotlisted, the cardholder will need a new card from their issuer (unlike with a temporary block or freeze).

hot wallet A type of *crypto wallet* that keeps the *private keys* online and connected to the internet, allowing for quick and easy access to funds for transactions. Hot wallets are typically software-based applications or online services that provide convenient access to cryptocurrencies but are more vulnerable to potential security threats due to their constant internet connection. They are often used for day-to-day transactions and storing smaller amounts of cryptocurrency. Also referred to as "hot storage". See also *cold wallet*.

Howey Test A legal framework established by the US Supreme Court in 1946 to determine whether a transaction qualifies as an "investment contract" and therefore is considered a *security* subject to disclosure and registration requirements. The test consists of four criteria: (1) an investment of money, (2) in a common enterprise, (3) with the expectation of profit, and (4) derived primarily from the efforts of others. The Howey Test has gained recognition and influence beyond the United States, though its application and interpretation may vary in different jurisdictions. European regulations tend to be more prescriptive and detailed, leaving less room for discretionary interpretation compared to the Howey Test. As the crypto industry has gained traction globally, regulators in various countries have turned to principles similar to the Howey Test to determine whether *cryptocurrencies* and *Initial Coin Offerings (ICOs)* should be classified as securities.

HSM See *Hardware Security Module.*

HTML HyperText Markup Language. The standard markup language for creating and structuring web pages. It provides a way to define the content, layout, and semantics of a webpage using a series of elements denoted by tags, which are enclosed in angle brackets (e.g. <p>, <h1>, and <img>). HTML elements can include text, images, videos, links, and other content, and they are interpreted by web browsers to render the final webpage. HTML works in conjunction with other technologies like CSS for styling and *JavaScript* for interactivity to create dynamic and visually appealing websites.

Hundi A *barter system* used in India and South East Asia.

hybrid blockchain A *blockchain* offering features from both a *permissioned blockchain* and a *permissionless blockchain*. It is controlled by a central authority but also offers some permissionless elements. The controlling entity can make the blockchain accessible to everyone (through a public blockchain), whilst a permissioned blockchain controls ledger updates. See also *private blockchain* and *consortium blockchain*.

hybrid CBDC A *Central Bank Digital Currency* (CBDC) model that combines elements of both a *direct CBDC* and an *intermediated CBDC*. In this approach, the central bank issues the CBDC and maintains a central ledger, whilst also directly handling distribution for large organisations such as government agencies and major corporations. Financial institutions manage distribution and customer-facing services for retail customers and small businesses. This model aims to balance the benefits of central bank control with the efficiency of private sector involvement in retail banking services.

Hyperledger Fabric[2] A *permissioned blockchain platform*. Created by the Linux Foundation, it is designed for building permissioned blockchains with a focus on scalability and security. Often used in enterprise settings.

hyper-personalisation The use of real-time data, advanced analytics, and *artificial intelligence* to deliver highly tailored and contextually relevant financial products, services, and experiences to individual customers. This approach goes beyond basic segmentation, leveraging a customer's transaction history, spending patterns, lifestyle preferences, and real-time behaviours to offer personalised recommendations, dynamic pricing, customised rewards, and proactive financial advice. The goal is to provide each customer with a uniquely optimised payment experience that anticipates their needs and preferences, ultimately enhancing engagement, satisfaction, and loyalty.

Notes

1 Hedera. https://hedera.com/ (Accessed 12 January 2024)
2 Hyperledger Fabric. https://hyperledger-fabric.readthedocs.io/en/release-2.5/ (Accessed 29 September 2024)

I

I IS FOR...

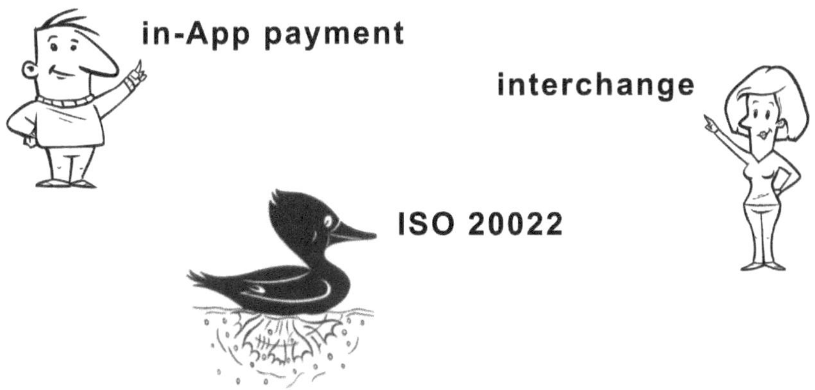

IBAN See *International Bank Account Number.*

Iberpay[1] Spain's operator of the national bank *payment schemes.*

IBPS[2] A real-time payment system (RTP system), retail payment system (RPS) in China, operated by China NCC.

iCVV See *Integrated Chip Card Verification Value.*

IDE See *Integrated Development Environment.*

DOI: 10.4324/9781003571131-10

iDeal[3] An *account-to-account payment* service in The Netherlands.

Identity Check[4] The Mastercard implementation of *3D Secure* version 2.

identity theft A type of *cybercrime* where fraudsters steal and use a victim's personal information to commit a variety of crimes, such as opening accounts in the victim's name, unauthorised use of existing accounts, and illegally obtaining goods or services. Also referred to as "ID theft".

IIN Issuer Identification Number. See *Bank Identification Number.*

immutability The state of not being able to change or be changed once created. A term used in the context of *blockchain* infrastructures where, once transactions are added to the blockchain, they become immutable. See also *blockchain settlement, finality.*

impermanent loss A financial concept that refers to the potential opportunity cost incurred when holding a volatile asset rather than holding a stable asset like cash. In the context of *decentralised crypto exchanges (DEXs)*, it refers to the loss in value experienced by *liquidity* providers when the price of the assets they contribute to a *liquidity pool* changes significantly compared to when they initially deposited them. This loss is realised when the liquidity provider withdraws their assets from the pool.

improvement proposal (IP) A *blockchain* improvement proposal is a formalised suggestion for changes or upgrades to a *blockchain protocol*, aimed at enhancing its functionality or addressing issues. Prominent improvement proposal processes include Bitcoin Improvement Proposals (BIPs), which outline changes to the Bitcoin protocol; Ethereum Improvement Proposals (EIPs), which suggest modifications to the Ethereum network; Cardano Improvement Proposals (CIPs) for the Cardano blockchain; Zcash Improvement Proposals (ZIPs) focused on Zcash enhancements; and the Tezos amendment process, which facilitates on-chain governance for protocol updates. These proposals typically undergo community discussion, peer review, and a consensus mechanism for adoption.

in-app payment A payment made by a payment account holder through a mobile app without having to leave the app. See also *micropayment.*

Independent Sales Organisation (ISO) An organisation that markets and sells card payment processing products and services directly to merchants, in partnership with one or more *acquirer(s)*. They can also be referred to as *Merchant Services Providers (MSPs)*. Acquirers may contract with ISOs to bring merchant transaction volumes.

Independent Software Vendor (ISV) A business that develops and sells software products that may run on physical hardware devices, virtual machines, or in the cloud. They supply technology enablers for specific markets, industries, etc. In a payments context, an ISV will sell software to integrate within a stakeholder's payment technology environment. Sometimes called "Integrated Software Vendor".

indirectly connected participant A bank *payment scheme* participant that is not directly connected to the payment scheme nor able to settle directly through the *settlement agent*. These participants will connect and settle funds through *directly connected settling participants*. This model is referred to as "agency banking" and gives financial services institutions the ability to offer payment services to their customers in locations where they don't have a physical presence or where they are unable to meet the regulatory requirements for direct access to a payment scheme. Also referred to as "indirect participant".

indirect participant See *indirectly connected participant*.

indirect payment instruction See *payment instruction*.

Informal Value Transfer System (IVTS) See *barter system*.

information asymmetry A situation in which one party in a transaction or relationship has more or better information than the other party. This imbalance in access to relevant information can lead to unfair advantages, market inefficiencies, or suboptimal decision-making. In economics and finance, information asymmetry can result in adverse selection, moral hazard, or market failure. It is a key concept in understanding market dynamics, contract theory, and the design of regulatory frameworks aimed at promoting fairness and efficiency in various contexts, including financial markets, insurance, and corporate governance.

Ingenico[5] A French technology company providing *merchant services* that expanded from manufacturing *Point-of-Sale* (POS) payment terminals to also include complete merchant payment SaaS and related services.

Initial Coin Offering (ICO) The *cryptocurrency* version of crowdfunding where anyone can invest, usually launched on the *blockchain* project's website. See also *tokenomics*, *Initial Exchange Offering*, *Security Token Offering*, and *airdrop*.

Initial DEX Offering (IDO) A fundraising method in which a cryptocurrency project launches its token directly through a *decentralised* *exchange* (*DEX*). IDOs allow projects to raise capital and provide immediate liquidity by creating a trading pair with the newly minted token. This model offers a more decentralised, accessible, and often faster alternative to traditional *Initial Coin Offerings* (*ICOs*) or *Initial Exchange Offerings* (*IEOs*), typically with lower barriers to entry for both projects and investors. See also *tokenomics*, *Security Token Offering*, and *airdrop*.

Initial Exchange Offering (IEO) A fundraising method in the *cryptocurrency* industry where a new project sells its tokens directly through an established cryptocurrency exchange. The exchange vets the project, manages the token sale process, and typically lists the tokens for trading immediately after the sale. IEOs aim to provide enhanced security and credibility compared to *Initial Coin Offerings* (*ICOs*) by leveraging the exchange's reputation and user base. See also *tokenomics*, *Security Token Offering*, and *airdrop*.

instalment payment A type of debt payment made on a periodic, regular basis in which the total amount of the payment transaction (including *principal* and *interest* if applicable) is divided into smaller amounts, usually of equal value, over a period of time. Applies to loans, debt, *credit*, etc. A form of *recurring payment*.

instant payment See *real-time payment*.

integer overflow A programming error where the result of calculations is too big or too small for the data type storing it. Imagine a counter that only goes up to 99, but you try to add 1. Instead of 100, it overflows and flips back to 0. In *smart contracts*, this error can lead to unexpected behaviour, like accidentally resetting a user's balance to 0 instead of adding funds. Using bigger data types and checking for potential overflows can help prevent these issues.

Integrated Chip Card Verification Value (iCVV) An alternative *Card Verification Value* (*CVV*) found on *EMV cards*, stored on the *EMV* chip. The iCVV is generated by the chip and the card payment terminal for each transaction (i.e. it is dynamic) using a different calculation from the one used for the *CVV1* on the magstripe. *Issuers* use the iCVV to identify fraudulent use of *chip cards* in magstripe-read transactions. Also known as the CVV3.

Integrated Circuit Card (ICC) See *chip card*.

Integrated Development Environment (IDE) A software application combining a variety of tools to help programmers develop software efficiently. IDEs may include features such as code editors, debuggers, compilers or build automation tools, version control, graphical user interface builders, and testing tools. They aim to improve productivity, reduce errors, increase code quality, and simplify collaboration. Popular IDEs include Visual Studio, Android Studio, and PyCharm.

Interac[6] A Canadian financial services business that serves multiple purposes. They operate the domestic debit *card scheme* Interac Debit (for which most Canadian banks are *issuers*) and *ATM* network throughout Canada, and through their partnership with NYCE terminals, Canadian Interac Debit cardholders can use their cards at two million US retailers. Interac is also the operator of three bank payment schemes: Interac e-Transfer for consumers and businesses, Interac e-Transfer Bulk (payables and receivables) for businesses, and Interac Bulk Disbursements, also for businesses. Interac also provides identity verification services, such as "Interac sign-in" for access to government services, "Interac verification services" for access to financial services, and the "Interac document verification" service for personal information verification using government-issued photo ID and advanced *biometrics* from participating service providers, eliminating the need for in-person visits to access online services that require proof of identity. Interac has also been selected by Payments Canada to provide the infrastructure for Canada's A *real-time payment system (RTP system)*.

Interac Debit[7] An *account-to-account payment* service in Canada.

Interactive Voice Response (IVR) A telephony technology that enables a computer to interact with a consumer through the use of voice commands and keypad functions. In payments IVR is the basis for menus enabling identification, segmentation, and routing of inbound callers to specific agents in contact centres or for self-service resolution.

interbank settlement Traditionally, a centralised function coordinated by the *payment scheme* concerned with the *settlement* of a large variety of payment types (e.g. *retail payments* and *wholesale payments*), sizes (e.g. high value and low value), and settlement times. On the *card rails*, interbank settlement is the process of moving funds between *issuers* and *acquirers* and is managed by the *card scheme* through their *settlement agents*. This is the first step of the settlement process for card payments (the second step being *merchant settlement*). On the bank rails, interbank settlement happens between banks through the *settlement agent* (a *central bank*) for a given bank *payment scheme*. More recently, interbank settlement can be performed using stablecoins, and traditional players may partner with *blockchain* service providers or *stablecoin issuers* for this. See also *retail settlement* and *wholesale settlement*.

interchange An *ecosystem* funding mechanism used on the *card rails*. It is a percentage of the card transaction value. In the *four-party model*, this amount flows from the *acquirer* to the *issuer* for card transactions. In some countries, such as the EU, interchange is regulated, but the interchange rules are specified by the *card schemes* (within applicable regulations). For ATM transactions, the interchange fee is paid to the ATM operator that processes the transaction on the ATM network by the issuer of the card. Also referred to as "interchange fee".

interchange + A pricing model by which a *merchant* will be able to see the *Merchant Service Charge* (MSC) split between the interchange and the rest, but both *card scheme* fees and *acquirer* margin will be amalgamated into a fixed percentage on top on the interchange fee. This model offers less transparency than *interchange++*, but the merchant still sees the interchange. This is typically used for larger merchants.

Interchange ++ A pricing model by which a *merchant* will be able to see the *Merchant Service Charge* (MSC) split between interchange, *card scheme* fees, and *acquirer* margin. This is the most transparent of pricing model. This is typically used by acquirers for larger merchants, although regulations in some geographies may force acquirers (and others) to use this pricing model for all merchants.

Interchange Fee Regulation (IFR)[8] A European regulation that caps *interchange* fees on some cards.

interchange optimisation A strategic approach used by *merchants* and *payment service providers* to reduce the *interchange* fees associated with card transactions. It involves analysing transaction data, adjusting processing methods, and implementing techniques to qualify for lower interchange rates. These techniques may include properly categorising transactions, using the most advantageous *Merchant Category Codes* (MCCs), providing additional transaction data, and routing transactions through optimal payment networks. The goal is to maximise the number of transactions that qualify for lower interchange rates, thereby reducing overall payment processing costs for the merchant. See also *payment optimisation*.

interest A term used in the context of *credit*. A fee representing the cost of borrowing the *principal*.

intermediated CBDC (sCBDC) A *Central Bank Digital Currency* (*CBDC*) architecture model by which a *central bank* issues one CBDC, maintains the ledger, and performs wholesale *settlement* (direct liability). Private *issuers* (e.g. commercial banks and *non-bank PSPs*) issue a synthetic CBDC (sCBDC) and distribute it to consumers and businesses by offering accounts and services. Here, commercial banks and non-bank PSPs offering services hold CBDC accounts at the central bank and perform *retail settlement*. The central bank needs to honour claims of which it has no record since it has no visibility of retail balances. There is a variant of this model, where the central bank would periodically record retail balances. Although this offers protection for businesses and consumers, it creates similar problems for the central bank as in the *direct CBDC* architecture model, as the central bank would have to rely on the intermediaries to consistently report the retail balances. An sCBDC is used for retail purposes and its operation is similar to how *eMoney* works. This model is also referred to as "indirect", "synthetic", or "two-tier". Also see *direct CBDC* and *multi-CBDC*.

International Electrotechnical Commission (IEC)[9] The International Electrotechnical Commission is an international standards organisation that prepares and publishes international standards for all electrical, electronic, and related technologies. The standards collection addresses product development, performance, compatibility, and related topics in order to ensure product compatibility and environmental safety.

Internal Security Assessor (ISA) A qualified security professional who can be used as an alternative to a *Qualified Security Assessor* (*QSA*) for validating *PCI DSS* compliance. ISAs are listed on the *PCI SSC* website and must renew their certification annually. ISAs are generally used by larger companies. See also *Payment Card Industry Data Security Standard*.

International Bank Account Number (IBAN) An internationally agreed-upon system (ISO 13616) of identifying bank accounts across national borders to facilitate the communication and processing of *cross-border* transactions with a reduced risk of transcription errors. *SWIFT* is the designated registration authority for IBANs.

International Organization for Standardization (ISO) An organisation that prepares and publishes international standards intended to ensure that products and services are safe, reliable, and of good quality. ISO standards cover a broad range of topics, unlike IEC standards, which are specific to electrical and electronic technologies.

Internet of Things (IoT) Describes the network of physical objects – things – that contain sensors, software, and other technologies, enabling them to connect and exchange data with other devices and systems over the internet.

intrabank settlement See *on us*.

intraday liquidity A term used to describe funds accessible during the business day, usually to enable financial services institutions to make payments. Also see *liquidity*, *liquidity risk*, and *settlement*.

invisible payments This term refers to the idea that payments can be processed seamlessly without the customer having to interact with any payment instrument or device. Typically, in the background, the customer would need to set up an account and provide credentials in advance, but any subsequent payment interactions, through the use of technology such as *artificial intelligence* and *biometrics*, will seem invisible.

invoice factoring See *factoring*.

imprinter See *card imprinting machine*.

imprinter voucher A sales paper slip that must be signed by a cardholder when making a card transaction using a *card imprinting machine*. The embossed elements on a card are transferred to the imprinter voucher by the card imprinting machine.

IMPS[10] Immediate Payment Service. A *real-time payment system (RTP system)*, *retail payment system* (RPS) in India, operated by NPCI.

IoT See *Internet of Things*.

IPN[11] A *real-time payment system (RTP system)*, *retail payment system* (RPS) in Egypt.

IRIS[12] A real-time payment system (RTP system), retail payment system (RPS) in Greece.

IRS reporting fee In the US, a fee charged to a merchant by a payment processor for reporting payment processing information directly to the Internal Revenue Service (IRS).

ISA See *Internal Security Assessor*.

ISO See *International Organization for Standardization* or *Independent Sales Organisation*.

ISO 13616 A standard by which an *IBAN* is constructed.

ISO/IEC 14443 A standard for *contactless card* transactions. Applied as an *EMV* standard for the EMV chip structure for *contactless transactions*.

ISO 18092 A standard for *near-field communication* (NFC). Information Technology – Telecommunications and Information Exchange between Systems – Near Field Communication – Interface and Protocol (NFCIP-1). 2013.

ISO 18245 A standard for *Merchant Category Codes* (MCCs).

ISO 20022 A modern messaging standard for data interchange between financial institutions, and prior to its release in 2004, *large-value payment systems* (*LVPS*) used SWIFT messaging, and *retail payment systems* (RPSs) used ISO 8583. Unlike ISO 8583, ISO 20022 data is machine-readable (not sequential) and uses XML (Extensible Markup Language) and ASN.1 (Abstract Syntax Notation). It can significantly streamline payment messaging by providing richer data, more transparency, better interoperability (e.g. standardising non-Latin alphabets), and adapting to changing needs and business models. ISO 20022 involves the processing of much larger data volumes, and payment *ecosystem* actors need to update their infrastructures to manage the additional information, which means substantial investment. ISO 20022 is particularly fundamental to modern *real-time payment system* infrastructures. See also *Electronic Data Interchange*.

ISO 21481 A standard for *Near field communication* (NFC). Information Technology – Telecommunications and Information Exchange between Systems – Near Field Communication Interface and Protocol 2 (NFCIP-2). 2021.

ISO/IEC 7812 The standard by which a *Primary Account Number* (*PAN*) is constructed for six-digit *BIN* cards. ISO 7812-2 is the standard for eight-digit BIN cards.

ISO 7813 The standard by which the *magnetic stripe* on a payment card is constructed. A magnetic stripe contains two tracks commonly referred to as "*Track 1*" and "*Track 2*".

ISO/IEC 7816 A standard for contact card transactions. Applied as an EMV standard for the *EMV* chip structure for *contact transactions*.

ISO 8583 The payment messaging standard used to communicate between card payment *ecosystem* actors. This legacy messaging standard is also used by other payments ecosystems (bank *payment schemes*). ISO 8583 is an old standard and uses a bitmap format, where each data element is assigned a specific position and is processed sequentially (i.e. as it is being read). It has been used since 1987 and is now on its third version (2003). ISO 8583 is now considered a legacy standard, although *card schemes* use this protocol, and there is no evidence that they are planning to move away from it (for card transactions). See also *Electronic Data Interchange*.

issuer In traditional financial services, this is an *Account Servicing PSP (ASPSP)* on the *card rails*. They provide and manage the cardholder account. An issuer can be a *bank* or a *non-bank Payment Service Provider* (PSP). In decentralised (e.g. *blockchain*) systems, the term refers to the organisation issuing the *coins* or *tokens*.

Issuer Identification Number See *Bank Identification Number*.

issuer processor A card payment *ecosystem* actor which connects *issuers* to *card schemes*. The issuer processor is not a bank or an issuer. In a similar fashion to a bank wanting to provide *acquiring* services and outsourcing the processes to a non-bank *acquirer* (hence the term "processor" sometimes being used for these entities). Issuer processors are an important part of the ecosystem, and they have facilitated quick time to market for many fintechs and new entrants, as well as incumbent issuers plagued by old technology.

issuing Typically, the process of creating and managing card products for cardholders. These products can be physical or virtual and may take many forms, including consumer credit cards, commercial cards, and debit cards. The term "issuing" is also used for the creation and management of currency (e.g. *fiat currency* and *crypto asset*).

issuing bank An *issuer* that is also a *bank*.

issuing clearing file A file created by a *card scheme* during the *clearing* process. A *card scheme* collects all the *acquiring clearing files* from their acquiring members for that day, in line with their clearing and *settlement* processes. They will then collate and reconcile them to produce the issuing clearing files to send to each of their issuing members. A card scheme will produce as many issuing clearing files as there are issuing members for that scheme. *Issuers* will use these files to settle their positions with the *settlement agent*.

ISV See *Independent Software Vendor*.

IT[13] Immediate Transfer. A *real-time payment system (RTP system)*, *retail payment system* (RPS) in Argentina, operated by Redlink SA and Prisma SA.

itsme app[14] A privately led *digital identity* service in Belgium.

IVR See *Interactive Voice Response*.

IVTS Informal Value Transfer System. See *barter system*.

Notes

1 Iberpay. https://www.iberpay.com/es/iberpay/iberpay/somosiberpay/ (Accessed 21 November 2023)
2 The People Bank of China. http://www.pbc.gov.cn/en/3688241/3688663/3688666/index.html (Accessed 21 November 2023)
3 iDeal. https://www.ideal.nl/en/ (Accessed 21 November 2023)
4 Mastercard (Identity Check). https://www.mastercard.co.uk/en-gb/personal/safety-security/identity-check.html (Accessed 21 November 2023)
5 Ingenico. https://ingenico.com/en (Accessed 21 November 2023)
6 Interac. https://www.interac.ca/en/ (Accessed 21 November 2023)
7 Interac (Interac Debit). https://www.interac.ca/en/content/life/interac-debit-101-everything-you-need-to-know-about-using-interacdebit/ (Accessed 21 November 2023)
8 EUR-Lex (Interchange Fee Regulation). https://eur-lex.europa.eu/legal-content/EN/TXT/HTML/?uri=CELEX%3A32015R0751 (Accessed 21 November 2023)
9 IEC. https://www.iec.ch/homepage (Accessed 21 November 2023)
10 NPCI (IMPS). https://www.npci.org.in/what-we-do/imps/product-overview (Accessed 21 November 2023)
11 Central Bank of Egypt (IPN). https://www.cbe.org.eg/en/paymentsystems-and-services/instant-payment-network (Accessed 21 November 2023)
12 DIAS (IRIS). https://www.dias.com.gr/en/iris/ (Accessed 21 November 2023)
13 Banco Central de la Republica Argentina (Payment Systems). https://www.bcra.gob.ar/MediosPago/Politica_Pagos-i.asp (Accessed 21 November 2023)
14 Itsme. https://www.itsme-id.com/en-BE (Accessed 21 November 2023)

J

J IS FOR...

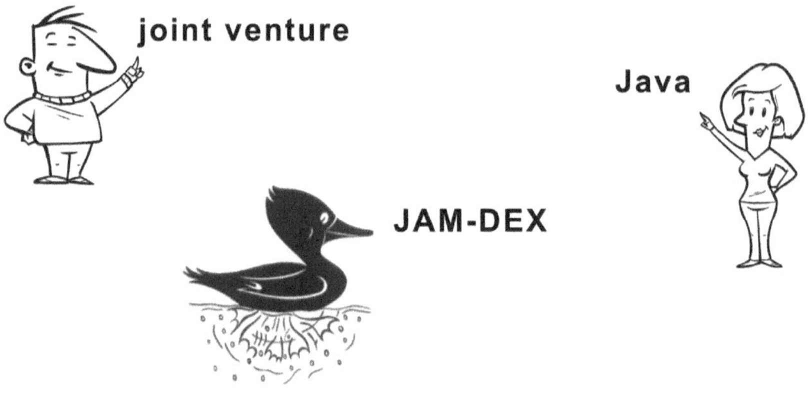

JAM-DEX The Jamaican *Central Bank Digital Currency* (*CBDC*).

Java A high-level, class-based, object-oriented programming language designed to have minimal implementation dependencies, enabling the principle of "write once, run anywhere" (WORA). Developed by James Gosling at Sun Microsystems and released in 1995, Java applications are typically compiled into *bytecode*, which can run on any system

DOI: 10.4324/9781003571131-11

equipped with a Java Virtual Machine (JVM). This portability makes Java a popular choice for developing a wide range of applications, from mobile and web applications to large-scale enterprise systems. Its syntax is similar to that of C and C++, but it includes features that enhance security and performance, making it suitable for various computing environments.

JavaScript A lightweight, interpreted, object-oriented language with first-class functions, known for its ability to add interactivity and dynamic behaviour to web pages. It is primarily used client-side in web browsers but is also employed on the server-side via platforms like Node.js. JavaScript supports multiple programming paradigms, including functional, imperative, and declarative styles. It features dynamic typing, automatic-type conversion, and prototype-based inheritance. With its versatility in web development, game development, and server-side scripting, JavaScript has become one of the most widely used programming languages on the web.

JCB[1] (Formerly Japanese Credit Bureau). A Japanese *card scheme* operating on the *three-party model.*

joint account A bank account held by two or more parties allowing all account holders to manage and operate the account.

joint and several liability A legal principle where each party in a group of two or more is individually responsible for the entirety of a debt or obligation.

joint liability A legal principle where two or more parties are responsible for settling a debt or fulfilling an obligation.

joint venture (JV) An enterprise entered into by two or more people for profit, for a limited purpose. A joint venture anticipates a specific area of activity and/or period of operation, so after the purpose is completed, bills are paid, profits (or losses) are divided, and the joint venture is usually terminated. JVs are common in the payments world.

JPM Coin A *stablecoin* issued by JPMorgan Chase for instantaneous transfer of payments between institutional clients. It is a permissioned, blockchain-based stablecoin pegged 1:1 to the US dollar. JPM Coin is designed to facilitate real-time value transfer, enhance settlement efficiency, and reduce counterparty risk in wholesale financial transactions. Unlike public cryptocurrencies, JPM Coin operates on a *private blockchain* and is only accessible to JPMorgan's institutional clients.

JP Morgan Chase[2] A financial services institution. Also an *acquirer* and *issuer.*

JPY The currency code for the Japanese Yen.

Notes

1 JCB. https://www.global.jcb/ (Accessed 21 November 2023)
2 JP Morgan. https://www.jpmorgan.com/payments#awardwinning-products (Accessed 21 November 2023)

K

KBA See *knowledge-based authentication*.

key exchange The process of securely sharing cryptographic keys between parties to enable encrypted communications. See also *public key*, *private key*, *public key cryptography*, *symmetric cryptography*, and *encryption*.

DOI: 10.4324/9781003571131-12

key fob A small portable device capable of generating a *one-time passcode (OTP)* or of providing access to secure applications, often used in *two-factor authentication*.

keylogger A type of *malware* or hardware device designed to record and log every keystroke made on a computer or mobile device with the intent of capturing sensitive information such as user names, passwords, card numbers, and PINs. Whilst a keylogger may be used for legitimate (but not necessarily ethical) purposes (e.g. monitoring children or employees), they are generally associated with fraud. See also *shimmer* and *skimmer*.

key pair A set of cryptographic keys, usually consisting of a *public key* and a *private key*, used for securing communications and authentication. See also *public key cryptography* and *encryption*.

keystroke encryption A security measure by which keystrokes on a keyboard are encrypted to protect the data that is being entered from being intercepted by a *keylogger* or other *malware*. See also *cryptography* and *encryption*.

kiosk A self-service machine or terminal that enables users to conduct various activities, including purchasing goods, making payments, etc. See also *unattended payment terminal*.

Klarna[1] A *Buy-Now-Pay-Later (BNPL)* service provider.

knowledge-based authentication (KBA) A method of verifying a user's identity by requiring them to answer questions based on personal information that only they should know. This can include static KBA, where users pre-select questions and answers during account setup, or dynamic KBA, which generates questions in real-time based on information from public records or other data sources. KBA is often used as an additional security layer for account recovery, password resets, or high-risk transactions. Whilst relatively easy to implement, KBA's effectiveness can be limited by the potential for answers to be researched or socially engineered, especially in the age of social media and data breaches. KBA is generally used as a component in *multi-factor authentication (MFA)*. See also *risk-based authentication*.

Know Your Business (KYB) A due diligence process used by financial institutions and other regulated entities to verify the identity, ownership structure, and legitimacy of business clients in order to comply with anti-money laundering regulations and mitigate financial crime risks. See also *money laundering*.

Know Your Customer (KYC) A process to verify a customer's identity through an independent, reliable source. See also *Customer Due Diligence*, *money laundering*.

Konbini[2] A *post pay* service used through convenience stores popular in Japan.

Kotlin A modern, *open-source*, statically typed programming language developed by JetBrains. It is fully interoperable with *Java* and runs on the Java Virtual Machine (JVM). Kotlin combines object-oriented and functional programming features, offering concise syntax, null safety, and enhanced expressiveness. It is the preferred language for Android app development and can also be used for server-side, web frontend, and native development. Kotlin's design focuses on pragmatism, safety, and tooling support, making it suitable for building a wide range of applications from mobile apps to large-scale enterprise systems.

Kraken[3] A centralised *crypto exchange*.

KYB See *Know Your Business*.

KYC See *Know Your Customer*.

Notes

1 Klarna. https://www.klarna.com/ (Accessed 21 November 2023)
2 Japan-guide.com (Convenience Stores). https://www.japan-guide.com/e/e2071.html (Accessed 21 November 2023)
3 Kraken. https://www.kraken.com (Accessed 21 November 2023)

L

L IS FOR...

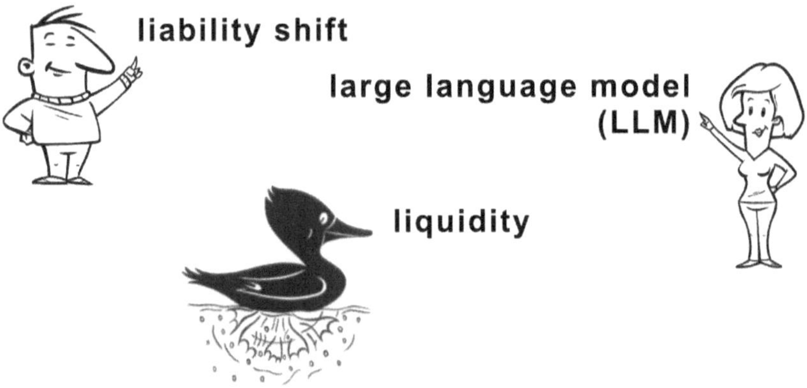

Lamport The smallest subdivision of a *Solana* (SOL) where 100,000,000 Lamports represent one SOL. The unit of measurement for SOL transaction costs. See also *gas price*.

large language model (LLM) A *deep learning* algorithm that can perform a variety of *natural language processing* (NLP) tasks through the use of large

DOI: 10.4324/9781003571131-13

datasets, enabling them to recognise, translate, predict, or generate text or other content. ChatGPT is an example. See also *Generative AI*.

large-value payment system (LVPS) A bank *payment scheme* that is designed for high-value payments. Sometimes referred to as large-value transfer system (LVTS) or high-value payment system (HVPS). See also *retail payment system*.

layer 1 blockchain The term layer 1 *blockchain* is generally accepted as representing the base layer in a *permissionless blockchain* ecosystem that is for general purpose use. It serves as the base infrastructure for building various applications serving various use cases. Some definitions might encompass the use of *open-source* technology for the underlying code and *consensus protocol*, whilst others might add the use of an established consensus protocol such as *Proof of Work* or *Proof of Stake*. The *Bitcoin*, *Ethereum*, and *Solana* blockchains are layer 1 blockchains. It is important to note that other interpretations exist: *Hyperledger Fabric* is often defined as a layer 1 blockchain although it is a framework used to develop *permissioned blockchains*, not a blockchain itself; Ripple is also sometimes defined as a layer 1 blockchain, although it is *permissioned blockchain*, with a proprietary consensus protocol, and is designed for a specific purpose (i.e. cross-border payments). In any instance, if we take the broad definition of a "base layer" blockchain, I think the industry agrees on the terms "mainchain", "mainnet", and "parent blockchain", regardless of whether they are classified as "layer 1" or not. See also *layer 2 blockchain*.

layer 1 scaling solution See *scaling solution*.

layer 2 scaling solution See *scaling solution*.

layering The process of distancing illegal proceeds from their source by creating complex levels of financial transactions in order to disguise the audit trail and provide anonymity. A technique used for *money laundering*.

Ledger Wallet[1] A hardware *crypto wallet*.

legal ownership The recognition in law of ownership of an asset or business. Also see *beneficial ownership*.

legal tender A form of *money* that a government recognises as the standard for the repayment of debt and that a court of law is required to recognise as a satisfactory payment of monetary debt. A *fiat currency* is made legal tender by the government that issues it. A *cryptocurrency* is not considered legal tender unless a government makes it so (e.g. El Salvador with Bitcoin).

Level 1 The first data level for card transactions. Level 1 data is typically associated with consumer transactions and provides limited purchase data. All merchants will be able to accept these transactions, physically or virtually, and all cards (e.g. consumer, commercial, corporate, and government) can be accepted that way.

Level 2 The second data level for card transactions. Level 2 data adds more information to benefit the corporate/government/industrial buyer. Commercial, corporate, purchasing, and government cards are eligible for Level 2 processing, but not consumer cards (which can only be processed at Level 1). Historically, the amount of extra data transmitted in a card transaction by a merchant has been limited only by the capabilities of hardware *Point-of-Sale* (POS) terminals.

Level 3 The third data level for card transactions. Level 3 data provides line-item detail equivalent to the information found on an itemised invoice. Historically, these transactions could only be accepted virtually (i.e. through a *payment gateway*) and often integrated with Enterprise Resource Planning (ERP) platforms such as SAP or Oracle NetSuite. This is because they were beyond the capabilities of traditional hardware POS terminals (as many of the data elements require text input, and standard card terminals have basic numeric keypads). Increasingly, modern card payment terminals offer Level 3 capability through touchscreen technology (see *smart POS*).

liability shift The process by which a liability is shifted from one party to the other. In the card payments industry, when fraud happens in the Card Present channel, the liability is shifted from the merchant to the *issuer*. When fraud happens in the e-commerce channel, liability will be shifted from the merchant to the issuer if the merchant has authenticated the transaction using *3D Secure*. There is no liability shift for the MOTO channel at the time of writing, although this may change with newer versions of *3D Secure*. A form of *contingent liability*.

Lightning Network[2] A *layer 2 scaling solution* built on top of the Bitcoin *blockchain* that enables fast, low-cost micropayments between participating nodes. It uses *smart contracts* to create payment channels, allowing users to conduct multiple transactions *off-chain* before settling the final balance on the main blockchain. This approach significantly increases transaction speed and reduces fees, making Bitcoin more viable for everyday transactions whilst maintaining the security of the underlying blockchain.

light node In *blockchain* networks, this is a type of *node* with special responsibilities and privileges. A light node doesn't store the entire blockchain transaction history, like a *full node* does, but only block headers and specific transaction information. However, a light node participates in the transaction validation process and perform the same steps as other validating nodes. If the transaction passes all validation steps, a light node sends the transaction to a full node for validation and inclusion on the blockchain ledger. Typically, light nodes are less resource-intensive than other nodes and can even be run on mobile devices, which is why they are considered more vulnerable to attacks than other nodes, but also more affordable to run for users that don't have the resources to run full nodes. As such, light nodes rely on full nodes for most functionality. Also referred to as "lightweight node" or "simplified payment verification (SPV)" node or "stateless clients". See also *miner*, *validator*, *full node*, and *master node*.

limited network Usually refers to *payment instruments* with limited capabilities. For example, those that can only be used on the premises of the issuing institution (e.g. a shopping centre) or for a limited range of goods (e.g. *fuel card* and *public transport card*) or service providers. These payment instruments may be subject to less stringent regulatory obligations.

Linden Dollar A *virtual currency* used in the game Second Life.

liquidation risk The potential for an asset or position to be forcibly sold or closed out due to the inability to meet financial obligations or maintain required collateral levels. In trading and lending, it refers to the risk of a position being automatically closed by a platform or lender when its value falls below a specified threshold, often resulting in significant losses for the holder. Liquidation risk is particularly relevant in leveraged trading, margin lending, and collateralised debt positions in both traditional finance and *decentralised finance (DeFi)* protocols.

liquid democracy A hybrid governance model that combines elements of direct and representative democracy. It allows participants to either vote directly on issues or delegate their voting power to trusted representatives on a granular, issue-by-issue basis. This flexibility enables voters to leverage the expertise of others when needed, whilst retaining the ability to participate directly in decisions they feel strongly about. Delegates can further pass on their voting power, creating a dynamic "liquid" flow of democratic decision-making that aims to balance participation and expertise.

liquidity A term describing the ease with which financial institutions can discharge their payment and *settlement* obligations. Financial institutions must ensure that they have sufficient funds at a reasonable cost to meet their obligations.

liquidity mining A *token* distribution mechanism used in *DeFi* protocols to incentivise users to provide *liquidity* to trading pools. Participants deposit their cryptocurrency assets into *liquidity pools* on *decentralised crypto exchanges* and, in return, receive rewards in the form of the protocol's native tokens or other cryptocurrencies. These rewards are typically proportional to the amount of liquidity provided and the duration of participation. Liquidity mining aims to bootstrap liquidity for new DeFi projects, increase trading volume, and distribute tokens to active users of the platform. This mechanism played a significant role in the growth of DeFi ecosystems by attracting users and capital to various protocols.

liquidity pool A collection of *cryptocurrency tokens* or assets locked in a *smart contract* on a *decentralised exchange* (*DEX*) to facilitate trading. It provides the necessary *liquidity* for users to trade directly with the pool rather than waiting for a matching counterparty. In traditional forex markets, large banks act as market makers, holding reserves of various currencies to facilitate exchanges. A liquidity pool in *DeFi* is similar to these bank reserves, but instead of being controlled by a central entity, it is managed by a smart contract and funded by multiple participants.

liquidity risk A type of risk that a financial institution may face if it will not discharge its payment and settlement obligations on the *due date*. This doesn't necessarily mean that the financial institution is insolvent as it may be able to settle at some later point.

Litecoin (LTC)[3] A *cryptocurrency*, also a *coin*. Litecoin also refers to the *layer 1 blockchain* infrastructure on which LTC operates (i.e. the Litecoin blockchain). A *permissionless blockchain*. See also *Litoshi*.

Litoshi The smallest subdivision of one *Litecoin* (*LTC*) where 100,000,000 Litoshis represent one LTC. The unit of measurement for LTC transaction costs on the Litecoin *blockchain*. See also *gas price*.

LLM See *large language model*.

load balancing In the context of payments, this usually refers to the practice of *merchants* sourcing, acquiring services from multiple *acquirers* with the aim to reduce their *chargeback ratio*. Using load balancing to reduce the chargeback ratio is not a good practice and could lead to merchants being blacklisted, but load balancing may be used for legitimate purposes (e.g. not putting all your acquiring eggs in one basket).

Lovelace The smallest subdivision of one *ADA* where 100,000 Lovelace represent one ADA. The unit of measurement for ADA (the *Cardano cryptocurrency*) transaction costs. See also *gas price*.

loyalty programme See *merchant loyalty*.

Luhn Algorithm Also known as Modulus 10. A mathematical formula used to validate a card number.

LVPS See *large-value payment system*.

Notes

1 Ledger. https://www.ledger.com/ (Accessed 21 November 2023)
2 Lightning Network. https://lightning.network/ (Accessed 29 September 2024)
3 Litecoin. https://litecoin.org/ (Accessed 26 May 2024)

M

M IS FOR...

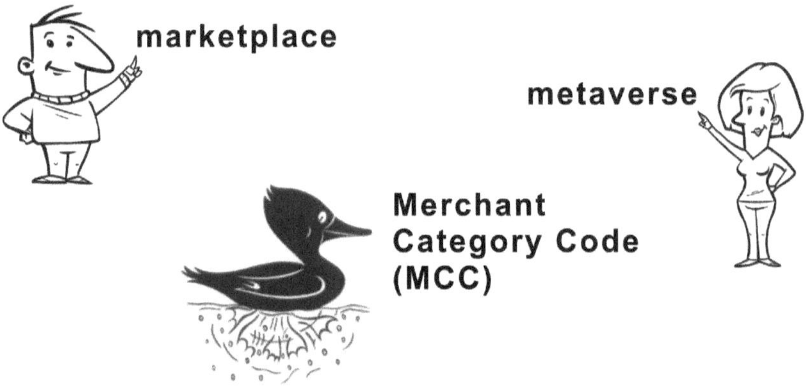

M1, M2, and M3 money See *money.*

M2M payments See *Machine-to-Machine payments.*

MaaS See *Mining-as-a-Service (MaaS).*

machine customer As defined by Gartner,[1] a machine customer is a non-human economic actor that autonomously engages in commerce

DOI: 10.4324/9781003571131-14

and financial transactions. These AI-powered entities can independently discover, evaluate, and purchase goods or services without direct human intervention. Machine customers use advanced technologies such as *artificial intelligence*, *machine learning*, and the *Internet of Things* (*IoT*) to make decisions, initiate payments, and manage transactions based on predefined parameters, real-time data, and adaptive algorithms. They represent a significant shift in the concept of "customer", extending beyond traditional human consumers to include smart devices, autonomous systems, and AI agents. As this technology evolves, machine customers are expected to play an increasingly important role in various industries, potentially transforming business models, supply chains, and customer engagement strategies. See also *digital twin* and *autonomous purchasing*.

machine learning (ML) A subset of *artificial intelligence* (*AI*) which encompasses techniques that enable machines to progressively improve their performance on specific tasks through experience without being explicitly programmed. This is achieved through the use of large datasets which are used to "learn" in order to inform predictions, decisions, or actions, leading to increased accuracy and/or efficiency over time. See also *deep learning*, *generative AI*, and *large language model*.

machine-to-machine payments (M2M payments) Financial transactions that occur automatically between two or more devices or systems without direct human intervention. These payments are typically facilitated by *Internet of Things* (*IoT*) technology, *APIs*, and *artificial intelligence*, enabling devices to communicate, make decisions, and execute transactions autonomously. M2M payments can involve various scenarios, such as smart devices ordering supplies, vehicles paying for tolls or parking, or industrial equipment settling usage-based fees. This technology streamlines processes, reduces human error, and enables new business models in sectors like manufacturing, logistics, utilities, and smart cities. M2M payments represent a significant evolution in the payments landscape, supporting the growing trend of automation and interconnected devices in the digital economy. See also *machine customer*, *autonomous purchasing*, and *digital twin*.

magnetic stripe A data container in a physical card constructed in accordance with ISO/IEC 7813 and embodied in two magnetic tracks used for data storage: Track 1 and Track 2. Also known as "magstripe".

magnetic stripe reader (MSR) A type of *Point-of-Sale* (POS) card terminal that can read the magnetic stripe on a card.

magstripe See *magnetic stripe.*

Mail Order/Telephone Order (MOTO) The term used to describe card payment transactions conducted over the telephone or via mail order.

mainchain See *layer 1 blockchain.*

mainnet See *layer 1 blockchain.*

Major Industry Identifier (MII) The first digit in the card number. It identifies the industry or type of card. (e.g. 1 = airlines). See also *Primary Account Number (PAN).*

malicious payee A type of *authorised push payment fraud* where the payee is a fraudster, including purchase scams, investment scams, romance scams, and advance fee scams.

malicious redirection A type of *authorised push payment fraud* generally involving impersonation of official entities (e.g. bank, government, and police), including invoice and mandate scams, CEO fraud, law enforcement, or bank staff impersonation, and other impersonation.

malware A contraction of "malicious software". Any software designed to disrupt, damage, or gain unauthorised access to a computer system, leak private information, deprive access to information, or interfere with computer security and privacy. An example is *ransomware.*

MAMAA An acronym for Meta (Facebook's parent company), Apple, Microsoft, Amazon, and Alphabet (Google's parent company). These platforms are increasingly involved in payments and financial services. See also *Big Tech*, *BATX*, *GAFA*, *FAANG*, and *FANG*.

man-in-the-middle (MITM) attack A type of *cybersecurity* threat where an attacker secretly intercepts and potentially alters the communication between two parties who believe they are directly communicating with each other. The attacker positions themselves between the victims, acting as a proxy to relay messages whilst having the ability to eavesdrop or modify the content. This attack can compromise the confidentiality and integrity of data transmission, potentially leading to information theft, unauthorised access, or the injection of malicious content. MITM attacks highlight the importance of secure, encrypted communications and proper *authentication* methods in digital interactions.

Manual Key Entry (MKE) See *PAN Key Entry.*

manual review A process by which transactions are flagged by *fraud prevention* software so that they can be manually reviewed to determine whether they should be accepted or rejected. Typically, these transactions fall into a grey area where the software hasn't determined them to be clearly fraudulent or clearly legitimate.

market capitalisation The total value of a publicly traded company's outstanding shares, calculated by multiplying the total number of shares by the current market price per share. In the crypto space, market capitalisation refers to the total value of a *cryptocurrency*, calculated by multiplying the *circulating supply* of coins or tokens by the current price per unit. For cryptocurrencies, this metric can be more volatile due to factors like token *burning*, *minting*, and varying circulating supplies and may not always accurately reflect the true value or adoption of a project.

Markets in Crypto Assets (MiCA) regulation A comprehensive regulatory framework implemented by the European Union in 2024 to govern *crypto asset* service providers and issuers. It aims to protect investors, maintain financial stability, and foster innovation in the crypto space by establishing clear rules for the issuance, trading, and custody of crypto assets. MiCA introduces licensing requirements, operational standards, and consumer protection measures for crypto businesses operating within the EU, whilst also addressing concerns related to market integrity, *money laundering*, and environmental impact.

marketplace Traditionally, a marketplace is a trading environment, such as eBay, Amazon, or Etsy, which connects buyers with multiple sellers and maintains complete control over the payment transactions, their fulfilment, and the end-to-end customer experience. With a marketplace, a cardholder intends to buy a product or service, and the marketplace will offer these products or services from multiple sellers. Marketplaces also come in other forms on different infrastructures (e.g. *Web* 3.0 and *blockchain*), such as NFT marketplaces.

markup fee See *acquirer margin*.

master merchant See *merchant of record*.

masternode A type of *full node* in specific *blockchain* networks, particularly those using *Proof-of-Stake* or hybrid consensus protocols. Masternodes perform specialised functions beyond transaction validation, such as enabling instant or private transactions, voting on governance decisions, and treasury system management. They typically require operators to stake a significant amount of cryptocurrency as collateral, incentivising network stability and security. See also *consensus node* and *validator node.*

Mastercard[2] A *card scheme* operating on the *four-party model.*

MATCH™ list[3] The Member Alert to Control High-Risk Merchants list is maintained by Mastercard and identifies *high-risk merchants* and those that have been terminated within the last five years. Sometimes called the Terminated Merchant File (TMF).

Maximum Extractable Value (MEV) In a *blockchain* context, this is the maximum additional profit a block producer (e.g. *miner* and *validator*) can extract from a block, beyond the standard *block reward* and transaction fees, by manipulating the order in which transactions are included within that block.

MCC See *Merchant Category Code.*

mCBDC See *multi-CBDC.*

mCommerce See *mobile commerce.*

MD-5 A legacy *hashing* algorithm now considered unsafe. See *cryptography, encryption*, and *hash.*

MDR Merchant Discount Rate. See *Merchant Service Charge.*

meme coin A type of *cryptocurrency* that is often created as a joke or parody, typically inspired by internet memes and social media trends. Meme coins gain popularity through community engagement and speculative trading rather than inherent technological value or *utility*. The most notable example is Dogecoin (DOGE), which started as a joke based on the "Doge" meme featuring a Shiba Inu dog but has since gained significant market value and community support. Meme coins are generally considered high-risk investments due to their *volatility* and lack of fundamental backing.

mempool A staging area used in *blockchain* infrastructures, where validating nodes verify transactions and build candidate blocks for addition to the blockchain. Think of it as temporary storage of pending transactions. After a node has verified the validity of a transaction, they pass it on to the other validating nodes, who also verify the transaction and add it to their mempool (depending on how they prioritise transaction processing). Transactions in the mempool are called "unspent" because they have not yet been added to the blockchain (i.e. they are pending). The mempool is slightly different in *Proof-of-stake* blockchains, and whilst the concept is similar (i.e. a staging area for unspent transaction), the transactions within are not validated. Sometimes referred to as the "transaction pool". As a parallel with centralised systems, the transaction in a mempool is partly "authorised" and partly "cleared", but not yet "settled". Each validating node maintains its own mempool and decides on their own computing configuration. See also *clearing*, *validation*, and *settlement*.

merchant A term generally describing an entity that provides goods or services and is able to accept card payments. A merchant can be virtual (e.g. *e-commerce*) or physical (e.g. a *brick-and-mortar* shop). Increasingly, this term is also used to describe businesses that accept bank payments or other types of payments.

merchant acquirer See *acquirer*.

merchant aggregator See *payment aggregator*.

merchant agreement The contract between a *merchant* and a *Payment Service Provider (PSP)* (e.g. *acquirer*, ISO, payfac).

merchant bank See *acquirer*.

Merchant Category Code (MCC) Used to classify a business by the types of goods or services they provide. Good News! In an attempt to provide consistency across the card payments *ecosystem*, an international standard (ISO 18245) is used for this four-digit identifier, but there may be variations across *card schemes*.

Merchant Discount Rate (MDR) See *Merchant Service Charge*.

merchant financing A value-added service that has seen a resurgence of popularity during the pandemic and can be offered to merchants on the *card rails*. There are two forms of merchant financing. A merchant cash advance is a form of debt financing that involves a merchant borrowing money based on their projected sales. Providers of such services include YouLend,[4] 365 Finance,[5] Nucleus Commercial Finance,[6] and Liberis Ltd,[7] to name but a few. Factoring (aka invoice factoring) is another form of merchant financing, and it involves the sale of unpaid invoices to a third party at a discount. Providers include Aldermore,[8] eCapital,[9] and Kriya,[10] and some mainstream banks also provide this service. Merchant financing is a form of *alternative finance* or *embedded finance*.

Merchant ID (MID) An identifier given to a business when they are onboarded directly by an *acquirer* or by an *Independent Sales Organisation (ISO)*. This is, in effect, their customer number and is a unique code linked with the merchant's bank account. The MID identifies a merchant to their acquirer (either directly, or indirectly through their partner ISO).

Merchant-Initiated Transaction (MIT) A payment that is initiated by the merchant, according to the agreement they have with the cardholder, which allows them to initiate a payment on the cardholder's behalf. A form of *pull payment*.

merchant level This term is generally used in the context of the *Payment Card Industry Data Security Standard* (PCI DSS), and there are three merchant levels:

Level 1: those who process more than six million transactions annually per *card scheme*

Level 2: those who process between one and six million transactions annually per card scheme

Level 3: e-commerce merchants who process between 20,000 and 6 million transactions per card scheme

Level 4: those who process less than 20,000 transactions annually per card scheme and all other merchants

There are different PCI DSS compliance validation requirements (e.g. *SAQ* and *ROC*), depending on the merchant level.

merchant loyalty A value-added service that can be offered to merchants by *Payment Service Providers (PSPs)* or *Independent Software Vendors (ISVs)*. The benefits offered to consumers through the *merchant loyalty* programme can either be funded by the merchant or the partner or the consumer (i.e. via membership).

merchant monitoring programme A *card scheme* programme to monitor merchant compliance with *operating regulations*. Generally associated with fraud monitoring.

Merchant of Record (MOR) A type of *payment aggregator* suited to smaller merchants who want to accept card payments but may not be able to afford (or be approved to get) payment services directly from an *acquirer* or an *Independent Sales Organisation* (ISO). Also referred to as "master merchant".

merchant onboarding A process involving assessing merchant risk and contracting with the merchant. This step is about ascertaining whether the merchant's potential value is worth the risk, and therefore the cost, prior to signing a contract. See also *underwriting* and *Customer Due Diligence*.

Merchant Plug In (MPI) See *3D Secure Server*.

merchant reserve An amount of funds, usually taking the form of a rolling reserve and amounting to a percentage of each transaction, that is held back by the merchant account provider (e.g. *acquirer*) to cover the cost of potential *chargebacks*. Usually associated with *high-risk merchants*. Also referred to as "holdback".

Merchant Service Charge (MSC) What a *merchant* pays an *acquirer* for processing card transactions.

MSC = *interchange* + *card scheme fees* + *acquirer margin*

There are various ways of presenting the MSC to merchants, depending on a number of factors (e.g. size and risk), some more transparent than others (see *interchange+*, *interchange++* and *blended pricing*). Also referred to as the "Merchant Discount Rate (MDR)", "discount rate", and "bank rate".

merchant services A generic term used to describe services provided to merchants to enable them to connect to a *card scheme*. Also referred to as *acquiring*.

Merchant Services Provider (MSP) A catch-all generic term that describes an organisation that provides *merchant services*, such as an *acquirer*, *ISO*, or a *payfac*.

merchant settlement Traditionally, the second and final step of the *settlement* process on the *card rails*, by which the *acquirer* will credit the merchant account according to their commercial contract. Acquirers may decide to defer merchant settlement as a risk management tool for certain industries (e.g. airlines and hospitality). As other payment infrastructures gain in popularity (e.g. account-to-account *payment* and *blockchain*), this term may also describe how any business will be paid. Also see *settlement* and *settlement cycle*.

merchant's PSP A *Payment Service Provider* (*PSP*) that provides technology to merchants to enable them to connect to a *card scheme* or other *payment scheme*. See *payee's PSP*.

Merkle root See *Merkle tree*.

Merkle tree A mathematical construct used in *blockchain* infrastructures commonly used to ensure block integrity in various blockchain implementations. This data structure summarises the transactions within a block by *hashing* each transaction individually, and then the individual hashes are hashed again in pairs, repeating the process until a single hash is obtained representing all the transactions. This final hash is known as the "Merkle root", which is included in the *block header*. When other validating nodes receive the proposed block, they verify its integrity by recalculating the Merkle root using the received transactions and then check whether it matches the Merkle root included in the block header. This is an efficient way of validating block integrity without having to re-validate each transaction.

metaverse A collective virtual shared space, created by the convergence of virtually enhanced physical reality and physically persistent virtual space, including the sum of all virtual worlds, augmented reality, and the internet. It's characterised by persistent, shared, 3D virtual spaces linked into a perceived virtual universe where users can interact, create, and exchange experiences and *virtual assets*. The metaverse is often associated with emerging technologies such as virtual reality (VR), augmented reality (AR), *Web 3.0*, and *blockchain*. Whilst still evolving, it's envisioned as a more immersive, interactive, and interconnected successor to the current internet.

MEV See *Maximum Extractable Value*.

MFA See *multi-factor authentication*.

MiCA See *Markets in Crypto Assets regulation*.

micropayment A financial transaction involving a very small amount of money, typically ranging from a few cents to a few dollars. Micropayments are often used for digital goods and services, such as online articles, music downloads, or *in-app payments*, where traditional payment methods may be impractical due to high transaction fees. This payment model enables consumers to pay for individual items or services rather than committing to larger subscription fees, making it particularly popular in the digital economy. Micropayments can enhance revenue streams for content creators and service providers by allowing users to access specific content or features on a pay-per-use basis.

MID See *Merchant ID*.

MII See *Major Industry Identifier*.

miner A *node* in a *Proof-of-Work (PoW)* blockchain network that participates in the transaction validation process. A miner listens to the network and gathers valid transactions to fit in a block. Miners ensure the integrity and security of the blockchain network by completing tasks including verifying and processing transactions, ensuring consensus, and preventing *double-spending*. As miners do this all at the same time for all transactions, which blocks get added to the chain is determined by the *consensus protocol*. Miners are incentivised with *cryptocurrency* for their participation. See also *mining*, *validator*, *master node*, *full node*, and *light node*.

mining A process commonly associated with *Proof-of-Work (PoW)* consensus in *blockchain* networks through which new transactions are added to a blockchain. It involves solving complex mathematical problems or cryptographic puzzles to validate and confirm transactions. See also *miner*, *staking*, and *validator*.

Mining-as-a-Service (MaaS) In a *Proof of Work (PoW) blockchain* context, a *mining* model where service providers rent out their own *hashing power* (including hardware and software) to individuals or businesses interested in earning mining rewards. The fees charged to users and cryptocurrencies supported will depend on the service provider. For example, they may require an initial deposit representing the hashing power to be rented or offer pay-as-you-go options. The individual or business can then start mining in the usual way without having to incur the infrastructure outlay. Rewards are then paid out regularly, after service fees are deducted. Also known as "cloud mining".

mining farm In a *Proof of Work (PoW) blockchain* context, a type of mining model where a business creates a dedicated facility with specialised equipment (*mining rigs*) dedicated to mining cryptocurrencies in PoW networks. Unlike *mining pools* and *MaaS* providers, which are targeted at those with no or little access to resources, these primarily attract investors as they require a high initial investment and could potentially give high returns. Farms may also join mining pools to leverage collective power.

mining pool In a *Proof of Work (PoW) blockchain context*, a type of cooperative construct where individual miners combine their individual computing resources, known as their *hashing power*, into one pool that competes as one entity to solve the cryptographic puzzle. The more hashing power, the more chance the mining pool has to solve the puzzle faster and earn the block reward. Rewards are then distributed amongst the pool members according to their hashing power contribution.

mining rig A specialised computer specifically designed to help *Proof of Work (PoW) miners* solve the complex cryptographic puzzles required by the *consensus protocol*.

minimum fee requirement A threshold for transaction fees that may be set by a blockchain protocol to manage network operations.

Minimum Monthly Service Charge (MMSC) This is a charge levied on merchants by acquirers if they don't process a minimum monthly value of card transactions that has been agreed in their *merchant agreement*.

minting The process of manufacturing or producing coins or other forms of currency. Traditionally, this refers to the creation of physical coins by stamping metal blanks with designs. In the context of *blockchain*, minting refers to the creation of new coins or tokens or crypto assets. This can involve generating new coins as block rewards in *Proof-of-Work* blockchains, creating tokens in *Proof-of-Stake* networks, or producing *non-fungible tokens* (NFTs). Blockchain minting is typically governed by the blockchain protocol, ensuring controlled issuance and distribution of digital assets. See also *seigniorage*, *tokenomics*, and *burning*.

MIT See *Merchant-Initiated Transaction*.

MitID[11] A *digital identity* framework in Denmark which replaced the NemID framework in June 2023.

MITM attack See *man-in-the-middle attack*.

MKE Manual Key Entry. See *PAN Key Entry*.

ML See *machine learning*.

MLRO See *Money Laundering Reporting Officer*.

MMSC See *Minimum Monthly Service Charge*.

MNO See *Mobile Network Operator*.

Mobiilivarmenne[12] A *digital identity* framework in Finland which is a partnership between telcos.

mobile banking The use of mobile devices, such as smartphones and tablets, to access and manage banking services and financial transactions through dedicated applications or mobile-optimised websites. It allows users to perform a variety of tasks, including checking account balances, transferring funds, paying bills, depositing cheques, and monitoring transaction history, all from the convenience of their mobile devices. Mobile banking enhances accessibility and convenience for customers, enabling them to conduct financial activities anytime and anywhere, whilst also incorporating security features such as *biometric authentication* and *encryption* to protect sensitive information.

mobile commerce (mCommerce) The purchase of goods or services through mobile devices.

mobile money A way to store and manage money in an account linked to a mobile phone, similar to a bank account. Most mobile money services allow users to purchase items in shops or online, pay bills, school fees, and top-up mobile airtime. Cash withdrawals can also be carried out at authorised agents. Most mobile money services are offered by local mobile telecom operators. A type of mobile payment that doesn't rely on a formal financial services infrastructure (e.g. bank accounts). Popular in developing countries. See also *e-money.*

Mobile Network Operator (MNO) A telecommunication service provider that supplies wireless voice and data communication to its subscribed mobile users. Also referred to as a "carrier service provider", "mobile phone operator", "mobile network carrier", "mobile carrier", or, simply, "carrier".

mobile payment A broad term to describe payment facilities that have a mobile element. It encompasses mobile banking, *mobile wallets*, *mobile money*, and even mobile *payment acceptance*. Mobile payments can be classified in two categories: those that necessitate a formal payment instrument as the underlying payment mechanism (e.g. card or bank account) and those that don't (e.g. use of cash).

Mobile *Point-of-Sale* (mPOS) A physical device, usually proprietary to its manufacturer, which can be either attached to a standard mobile phone (e.g. a dongle) or used on its own by a merchant to enable *payment acceptance* mobility (e.g. market traders) at a relatively low cost. mPOS solutions have evolved in recent years and may take many forms: tablet-based systems, mobile-phone-based systems, terminal-based systems, etc.

mobile wallet A payment facility tied to a mobile hardware device that usually uses cards as the funding option.

MobilePay[13] An *account-to-account payment* service in Denmark.

Modulr[14] An *API aggregator*, Authorised Electronic Money Institution (EMI), Account Information Service Provider (AISP), and Payment Initiation Service Provider (PISP) in the UK. See also *Open Banking*.

Modulus 10 See *Luhn algorithm*.

monetary policy The actions taken by a central bank or monetary authority to manage the money supply, interest rates, and overall economic conditions of a country. It aims to achieve macroeconomic objectives such as price stability, full employment, and economic growth. In traditional monetary systems, this involves tools like setting interest rates, adjusting reserve requirements, and conducting open market operations. In *blockchain* environments and *tokenomics*, *monetary policy* refers to the rules and mechanisms programmed into a *cryptocurrency*'s protocol to control its supply, distribution, and value. This can include predetermined issuance rates, token *burning* mechanisms, *staking rewards*, and governance decisions. Unlike traditional monetary systems overseen by central authorities, these policies are often decentralised and algorithmically enforced, aiming to create a predictable and transparent monetary system within the cryptocurrency's ecosystem.

monetary system a framework established to manage a nation's *currency*, *money* supply, and interest rates, typically overseen by a *central bank*. It functions as a public good, serving the nation's interest by ensuring economic stability, facilitating trade, and promoting sustainable growth within the economy.

money Any medium of exchange that is accepted by people for the payment of goods and services and the repayment of debt. Historically, *barter systems* were used to exchange goods and services for other goods and services. But the lack of transferability and divisibility, as well as the variable desirability of goods and services when compared to other goods and services, led to the development of commodity money (e.g. dried pelts, grain, and gold). Especially in the case of gold, everybody agrees on its perceived value, making it a good medium of exchange. This is why national currencies were backed by gold until recently (in the history of money). Fast forward to more modern times, most currencies are no longer backed by gold, but rather on supply and demand and the stability of the government that issues it. The US dollar hasn't been backed by gold since 1971 and the British pound since 1931. A currency that isn't backed by gold is called a fiat currency or *fiat money*. Economists classify money into three categories:

M1 money: All physical representations including notes and coins; bank accounts where money can be withdrawn immediately (i.e. on-demand); traveller's cheques; any other form of liquid deposits and assets.

M2 money: All the M1 money, plus all time-related deposits, several types of retirement accounts, and non-institutional money market funds.

M3 money: All the M1 and M2 money, with the addition of all large time deposits, institutional money market funds, short-term repurchase agreements, and other larger liquid assets. M3 represents a country's total money supply.

In practice, the terms "money" and "currency" are often used interchangeably, and from the definition above, you'll realise that currency (i.e. notes and coins) is only one representation of M1 money...

Moneygram[15] A *Money Transfer Operator.*

money laundering Concealing the origin of money obtained from illegal activities such as drug trafficking, corruption, embezzlement, or gambling (where illegal) by converting it into a legitimate source. There are three stages of money laundering – placement, layering, and integration – that allow illicit funds to enter the legitimate financial system, obfuscate their origins, and then to reintegrate them so as to appear as legal tender. A form of *financial crime.*

Money Laundering Reporting Officer (MLRO) An employee appointed to oversee a firm's compliance with *Anti-Money Laundering (AML)* regulations and to alert the company where there is knowledge or suspicion of *money laundering.* A tough job.

money mule A person who uses a payment account (e.g. a bank account) in their control to transfer money (usually obtained illegally) to another account or set of accounts on behalf of others. Typically, money mules are duped by fraudsters through fake job offers, commissions, and other incentives, but some may act willingly. Money mules are liable for fraud and may be prosecuted as they facilitate *money laundering.* See also *financial crime, first-party fraud,* and *social engineering.*

money remittance A payment service by which funds are sent by a *payer* to a *payee* where no payment account needs to be opened in the name of either the payer or payee.

Money Service Business (MSB) Outside of Europe, this term is used to describe an *Electronic Money Institution (EMI)* or *Payment Institution (PI).*

Money Transfer Operator (MTO) A financial company (usually not a bank) engaged in *money remittance* including *cross-border* transfer of funds. MTOs use their internal systems and/or access to banking networks. The MTO will use their own banking relationships and each country's bank payment capabilities where they can.

Monzo[16] A UK *neo-bank.*

More Time System[17] A *real-time payment system (RTP system), retail payment system (RPS)* in Japan, operated by Zengin-Net.

MOTO See *Mail Order/Telephone Order.*

MOR See *Merchant of Record.*

Move A programming language developed for the Diem blockchain (formerly known as Libra) by Facebook, designed to enable secure and flexible *smart contract* development. It emphasises resource-oriented programming, allowing developers to express the ownership and lifecycle of digital assets directly in the code. Move features a strong static type system and formal verification capabilities, ensuring that smart contracts are safe from common vulnerabilities. Its design prioritises safety, efficiency, and composability, making it suitable for building decentralised applications that require robust asset management and complex transaction logic.

M-PESA[18] A *mobile money* service successful in Kenya and other African countries.

MPC See *secure multi-party computation.*

MPI Merchant Plug-In. See *3D Secure Server.*

mPOS See *mobile Point-of-Sale.*

MSC See *Merchant Service Charge.*

MSP See *Merchant Services Provider.*

MSR See *Magnetic Stripe Reader.*

MT message A legacy *SWIFT* message type (i.e. prior to ISO 2002). See also *MX message.*

MTO See *Money Transfer Operator.*

mule account See *money mule.*

multi-CBDC (mCBDC) A *CBDC* interoperability model that aims to tackle *cross-border* payments inefficiencies and frictions in today's *correspondent banking* system, such as differences in *payment systems* opening hours, varying communication standards, and lack of transparency around exchange rates or fees. There are three implementation models for mCBDCs:

Enhanced compatibility: the different jurisdictions agree on compatible regulatory technical standards, and there is a multitude of privately offered correspondent banking and *clearing* services. Each jurisdiction has its own CBDC regulation.

Interlinking: the different jurisdictions agree to connect their separate CBDC infrastructures through shared technical interfaces or by use of a common *clearing* mechanism (centralised or decentralised). Each jurisdiction has its own CBDC regulation.

Single-system integration: multiple CBDCs can be run on a single platform for all participating jurisdictions. There is a single set of regulations for all participants and a single infrastructure and ledger.

See also intermediated CBDC (sCBDC) and direct CBDC.

multi-factor authentication (MFA) The use of two or more *authentication* factors when authenticating payment account holders and users. See also *knowledge-based authentication*.

multi-function card A term used to describe cards that have multiple functions, such as payments online and in-person, and cash withdrawal at ATMs. Generally associated with *open-loop cards*. Also called "multifunctional card".

multi-party computation (MPC) See *secure multi-party computation*.

multi-rail A term used to describe payment services that enable operations across multiple payment channels, networks, or *payment schemes*.

MX message A *SWIFT* message type that complies with ISO 20022.

MyGov.be[19] A government-issued *digital identity* scheme in Belgium.

Notes

1 Gartner Urges Businesses to Join the Machine Customer Megatrend. *CX Today*, 17 March 2023. https://www.cxtoday.com/contact-centre/gartner-urges-businesses-to-join-the-machine-customer-megatrend/ (Accessed 29 September 2024)

2 Mastercard. https://www.mastercard.com (Accessed 21 November 2023)

3 Mastercard MATCH™. https://developer.mastercard.com/product/match/ (Accessed 21 November 2023)

4 YouLend. https://youlend.com/ (Accessed 19 January 2024)

5 365 Finance. https://www.365finance.co.uk/ (Accessed 19 January 2024)

6 Nucleus Commercial Finance. https://nucleuscommercialfinance.com/ (Accessed 19 January 2024)

7 Liberis Ltd. https://www.liberis.com/ (Accessed 19 January 2024)

8 Aldermore. https://www.aldermore.co.uk/business-finance/invoicefinance/ (Accessed 19 January 2024)

9 eCapital. https://ecapital.com/ (Accessed 19 January 2024)

10 Kriya. https://www.kriya.co/ (Accessed 19 January 2024)

11 MitID. https://www.mitid.dk/ (Accessed 21 November 2023)

12 Mobiilivarmenne. https://mobiilivarmenne.fi/ (Accessed 21 November 2023)

13 MobilePay. https://mobilepaygroup.com/ (Accessed 21 November 2023)
14 Modulr. https://www.modulrfinance.com/ (Accessed 21 November 2023)
15 Moneygram. https://www.moneygram.com/ (Accessed 21 November 2023)
16 Monzo. https://monzo.com/ (Accessed 21 November 2023)
17 Zengin-Net. https://www.zengin-net.jp/en/zengin_net/pdf/pamphlet_e.pdf (Accessed 21 November 2023)
18 M-PESA. https://www.vodafone.com/about-vodafone/what-we-do/consumer-products-and-services/m-pesa (Accessed 21 November 2023)
19 MyGov.be. https://mygov.be/ (Accessed 27 November 2024)

N

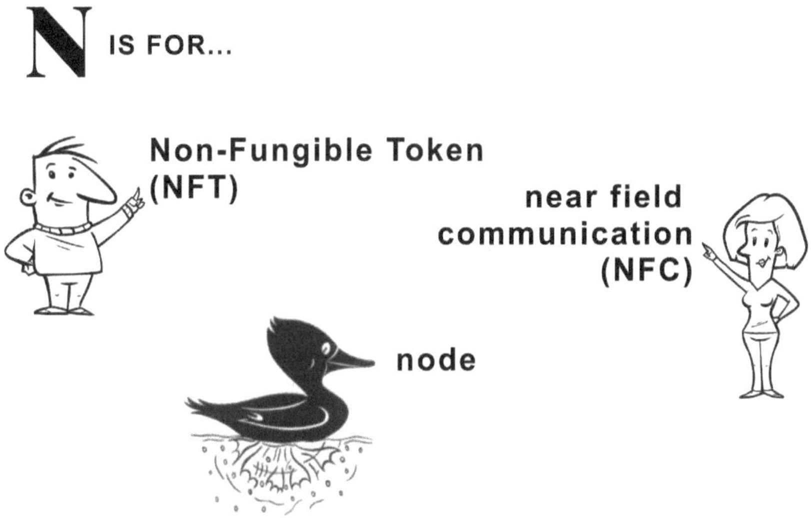

N26[1] A *neo-bank*.

National Automated Clearing House Association (NACHA)[2] The US governance body for US *ACH schemes*. NACHA is also an accreditation body.

Natural Language Processing (NLP) A branch of *artificial intelligence* that focuses on enabling computers to understand, interpret, and

DOI: 10.4324/9781003571131-15

generate human language in a valuable way. It combines computational linguistics, *machine learning*, and *deep learning* techniques to process and analyse large amounts of natural language data. NLP enables machines to perform tasks such as language translation, sentiment analysis, speech recognition, text summarisation, and question answering. In the context of payments and finance, NLP is used for *chatbots*, *voice-activated payments*, automated customer service, *fraud detection* through analysis of text data, and extracting insights from financial reports and news articles. By bridging the gap between human communication and computer understanding, NLP plays a crucial role in making financial services more accessible and user-friendly.

near field communication (NFC) A *contactless* interface. Contactless-enabled cards and contactless-enabled card payment terminals use this interface. It is defined in *ISO/ IEC 18092* and *ISO/ IEC 21481*.

NemID[3] A *digital identity* framework in Denmark.

neo-bank A digital-only bank. A *fintech* firm that offers mobile apps, software, and financial services with only an online presence and no physical branches. Also referred to as a "digital bank".

network vulnerability scan A software facility provided by *Accredited Scanning Vendors (ASVs)* which inspects the potential points of exploit on a computer or network to identify security holes. A vulnerability scan detects and classifies system weaknesses in computers, networks, and communications equipment and predicts the effectiveness of countermeasures. Also referred to as an "ASV scan". Particularly relevant in the context of *PCI DSS* compliance.

new account fraud A type of *unauthorised fraud* where a fraudster or *money mule* has been successfully onboarded by a financial institution after applying using their own identity (*first-party fraud*), a stolen identity (*third-party fraud*), or a synthetic identity (i.e. identity created from real and fake identity information over time). Also referred to as "application fraud".

Nexi (formerly Sia)[4] A financial services institution who operates bank payment schemes in Europe and is also an *acquirer*. See also *payment scheme*.

NextGenPSD2[5] An *Open Banking* standard originally proposed by the *Berlin Group* and on which all national EU Open Banking standards are based.

NFC See *Near Field Communication*.

NFT See *Non-Fungible Token*.

NIBSS Instant Payment (NIP)[6] An *account-to-account payment* service in Nigeria.

NKS-Inst[7] A *real-time payment system (RTP system)*, *retail payment system (RPS)* in Croatia.

No CVM A card transaction where there is no cardholder verification. No CVM payments have low transaction limits. See *Cardholder Verification Method (CVM)*.

node A term used in computing to refer to a physical device or *virtual machine* connected to a network capable of processing and/ or transmitting data. In *blockchain* infrastructures, a node is a computer that participates in the management and operation of the network by maintaining a copy of the distributed ledger and validating transactions. See also *blockchain*, *miner*, *validator*, *full node*, *master node*, and *deep learning*.

non-bank financial institution A financial institution that doesn't come under the definition of a *bank*, which means other than a credit institution in Europe or a depository institution in the US. Sometimes referred to as "non-bank PSP".

non-bank PSP Non-bank Payment Service Provider. See *non-bank financial institution*.

nonce A contraction of "number used once". In a *blockchain* context, the nonce is a number that can only be used once, is included as a transaction input, and used as a security measure in the transaction validation process. It is commonly used in computer science and *cryptography*, particularly in the context of *hashing* and *cryptography protocols*. In some *blockchain* implementations, a nonce may be included in individual transactions by the user's crypto wallet (or other facility used to interact with the blockchain). The user's wallet keeps track of the nonce associated with their address (*public key*) and ensures that each transaction has a unique and sequentially increasing nonce. By having users include a nonce, blockchain networks ensure that transactions are processed in the correct order and prevent *replay attacks*. A nonce may also be used for a different purpose in *Proof of Work (PoW)* blockchains where it is a field in the block header. Here, validating nodes must find a value for the nonce that, when combined with the other block header data, produces a hash that meets certain criteria (specified by the blockchain *consensus protocol*). Miners adjust the nonce repeatedly (this is resource-intensive) until a valid hash is found (i.e. below the *difficulty target*), signifying that they have successfully mined a block. See also *hash*.

non-custodial wallet See *crypto wallet*.

Non-Fungible Token (NFT) A type of *crypto asset* that has been tokenised on a *blockchain* and assigned a unique identification. Non-fungible means "unique" and therefore can't be replicated. An NFT is different from other crypto assets, or *fiat currencies*, which are interchangeable. NFTs are largely unregulated, unless they come in the scope of securities regulations.

nostro account See *correspondent banking*.

NPP[8] A *real-time payment system (RTP system)*, *retail payment system (RPS)* in Australia, operated by NPPA.

Notes

1 N26. https://n26.com/ (Accessed 21 November 2023)
2 NACHA. https://www.nacha.org/ (Accessed 21 November 2023)
3 NemID. https://lifeindenmark.borger.dk/apps-and-digital-services/nemid (Accessed 21 November 2023)
4 Nexi. https://www.nexigroup.com/ (Accessed 21 November 2023)
5 Berlin Group (NextGenPSD2). https://www.berlin-group.org/nextgen-psd2-downloads (Accessed 21 November 2023)
6 NIBSS. https://nibss-plc.com.ng/nibss-instant-payment/ (Accessed 21 November 2023)
7 Croatian National Bank. https://www.hnb.hr/en/-/announcementon-the-beginning-of-operation-of-the-nksinst-payment-system (Accessed 21 November 2023)
8 Reserve Bank of Australia. https://www.rba.gov.au/paymentsand-infrastructure/new-payments-platform/about-npp.html (Accessed 21 November 2023)

O

O IS FOR...

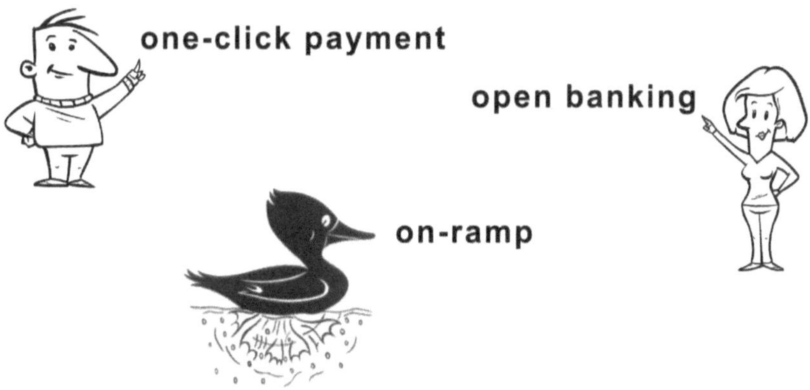

off-chain Refers to processing that is not conducted on a *layer 1 blockchain*. Processing may include processing transactions, record-keeping, computation, data storage, dispute resolution, security, governance, and much more. See also *layer 2 scaling solution* and *on-chain*.

off-chain governance A decision-making process for *blockchain* networks that occurs outside the blockchain itself. It involves discussions,

DOI: 10.4324/9781003571131-16

debates, and voting mechanisms conducted through external channels such as forums, social media, or in-person meetings. This approach allows for more flexible and nuanced decision-making but may lack the transparency and immutability of *on-chain governance*.

offline A state in which a device, system, or application is not connected to the internet or a network, preventing real-time communication or data exchange. In this context, offline can refer to the inability to access online services, resources, or updates and may also indicate that data is stored locally rather than in the cloud. Offline functionality is often designed to allow users to perform tasks without an internet connection, with changes synchronised once connectivity is restored.

offline bank transfer A *payment method* that breaks the payment process into two stages. First, the user would complete a transaction on the platform used and will be given the destination bank account details and other information, including a transaction identifier. Second, the user will make a payment through their bank to the platform with the details provided. They could also pay cash later at an affiliated outlet or store. Once the second stage is completed, the transaction would be considered complete on the platform. This is a form of *delayed payment*. Many PSPs offer this payment method to merchants, and it is popular in some geographies. An example is safetypay.[1]

off-ramp A service that allows users to convert *cryptocurrency* into *fiat money*. These services are typically provided by entities such as *crypto exchanges*, where they base the amount of the crypto-to-fiat transaction on current market rates. Essentially, off-ramp means leaving the decentralised, *blockchain*-based monetary system and entering into the traditional fiat monetary system. Also spelled "off ramp" and sometimes referred to as "crypto off ramp". See also *on-ramp*.

offline transaction On the *card rails*, the term is used to describe *card acceptance* where no network connection is available at the time of the transaction. This means that the *issuer* cannot be contacted for *authorisation*.

omnibus account An account held at a *central bank* that streamlines how financial institutions hold reserves at the central bank. Instead of each institution having its own separate account, they can all deposit funds into a single, consolidated account managed by the central bank. The central bank then keeps detailed records of how much each institution has deposited, ensuring everyone has access to their reserves, whilst benefiting from a more efficient system.

omnichannel A term used to describe the seamless integration of all the different methods of interaction that a business has with its customers: physical, online, mobile, social media, etc. Usually associated with the term "strategy" when associated with the retail industry, as in "Business X has an omnichannel strategy".

onboarding The process consisting of all activities involved in introducing a new customer to a business's products and services. This process ensures regulatory, legal, and credit-related *due diligence* obligations. It includes KYC checks and procedures such as identity verification and document collection. Also referred to as "customer onboarding". See also *merchant onboarding* and *underwriting*.

on-chain Refers to processing that is conducted on a *layer 1 blockchain*. Processing may include processing transactions, record-keeping, computation, data storage, dispute resolution, security, governance, and much more. See also *off-chain*.

on-chain analysis A service which provides *cryptocurrency* investors with charts and dashboards to better help them visualise *blockchain* data and track the movements of cryptocurrencies and individual wallets. See also *chain analysis*.

on-chain governance A decision-making process for *blockchain* networks where proposed changes and voting occur directly on the blockchain itself. Stakeholders (typically token holders) can propose and vote on protocol upgrades, parameter changes, or other decisions using transactions recorded on the blockchain. This approach aims to provide transparency, immutability, and automation to the governance process. See also *off-chain governance*.

one-click payment A type of card payment transaction that allows returning shoppers to make a payment without re-entering their full card details and address information. Also referred to as one-click checkout. See also *delegated authentication*.

one-leg out transaction In the context of the EU *Second Payment Services Directive (PSD2)*, this is a transaction where one of the PSPs (either the payer's or the payee's) is based outside of the EU. One-leg out transactions are not subject to the *Strong Customer Authentication (SCA)* requirements.

One-Time Passcode (OTP) A one-time authorisation code or dynamic password that is valid for only one login session or transaction, on a computer system or other digital device. Sometimes referred to as One-Time Password, One-Time PIN, or One-Time Authorisation Code (OTAC).

online PIN Describes the process by which the *PIN* entered by a cardholder for a card payment transaction is sent to the *issuer* online for verification. The entered PIN is encrypted before it is sent.

on-ramp A service that allows users to convert *fiat money* into *cryptocurrency*. These services are typically provided by providers such as *crypto exchanges* (the more commonly used) and third-party service providers (which may also offer services such as *crypto debit cards*), where they base the amount of the fiat-crypto transaction on current market rates. Essentially, on-ramp means leaving the traditional fiat monetary system and enter into the decentralised, *blockchain*-based monetary system instead, just like entering a motorway or highway. Also spelled "on ramp" and sometimes referred to as "fiat on-ramp". See also *off-ramp*.

on us When a payment instruction is issued to one bank and credited to a different account within the same bank. On us payments don't require the use of a *payment scheme*, and settlement is performed using the bank's own infrastructure. Also referred to as "intrabank settlement".

open API A communication interface that follows a public standard or set of standards that are publicly available for developers to use.

Open Banking A term referring to the use of *open application programming interfaces (APIs)* that enable *third-party PSPs (TPPs)* to build and provide account information or payment initiation services through data access to payment accounts managed by *Account Servicing PSPs (ASPSPs)*. Usually capitalised, but sometimes written as "open banking".

open banking payment A type of account-to-account *(A2A) payment* that follows agreed standards of interoperability, such as *open APIs*.

Open Economy An evolution of *Open Finance* where data sharing extends beyond financial services to all walks of life (e.g. travel, utilities, health, social, lifestyle, and property government). Usually capitalised, but sometimes written as "open economy".

Open Finance An evolution of *Open Banking* where data sharing extends beyond payment account data into wider financial services. Usually capitalised, but sometimes written as "open finance".

open loop An economic model that promotes competition. An open-loop *payment instrument* enables the account holder to make payments without having to be part of the system itself, such as a public transport card that may only be used on a specific public transport network. See *four-party model*, *three party model*, and *closed loop*.

open-loop card A card issued by *issuers* in the *four-party model*.

open source A term related to software development to describe an approach whereby something (e.g. a project, a product, an initiative, and software) can be shared and modified by anyone because it is publicly accessible, following the principle of open exchange. Nowadays, it primarily refers to open-source software, which is a computer code that anyone can inspect, modify, or otherwise enhance. This is different from proprietary software where only the original authors can inspect, modify, or enhance the code, and users of the software must agree that they will not do anything with it that is not expressively permitted by the authors/owners. Users of open-source software must also agree to the terms of a licence agreement, but the terms are very different from those applying to proprietary software as they are usually related to how users may use, study, modify, or distribute the software. *Permissionless blockchains* use open-source software. See also *blockchain*.

open standard A publicly available and universally accepted set of guidelines or specifications that allows different systems, products, or services to work together seamlessly. Open standards are developed collaboratively and are intended to foster interoperability, innovation, and competition. In the payments space, two prominent examples include the *ISO 20022* standard for electronic data interchange between financial institutions and the *EMV* standard for chip-based payment cards and terminals. These standards ensure compatibility and security across different payment systems globally.

OpenSSL A mature and widely used *open-source cryptography* library.

optimistic rollup (ORU) A *blockchain layer 2 scaling solution*. A type of *rollup*.

open wallet See *pass-through digital wallet*.

operating regulations This usually refers to the rules set by a *card scheme* for the operation and governance of their network. Sometimes referred to as "operating rules".

oracle A data feed that connects a *blockchain* to *off-chain* (real-world) information so that *smart contracts* can query real-world data. For example, a prediction market *dApp* may use oracles to settle payments based on events, such as asking users to bet *cryptocurrency* on who will become the next president of the United States. They'll use an oracle to confirm the outcome and payout to the winners.

ordering service node A type of *node* in some *permissioned blockchain* networks, particularly *Hyperledger Fabric*, responsible for ordering transactions into blocks and maintaining the shared ledger. These nodes play a crucial role in the consensus process by establishing the chronological order of transactions and ensuring consistency across the network.

Order Insight[2] A service offered by Visa allowing *issuers* and merchants to retrieve detailed card transaction information when a customer questions or disputes a transaction. Through integration within the merchant's environment, transaction details can be made available that may help a cardholder recognise a transaction. This can help with minimising *retrievals* or prevent retrievals from turning into *disputes*. Order insight was created by Verifi, which is a subsidiary of Visa.

orphan block A valid block in a *blockchain* that is not part of the main chain due to being mined simultaneously with another block. It is temporarily accepted but ultimately discarded when the network reaches consensus on a longer chain, resulting in the orphan block's transactions returning to the mempool for inclusion in future blocks. See also *accidental fork*.

ORU See *optimistic rollup*.

OTAC One-Time Authorisation Code. See *One-Time Passcode*.

OTP See *One-Time Passcode*.

outlet A term referring to one physical location of a retail chain in the network of a merchant's business.

overcapture A term used to describe the capture of a card payment for an amount higher than the amount authorised. *Card schemes* may allow overcapture but have limits such as percentage of transactions or types of businesses.

over-collateralisation A risk management practice where the value of collateral exceeds the value of the asset or loan it secures. In *crypto assets*, particularly for *crypto-backed stablecoins*, over-collateralisation involves maintaining a higher value of cryptocurrency collateral than the value of *stablecoins* issued. This excess collateral acts as a buffer against price *volatility*, helping to maintain the stablecoin's *peg* even during significant market fluctuations. For example, a crypto-backed stablecoin might require $150 worth of cryptocurrency collateral for every $100 of stablecoins issued, representing a 1.5:1 collateralisation ratio.

overlay service A term generally used in the bank payment context but also applies to the *card rails*. These are services implemented on top of an existing *payment scheme*. Some bank payment examples are *Confirmation of Payee*, *Request-to-Pay*, and *Variable Recurring Payment*. On the card rails, *3D Secure* can be considered and overlay service. In decentralised infrastructures such as *blockchain*, you could say that a *smart contract* is technically an overlay service on top of a blockchain *settlement* infrastructure.

Notes

1 Safetypay. https://www.safetypay.com/en/ (Accessed 6 December 2023)
2 Visa Developer Center. https://developer.visa.com/capabilities/visa-cardholder-purchase-inquiry (Accessed 21 November 2023)

P

P IS FOR...

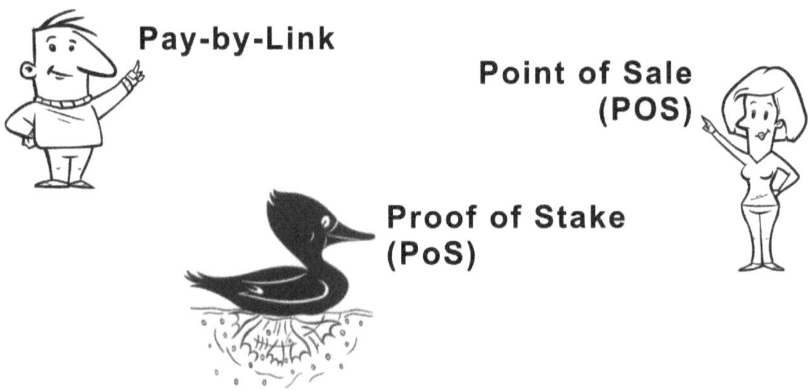

P27[1] The P27 *cross-border, real-time payment system* aimed to combine eight bank *payment schemes* across the Nordics into one integrated real-time payment system, but it collapsed in April 2023 due to a lack of political alignment and critical mass, as well as conflicts of interest. Also see *European Payment Initiative* (EPI).

DOI: 10.4324/9781003571131-17

P2P See *peer-to-peer.*

P2PE See *Point-to-Point Encryption.*

PaaS See *Payment-as-a-Service* or *Platform-as-a-Service.*

packet tampering A type of *cyberattack* where an unauthorised party intercepts, alters, or injects malicious data into network packets as they travel between a source and destination. This technique exploits vulnerabilities in network protocols or inadequate *encryption* to modify the content, routing information, or other attributes of data packets. Packet tampering can lead to various security breaches, including data theft, *man-in-the-middle attacks*, or service disruptions. It underscores the importance of secure communication protocols and encryption in maintaining data integrity and confidentiality across networks.

PAN See *Primary Account Number.*

PancakeSwap[2] A decentralised *crypto exchange.*

PAN Key Entry (PKE) A *Card Not Present* (CNP) payment transaction by which a merchant enters the cardholder details into a payment terminal. This is a type of *Merchant-Initiated Transaction* (MIT) usually associated with MOTO. These transactions are not authenticated and therefore expensive to process for merchants. Sometimes called Manual Key Entry (MKE), Manual PAN Key Entry, or keyed transaction.

paper wallet A physical form of *crypto wallet* where the public and private keys are printed on paper, often as *QR codes.* This offline storage method provides enhanced security against online threats and hacking attempts. Paper wallets are considered a type of "cold storage" as they are not connected to the internet, making them suitable for long-term storage of cryptocurrency. However, they require careful handling to prevent physical damage or loss, and users must exercise caution when generating and printing the keys to ensure security.

parent blockchain See *layer 1 blockchain.*

partial authorisation When a card purchase transaction exceeds the cardholder's limit, the *issuer* may return a partial authorisation for funds up to the amount of the limit. At the *Point of Sale* (POS), a merchant may request an additional method of payment to cover the outstanding balance.

passport arrangement See *passporting arrangement.*

passporting arrangement A term used in Europe to describe the process by which a payment firm authorised to conduct business by one country's regulator is able to conduct business in all countries in the EU block without having to be authorised by the other regulators. Also referred to as "passport arrangement".

pass-through digital wallet A *mobile wallet* where the card payment information is passed on directly to the *Account Servicing PSP (ASPSP)* (e.g. *issuer*) through the *payment scheme* (e.g. *card scheme*) to perform a payment transaction. Funds are never stored on this type of wallet. For example, if a Visa card is attached to a pass-through wallet, the payment transaction would be like any other Visa transaction. Technically, this type of wallet is not a *payment instrument* (i.e. the Visa card is), but only a technical service (i.e. a container or the digital equivalent of a leather wallet). Apple Pay, Venmo, and Samsung Wallet are pass-through digital wallets. Also referred to as "open wallet".

PAX[3] A Chinese multinational corporation providing merchant services technology including *Point-of-Sale* card terminals and value-added services.

pay-by-link A *payment method* by which a customer is able to make a payment through a web payment link sent to them whilst they're on the phone, chat, or social media channel. This means that card details don't have to be shared during the interaction. Pay-by-link is a value-added service that can be offered by a *Payment Service Provider (PSP)* or *Independent Software Vendor (ISV)* for merchants to integrate within their environment. Sometimes called a "payment link".

payee The entity or person that gets paid. See also *Payment Service User*.

payee's PSP The payment *ecosystem* actor which enables a *payee* to accept payments. On the *card rails*, they provide merchants with the connectivity to the *acquirer*. They can be either physical (e.g. payment terminal provider) or virtual (e.g. e-commerce payment gateway) and are often referred to as the merchant's PSP. Sometimes, these PSPs are also referred to as *Payment Service Providers (PSPs)* or *Merchant Service Providers (MSPs)*, which can be a bit confusing! Context is important. On the bank rails, it can be any entity that provides payment functionality, enabling a business to accept bank payments.

payer The entity or person who pays. See also *Payment Service User*.

payer's PSP A *Payment Service Provider (PSP)* that provides a payer with a payment account. Also referred to as an *Account Servicing PSP (ASPSP)*. On the *card rails*, they provide the payer with a card account and are also referred to as an "*issuer*". On the bank rails, this entity is a bank, and they provide a payer with a bank account. This term may also refer to technology providers such as *digital wallets*.

payfac See *payment facilitator*.

payment A transfer of value from one party to another.

payment acceptance The process by which merchants take payments by card. Also referred to as "card acceptance".

payment aggregator An aggregator of payment services. This is a generic term, and to understand its nuances, you need to look at specific models, such as *merchants of record*, *payment facilitator*, and ISO. Also referred to as "merchant aggregator".

Payment-as-a-Service (PaaS) A cloud-based delivery model that enables businesses to outsource their payment processing infrastructure and services to third-party providers. It allows organisations to offer advanced payment products and services to their customers without the need for significant upfront investment in hardware, software, or internal development. PaaS providers handle various aspects of payment processing, including *authorisation*, *settlement*, security, compliance, and maintenance, typically on a subscription basis. This model offers benefits such as cost efficiency, scalability, enhanced security, and access to cutting-edge payment technologies, allowing businesses to focus on their core competencies whilst leveraging modern payment capabilities.

payment card A *card* used for payments.

Payment Card Industry Data Security Standard (PCI DSS) A *data security* standard developed and maintained by the *Payment Card Industry Standards Security Council*. It applies to all organisations which store, process, or transmit cardholder information, either electronically or manually. *Card schemes* include PCI DSS compliance in their *operating regulations* and may levy penalties on their members and stakeholders for non-compliance. *Acquirers* are responsible for ensuring the PCI compliance of their merchant portfolios. Card schemes manage the compliance of service providers directly.

Payment Card Industry Standards Security Council (PCI SSC)[4] The PCI Standards Security Council was founded by American Express, Discover, JCB International, Mastercard, and Visa, and UnionPay is a strategic member. The PCI SCC is a body similar to EMVCo and is responsible for the development and maintenance of PCI standards. It encourages industry participation through various programmes, including "Participating Organisations", "Affiliate Members", and "Special Interest Groups".

payment facilitator (payfac) A type of *payment aggregator*. A payment facilitator, such as Stripe or PayPal, connects one buyer with one seller. The cardholder intends to buy from the seller and may not even know that a payfac is involved, as they only facilitate the payment. With a payfac, the seller is responsible for the fulfilment and end-to-end customer experience. This is a payment aggregation model that offers merchant services on a *sub-merchant* platform. Those sub-merchants then no longer have to get their own *Merchant ID (MID)* and can instead be boarded under the master *MID* of the payment facilitator. Payment facilitation differs from *payment orchestration*, in that payment orchestration focuses on managing and optimising multiple payment providers and methods for a single merchant, whilst payment facilitation is about enabling multiple sub-merchants to process payments under a single master account.

payment gateway The technology that enables merchants to accept online card payments on their websites. Provided by a *merchant's PSP* on the *card rails* (e.g. a payment gateway provider, an *acquirer*). Also see *payee's PSP*.

Payment Initiation Service Provider (PISP) A *Third-Party PSP (TPP)* which initiates payments on behalf of a payer. Sometimes called a "payment originator".

payment institution (PI) In Europe, a regulated payment business that is able to receive payments, remit money, issue cards, but can't store value. There are two types of payment institutions, the small payment institution (SPI) and the authorised payment institution (PI). In some geographies, it may be referred to as a "money service business (MSB)".

payment instruction A directive provided by a payer detailing the specifics of a payment to be executed, including the amount, recipient's account details, and payment method. A direct payment instruction is given directly to the organisation holding the *payer's* financial account (e.g. a bank), whilst an indirect payment instruction is given to an intermediary (such as a payment service provider or fintech company) authorised to execute the payment on behalf of the account holder. Indirect instructions often involve additional steps or processes before the actual account-holding institution receives the instruction to move funds. Sometimes called "payment order".

payment instrument A physical or virtual facility allowing the payment account holder to transfer funds. Examples of payment instruments are cards, money orders, cheques, etc.

payment message A communication message that typically contains information related to a payment, such as the identities of the parties involved, account information, and the payment amount.

payment method A facility that a *payer* (e.g. cardholder or bank account holder) will use to make payments.

payment optimisation The process by which a merchant optimises their payment processes, conversion rates, and card payment acceptance fees. *Acquirers*, other *merchant's PSPs*, and professional services firms may offer this service. Also referred to as card optimisation.

payment orchestration The process of integrating and managing several stakeholders in the payments value chain to simplify integration into merchant environments and payment processing. Payment orchestration platform providers typically offer these services through a single *API*, enabling businesses to connect to multiple payment gateways, *acquirers*, various PSPs, as well as providing other services such as risk management, CRM, and KYC. Increasingly, the term also applies to service providers offering payment services across multiple *blockchains*. See also *dynamic routing*.

payment order See *payment instruction*.

payment page The customer-facing part of a *virtual terminal* that is integrated into a merchant's environment (e.g. online shop). For telephone sales, a virtual terminal can be used by the merchant, and this is where they would enter the cardholder's details as supplied by the cardholder over the phone. See *payee's PSP*.

payment processing error In the cards world, this is a mistake made by a merchant when processing a card payment. Such mistakes often result in *chargebacks*, and common ones include processing a transaction twice, processing a cancelled transaction, or processing a transaction for the wrong amount.

Payment Request API A web standard introduced by the *World Wide Web Consortium (W3C)* in 2016 to streamline the checkout process on websites and web applications. It provides a consistent user interface for entering payment details, shipping information, and other transaction data across different devices and platforms. This *API* enables developers to create more seamless and secure payment experiences by leveraging browser-stored payment methods and user information, potentially reducing cart abandonment rates and improving conversion. The Payment Request API supports various payment methods, including credit cards, digital wallets, and other online payment systems, and aims to simplify the integration of payment functionality for web developers.

payment scheme Generally, this refers to the *ecosystem* actor which provides the centralised payment infrastructure and operating rules. For the *card rails*, examples of payment schemes are Visa, Mastercard, American Express, etc., and these are also referred to as *card schemes*, "card networks", or "card brands". For the bank rails, examples of payment schemes are UK FPS, US FedNow, etc. In Europe, however, a SEPA payment scheme only consists of the operating rules and technical specifications for the scheme (e.g. *SEPA credit transfer*). *SEPA* refers to the payment schemes mentioned above as *payment systems*.

payment security A subset of *data protection* concerned with the protection of payment-related data. Generally associated with the *Payment Card Industry Data Security Standard (PCI DSS)*.

Payment Services Provider (PSP) A very generic term referring to any entity providing a payment service in a payments *ecosystem*.

Payment Services Regulation (PSR)[5] The UK regulation for payment services. Also the EU regulation adjunct to PSD3.

Payment Service User (PSU) The payment *ecosystem* actor which uses payment services. If the actor makes a payment, they are referred to as a "payer", and if they receive a payment, they are referred to as a "payee". On the *card rails*, the PSU can be the actor who pays with a card, referred to as a *cardholder*, or the PSU who gets paid with a card, referred to as a *merchant*. On the bank rails, the PSUs are bank account holders.

payment system See *payment scheme*.

Payment Systems Regulator (PSR)[6] The UK regulator for *payment systems*.

payment terminal A payment facility to enable merchants to accept card payments. Payment terminals can be physical (hardware) or virtual (digital). See also *POS*, *EPOS*, *mPOS*, *SoftPOS*, *payment page*, *virtual terminal*, and *unattended payment terminal*.

Payment-versus-Payment (PvP) A common form of *settlement* used in foreign exchange transactions which guarantees the final transfer of one currency only happens after the final transfer of another currency also happens, alleviating *settlement risk*. See also *Delivery-versus-Payment (PvP)*, *atomic settlement*, and *atomic swap*.

PayNow[7] An *account-to-account payment* service in Singapore.

pay out A broad term used to describe a sum of money paid in one go to an individual or a business. Also spelled "payout".

PayPal[8] An *e-wallet*, a *staged digital wallet*.

PayTech A term used to describe technology used in the payments *ecosystem*. A subset of *fintech*.

Paytm[9] A *mobile wallet*, a *stored value digital wallet*. One of India's leading payment apps.

PayTo[10] An *account-to-account payment* service in Australia.

Pay.UK[11] The operator of the UK *retail payment systems*.

P card See *purchasing card*.

PCI DSS See *Payment Card Industry Data Security Standard*.

PCI SSC See *Payment Card Industry Security Standards Council*.

PDQ Process Data Quickly. A PDQ machine is also referred to as a *Point-of-Sale (POS)* terminal or card reader/ terminal.

PED PIN Entry Device. See *Point of Sale (POS)*.

peer-to-peer (P2P) A generic term used to describe services, platforms, or facilities that seemingly enable interactions between peers. It is used interchangeably with person-to-person.

peer-to-peer money exchange A type of *fintech* company challenging traditional *Money Transfer Operators (MTOs)* and bank *wire transfers*. Instead of using *correspondent banking* and *cross-border* transactions, they "crowd-source" fund transfer matches in each of the countries involved in a fund transfer. And then, theoretically, they only need to perform *domestic* bank transactions at each end, making them cheaper.

peer-to-peer networking A principle by which peers communicate with each other without the need for a central authority or intermediary.

peer-to-peer payment (P2P payment) A misnomer. Used to describe digital payment apps such as Venmo or Zelle. To the users, it looks like they're making a payment directly to their friend (or supplier, etc.) without intermediaries (hence peer-to-peer). This is not the case. Regardless of the rails used (i.e. card or bank), these payments still need to go through the existing mechanisms (i.e. *Authorisation*, *Clearing*, and *Settlement*), and therefore through intermediaries. For true "Peer-to-Peer" payments, you must look at decentralised rails. See also *real-time payment*, *invisible payment*, and *frictionless payment*.

peg A fixed exchange rate between two currencies or assets. In the context of *stablecoins*, a peg refers to the intended fixed value of the stablecoin relative to its target asset, typically a *fiat currency* like the US dollar. Stablecoins can have a *hard peg*, which aims to maintain a strict 1:1 ratio, or a *soft peg*, which allows for minor fluctuations around the target value. The peg is crucial for ensuring the stablecoin's stability and utility as a medium of exchange and store of value in the *cryptocurrency* ecosystem.

PEI[12] A real-time payment system (RTP system), *retail payment system* (RPS) in Argentina.

PEP See *Politically Exposed Person*.

permissioned blockchain A *blockchain* controlled by a central entity (or set of entities) where access is restricted to certain *nodes*, and rights also can be restricted. See also *consortium blockchain*, *private blockchain*, and *hybrid blockchain*.

permissioned blockchain platform A development environment specifically designed to address the needs of permissioned blockchain development to control access, maintain privacy, and use consensus mechanisms suited for smaller groups of known participants, features which are often absent in frameworks built for open access and transparency.

permissionless blockchain A *blockchain* where any user can join (i.e. become a *node*). A public blockchain.

Personal Identification Number (PIN) This is an *authentication* factor consisting of a number of digits that only a payment account holder should know.

personalisation The phase in physical payment card manufacturing where the cardholder information is loaded into the card.

Personal Finance Management (PFM) In a *fintech* context, this refers to digital tools, applications, and platforms that leverage technology to help individuals monitor, analyse, and optimise their financial activities. These solutions typically aggregate data from various financial accounts, provide real-time insights, automate budgeting processes, offer personalised financial advice, and facilitate goal-setting and tracking. PFM fintech solutions often incorporate *artificial intelligence*, *machine learning*, and data analytics to deliver tailored recommendations, predict future financial scenarios, and enhance financial decision-making. By providing user-friendly interfaces and advanced features, PFM in fintech aims to democratise financial management, making it more accessible, efficient, and effective for consumers in the digital age.

PesaLink[13] *A real-time payment system (RTP system), retail payment system (RPS)* in Kenya.

PFM See *Personal Finance Management.*

phishing A type of *social engineering* attack where fraudsters or cybercriminals deceive victims into revealing sensitive information, sending money, installing malicious software (e.g. *ransomware*), etc. Through phishing, malicious actors may pose as legitimate institutions, trusted individuals, etc. Usually conducted via email or other messaging services.

phone-to-phone payment Phone-to-phone payment, also known as peer-to-peer (P2P) mobile payment, is a digital transaction method that allows users to transfer money directly from one mobile device to another using a dedicated app or service, using *NFC* technology. This technology enables individuals to send and receive funds instantly. A prominent example of phone-to-phone payment is Apple's Tap to Pay on iPhone or Tap to Pay on Android.

Phoe Kuan A *Barter system* in Thailand.

PHP Hypertext Preprocessor. A widely used, *open-source* server-side scripting language specifically designed for web development. Created by Rasmus Lerdorf in 1994, PHP can be embedded directly into HTML code and is executed on the server, generating dynamic web content before sending it to the client's browser. It supports multiple programming paradigms, including procedural, object-oriented, and functional programming, and offers extensive database integration capabilities. PHP is known for its ease of use, cross-platform compatibility, and large community support, making it a popular choice for developing dynamic websites, web applications, and content management systems.

PI See *payment institution.*

PIN See *Personal Identification Number.*

PIN bypass A feature of card terminals that may be used by merchants to bypass the PIN entry for the cardholder. Not recommended.

PIN Entry Device (PED) See *Point of Sale (POS)*.

PIN pad See *Point of Sale (POS)*.

PISP See *Payment Initiation Service Provider*.

Pix[14] A real-time payment system (RTP system), retail payment system (RPS) in Brazil, operated by BCB.

PKE See *PAN Key Entry*.

PKI See *Public Key Infrastructure*.

Plaid[15] An *API aggregator*, authorised payment institution (PI), *account information service provider (AISP)*, and *Payment Initiation Service Provider (PISP)*. See also *Open Banking*.

plasma chain In a *blockchain* context, a layer 2 *scaling solution* introducing a hierarchy of blockchains, with a parent chain and child chains. The main blockchain acts as a secure foundation and sets the rules for the whole network, whereas the child chains handle transaction execution. A variant is the "nested blockchains" involving child chains which are closely coupled with the mainchain, usually implementing a modified version of the mainchain's protocol, or one that is specifically designed to work with the main blockchain. Because of their complexity, these have lost favour to other layer 2 scaling solutions. See also *rollup*, *side chain*, and *state channel*.

Platform-as-a-Service (PaaS) A cloud computing model that provides developers with a complete platform for building, running, and managing applications without the complexity of maintaining the underlying infrastructure. PaaS offerings typically include hardware, operating systems, development tools, databases, and other middleware, all hosted and managed by the service provider. This model allows developers to focus on writing code and creating applications, whilst the PaaS provider handles tasks such as server management, storage, networking, and scalability. PaaS enables faster development, easier deployment, and more efficient resource usage, making it a popular choice for businesses looking to streamline their application development processes.

play-to-earn (P2E) A gaming model in *blockchain*-based games where players can earn *cryptocurrency* tokens or other digital assets with real-world value by participating in gameplay activities. These rewards can be traded, sold, or used within the game ecosystem, allowing players to potentially generate income through their gaming engagement. See also *GameFi*.

Plutus A *smart contract* development platform and programming language for the *Cardano* blockchain. Based on Haskell, it allows developers to write *on-chain* code (*validators*) and *off-chain* code for *decentralised applications (dApps)*. Plutus features a compiler that translates Haskell-like code into Plutus Core, which runs on the Cardano blockchain. It emphasises security, formal verification, and predictable behaviour, making it well-suited for financial applications and complex smart contracts on Cardano.

Point-of-Sale (POS) A system used by businesses to manage sales transactions. In the past, a POS in a shop would consist of a cash register and a ledger to record purchases and sales. Today, we have dedicated electronic terminals and solutions to automate the processes – from customer purchases to inventory management. In the payments world, the term "POS" is used interchangeably with "POS terminal". Also called PIN Entry Device (PED) or PIN pad where PIN entry is available. Some merchants may have a separate device for cardholders to enter their *PIN*.

Point-of-Sale entry mode Describes the method by which the *Primary Account Number (PAN)* is propagated to the card payment terminal, such as keyed, swiped, or contactless.

Point-to-Point Encryption (P2PE) A term used to describe card data that is encrypted for transmission from the beginning to the end of the card transaction.

PolishAPI[16] The Polish *Open Banking* standard.

Politically Exposed Person (PEP) Usually a member of government, Parliament, etc., their family members, and known close associates. The exact way PEPs should be treated with regard to *Anti-Money Laundering (AML)* regulation will depend on the specific jurisdiction. See also *Enhanced Due Diligence (EDD)*.

Polkadot[17] A multichain network protocol that enables interoperability between *blockchains*, using a central relay chain for shared security and parallel processing through parachains – specialised blockchains that connect to the relay chain and can have their own tokens, governance, and functionality within the Polkadot ecosystem.

PoS See *Proof of Stake*.

POS See *Point-of-Sale*.

Post Pay A *payment method* by which consumers order goods online and pay for them later at affiliated outlets or stores. The delay between the initial order and the payment means that this isn't suited for perishable goods and time-sensitive purchases. A form of *delayed payment*.

post-quantum cryptography See *quantum-resistant cryptography*.

POT See *Predominantly Offline Terminal*.

PoW See *Proof of Work*.

Pre-Auth A process that allows a merchant to obtain advance *authorisation* or verification that funds are available for a card transaction. Often used as an alternative to deposits.

predicate offence A crime that forms part of a larger crime.

predictive analytics A branch of advanced analytics that uses historical data, statistical algorithms, and *machine learning* techniques to identify the likelihood of future outcomes. It involves analysing current and past data to make predictions about future events or behaviours. In the payments industry, predictive analytics is applied to forecast consumer spending patterns, detect fraudulent transactions, assess credit risk, optimise pricing strategies, and personalise customer experiences. It enables payment providers and financial institutions to anticipate market trends, improve decision-making, enhance security measures, and develop targeted marketing campaigns. By leveraging predictive models, payment companies can proactively address potential issues, streamline operations, and create more value for both businesses and consumers. See also *prescriptive analytics*.

Predominantly Offline Terminal (POT) A card terminal that operates using a local server so that in the event of network outage, merchants can still continue to accept card payments. The data is transferred once connection is regained.

prepaid card Generally refers to open-loop prepaid cards which run on *card scheme* networks. They can be used in the same way as a debit card or credit cards. The key difference is that they need to be loaded up with funds in advance. A *stored value card*.

prepay card Cards which are not run on *card scheme* networks and are usually authorised immediately. Consumers need to buy a card or voucher before starting a transaction. These are a type of *stored value card* which will be denominated in the currency in use for the specified amount. Increasingly, these are delivered as *virtual cards*.

prescriptive analytics An advanced form of data analytics that goes beyond predicting future outcomes to recommend specific actions or decisions. It uses mathematical models, *machine learning* algorithms, and optimisation techniques to analyse complex data sets, consider multiple scenarios, and suggest the best course of action to achieve desired results. In the payments industry, prescriptive analytics can be applied to optimise pricing strategies, detect and prevent fraud in real-time, personalise customer experiences, streamline payment processing workflows, and manage risk. For example, it can recommend the most effective *fraud prevention* measures based on emerging patterns, suggest optimal payment routing to minimise costs and maximise success rates, or provide tailored offers and payment options to individual customers to increase conversion and loyalty. Prescriptive analytics differs from *predictive analytics*, in that predictive analytics forecasts what might happen in the future based on historical data, whilst prescriptive analytics determines the best actions to take in response to those predictions, offering specific recommendations rather than just probabilities.

Primary Account Number (PAN) The card number, which is constructed according to the ISO/IEC 7812 (identification cards) standard. Usually 16 digits but can be up to 19 digits. See *Major Industry Identifier (MII)*, *Bank Identifier Number (BIN)*, *cardholder account number*, and *checksum*.

principal An entity that acts on its own behalf to conduct business activities. See also *principal member*. This term is also used in the context of *credit*, where it refers to the money that a borrower originally agreed to pay back. See also *interest*.

principal member On the *card rails*, a principal member of a *card scheme* can conduct the following activities: issuing, acquiring, cash disbursement, BIN licensing, direct settlement, and ongoing fee payments. The principal member may sponsor affiliate members and is accountable to the card schemes for reporting, *settlement*, and ongoing fee payment (including for their sponsorees). A principal member must comply with card scheme *operating regulations* and needs to have the necessary regulatory credentials to be able to apply for membership (e.g. *authorised payment institution* or *authorised emoney institution* in Europe, or equivalent in other geographies).

privacy The right and ability of individuals to control access to their personal information and to maintain a state of seclusion from public attention. Unlike *anonymity*, which focuses on concealing one's identity entirely, privacy allows individuals to selectively reveal information about themselves. Privacy encompasses the protection of personal data, communications, and activities from unauthorised access or intrusion, whilst still allowing for identified interactions when desired or necessary. See also *data protection* and *anonymity*.

privacy coin A type of *cryptocurrency* used to perform private and anonymous *blockchain* transactions by obscuring their origin and destination. Some of the techniques used in these anonymous cryptocurrencies include hiding a user's real *crypto wallet* balance and address and mixing multiple transactions with each other to elude *chain analysis*. Monero[18] and Zcash[19] are examples. Aimed at ensuring *data privacy* for investors, but often associated with *money laundering* activities and increasingly attracting regulatory scrutiny. Also see *coin mixer*.

private API A communication interface specific to one organisation. Its use can only be granted by that organisation. See also *open API*.

private blockchain A type of *permissioned blockchain* controlled by one authority. An example is *Ripple*.

private key A code that may take several forms: a 256-character long binary code, a 64-digit hexadecimal code, a *QR code*, or a mnemonic phrase. A *cryptocurrency* transaction is encrypted using a *public key* but can only be decrypted by an associated private key. For a cryptocurrency transaction to be authenticated, the recipient must "sign it" with their private key, proving that they are the legitimate recipient of the funds. Through the *consensus protocol*, unauthenticated transactions will be rejected by the *blockchain* network. Conversely, authenticated transactions are irreversible. Public and private keys fit together and are known as "key pairs". Also see *cryptography*, *public key cryptography*, *encryption*, and *public key*.

processor See *issuer processor* and *acquirer*.

procurement card A term used in the UK. See *purchasing card*.

programmability A key feature of *Central Bank Digital Currencies (CBDCs)* that allows for the implementation of *smart contracts* and automated processes, enabling more efficient and innovative financial services. It can facilitate conditional transactions, automated compliance checks, and other customised functionalities, potentially enhancing the flexibility and *utility* of digital currencies.

programmable money *Digital currency* with embedded rules or conditions that automatically execute predefined actions when specific criteria are met. It allows for automated, conditional transactions without intermediaries. In the context of *Central Bank Digital Currencies (CBDCs)*, programmable money refers to the ability to incorporate *smart contracts* or automated processes into the digital currency. This feature enables central banks to implement conditional transactions, automated compliance checks, and other customised functionalities, potentially enhancing the flexibility and *utility* of the CBDC in various financial applications.

programme manager Generally associated with the *prepaid card* industry. A programme manager acts as an *aggregator* between the different parties in the card payments *value chain* through *BIN sponsorship* agreements with an *issuer*. Programme managers bring quick time to market for their clients as they bring market knowledge. A programme manager is different from an issuer *processor* as they build the card programme functionality and technology that will exist on the issuer processor platform. Some programme managers are also issuer processors.

PromptPay[20] An *account-to-account payment* service in Thailand.

Proof-of-Stake (PoS) A *blockchain consensus protocol* by which *validators* stake their own funds, a process referred to as *staking*. A *coin* or *token* is picked randomly from all staked funds. The owner of the "winning" coin gets to add their block to the *blockchain*. In order to discourage validators from misbehaving (e.g. being offline for too long and attacking the network), some blockchains implement a governance mechanism called *slashing* by which a predetermined percentage or a fixed quantity of the validator's stake is lost, the amount of which depends on the severity of the transgression. See also *Proof of Work (PoW)*.

Proof-of-Work (PoW) A *blockchain consensus protocol* by which *miners* compete to solve a cryptographic puzzle. Whomever solves the puzzle first gets to add their block to the chain. See also *Proof of Stake (PoS)*.

pruned full node A type of *blockchain* node that stores and verifies the complete blockchain history but discards older transaction data to save storage space. It maintains the full validation capabilities of a *full node* whilst reducing storage requirements by only keeping recent blockchain states.

PSD agent In Europe, a small business that acts as an *agent* of an authorised *payment institution (PI)*, the latter being referred to as the *principal*.

PSD2 See *Second Payment Services Directive*.

PSD3 The EU Third Payment Services Directive.

PSP See *Payment Services Provider.*

PSR See *Payment Services Regulation* or *Payment Systems Regulator.*

PSU See *Payment Service User.*

public blockchain A type of *permissionless blockchain*. The *Bitcoin* and *Ethereum* blockchains are examples.

public key A cryptographic code that allows a user to receive *cryptocurrency* transactions. Anyone can send transactions to a public key, which can be freely shared (a bit like an email address). The public key is generated from a *private key*, and there can be any number of public keys associated with a private key. A user needs a private key to "unlock" a received transaction and prove they are the owner of the cryptocurrency received in the transaction. Public and private keys fit together and are known as "key pairs". Also see *cryptography*, *public key cryptography*, *encryption*, and *private key*.

public key cryptography An *encryption* method that uses two mathematically related, but not identical, keys – a *public key* and a *private key* – where each key performs a unique function. Public key cryptography is considered more secure and easier to manage than *symmetric cryptography*, but slower. Used by *blockchain* networks and anywhere digital signatures are desirable. Also known as "asymmetric cryptography", "public key encryption", and "asymmetric encryption". Well-known public key cryptography algorithms include Rivest–Shamir–Adleman (RSA), Elliptic Curve Digital Signature Algorithm (ECDSA), Digital Signature Algorithm (DSA), and Diffie–Hellman key agreement protocol. See also *quantum cryptography*.

public key encryption See *public key cryptography*.

Public Key Infrastructure (PKI) A collective term representing the hardware, software, processes, policies, and procedures required to manage *public keys* for *digital certificates* and *encryption*, as commonly used for securing data transfers over the internet.

pull payment After prior *authorisation* from the *payer*, the *payee* instructs their payment account provider to draw funds from the payer's payment account (effectively "pulling" the payment). *direct debits*, *recurring transactions*, and *cheques* are examples of pull payments. Also see *account-to-account payment (A2A payment)*.

purchasing card A type of *commercial card* given by organisations to their employees to allow goods and services to be procured without using a traditional purchasing process. Purchasing cards allow employees to buy quickly and efficiently what they need, simplifying expenses processing for their employer. Sometimes abbreviated as "P card". In the UK, purchasing cards are usually referred to as "procurement cards". Also sometimes referred to as "acquisition cards".

push payment When a *payer* instructs (i.e. authorises) a payment from their payment account to the *payee's* payment account essentially "pushing" the payment. See also *account-to-account payment (A2A payment)*. Historically referred to as "giro payment", "giro", and "*credit transfer*".

PvP See *Payment-versus-Payment*.

Python A high-level, interpreted, general-purpose programming language known for its simplicity and readability. Created by Guido van Rossum and first released in 1991, Python emphasises code readability with its use of significant indentation. It supports multiple programming paradigms, including structured, object-oriented, and functional programming. Python features dynamic typing, garbage collection, and a comprehensive standard library, often described as "batteries included". Its design philosophy prioritises code readability and expressiveness, making it popular for web development, data analysis, artificial intelligence, scientific computing, and automation tasks. Python's syntax allows developers to express concepts in fewer lines of code than languages like *Java* or C++, and its interpreter system enables rapid prototyping and debugging.

Notes

1 P27. https://nordicpayments.eu/ (Accessed 21 November 2023)
2 PancakeSwap. https://pancakeswap.finance/ (Accessed 5 December 2023)
3 PAX. https://www.paxtechnology.com/ (Accessed 21 November 2023)
4 Payment Card Industry Standards Security Council. https://www.pcisecuritystandards.org/ (Accessed 15 December 2023)
5 Legislation.gov.uk (Payment Services Regulation 2017). https://www.legislation.gov.uk/uksi/2017/752/contents (Accessed 21 November 2023)
6 Payment Systems Regulator. https://www.psr.org.uk/ (Accessed 21 November 2023)
7 The Association of Banks of Singapore (PayNow). https://www.abs.org.sg/consumer-banking/pay-now (Accessed 21 November 2023)

8 PayPal. https://www.paypal.com/ (Accessed 21 November 2023)
9 Paytm. https://paytm.com/ (Accessed 21 November 2023)
10 PayTo. https://payto.com.au/ (Accessed 21 November 2023)
11 Pay.UK. https://www.wearepay.uk/ (Accessed 21 November 2023)
12 Banco Central De La Republica Argentina. https://www.bcra.gob.ar/MediosPago/Politica_Pagos-i.asp#c (Accessed 21 November 2023)
13 IPSL. https://www.ipsl.co.ke/ (Accessed 21 November 2023)
14 Banco Central do Brasil. https://www.bcb.gov.br/en/financialstability/pix_en (Accessed 21 November 2023)
15 Plaid. https://plaid.com/ (Accessed 21 November 2023)
16 PolishAPI. https://polishapi.org/en/ (Accessed 21 November 2023)
17 Polkadot. https://polkadot.com/ (Accessed 29 September 2024)
18 Monero. https://www.getmonero.org/ (Accessed 15 December 2023)
19 ZCash. https://z.cash/ (Accessed 15 December 2023)
20 Bank of Thailand (PromptPay). https://www.bot.or.th/en/financial-innovation/digital-finance/digital-payment/promptpay.html (Accessed 21 November 2023)

Q

Q IS FOR...

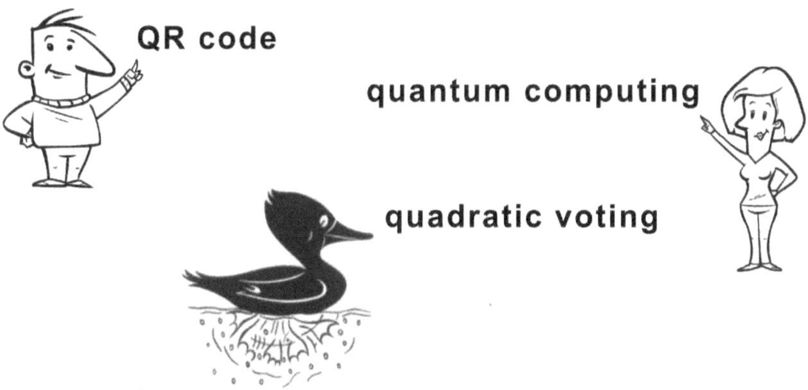

QR code Quick Response Code. QR codes are *contactless*, scannable matrix barcodes that direct consumers to websites, online checkouts, mobile apps, menus, and other digital channels. They can be used as an *authentication* method for payments. Particularly popular in Asia but gaining popularity in other parts of the world.

DOI: 10.4324/9781003571131-18

QR code fraud A type of fraud that occurs when a fraudster creates a QR code that links to a malicious website. The website may ask users to enter payment details, personal information, or click a button that downloads *malware.*

QR payment A payment, usually through a mobile device, made using a *QR code.*

QSA See *Qualified Security Assessor.*

QSAC See *Qualified Security Assessor Company.*

quadratic voting A collective decision-making method where participants can express the intensity of their preferences by allocating votes across different options. In this system, the cost of votes increases quadratically with the number of votes cast on a single issue, meaning that each additional vote costs more than the previous one. This approach aims to balance the influence of passionate minorities with broader majority preferences, potentially leading to more nuanced and representative outcomes in group decision-making processes. Some *blockchain* networks may use quadratic voting as part of their governance framework (e.g. to distribute funds).

Qualified Security Assessor (QSA) An individual employed by a *Qualified Security Assessor Company (QSAC)* who is certified by the *Payment Card Industry Security Standards Council (PCI SSC)* as a PCI compliance assessor. They need to have specific information security knowledge, and their certification must be renewed annually with the PCI SSC. QSAs are used by businesses to validate their compliance with the PCI standards. See also *Payment Card Industry Data Security Standard (PCI DSS).*

Qualified Security Assessor Company (QSAC) An independent security company that meets specific requirements and has been qualified by the PCI SSC to employ QSAs. QSACs are listed on the PCI SSC website.

quantum computing An emerging multidisciplinary technology field incorporating aspects of computer science, hardware research, physics, application development, and mathematics harnessing the laws of quantum mechanics in an effort to solve problems too complex for classical computers (including existing super-computers). In conventional computers, data processing is done in a Central Processing Unit (CPU), whereas in quantum computers, data processing is done in a Quantum Processing Unit (QPU), which consists of a number of interconnected *qubits*, the quantum equivalent of a "bit" in traditional computing. Use cases include drugs and chemical research, as well as *cryptography*, which is critical for securing digital transactions and communications. Amazon, Microsoft, Google, and IBM are dominant players in this market.

quantum cryptography A form of *cryptography* that uses the naturally occurring properties of quantum mechanics to secure and transmit data. Unlike traditional cryptography, which relies on mathematics, the security model of quantum cryptography relies on physics. Quantum cryptography should also remain safe against those using *quantum computing* to compromise data. See also *cryptography* and *encryption*.

quantum money A theoretical form of currency that leverages the principles of quantum mechanics and *quantum cryptography*, making impossible to forge. The concept was first proposed in 1983.[1] See also *money*.

quantum-resistant cryptography Cryptographic algorithms and systems designed to be secure against attacks by both classical and quantum computers. These algorithms aim to protect sensitive data and communications from potential threats posed by large-scale quantum computers, which could break many currently used encryption methods. Quantum-resistant cryptography typically relies on mathematical problems that are believed to be difficult for both classical and quantum computers to solve. It is distinct from *quantum cryptography*, which uses quantum mechanical properties to secure communications rather than relying solely on mathematical complexity. Also known as "post-quantum cryptography".

Qubit An abbreviation for "quantum bit". The basic unit of quantum data. Unlike classical bits, which can only have two states, 0 or 1, qubits can exist in multiple states at the same time, a condition described as "superposition", a key property of quantum computing. Another important property of qubits is "entanglement", which describes a state where two qubits become linked in such a way that the state of one is dependent on the state of the other. This property allows quantum computers to perform some calculations much faster than traditional computers.

Quorum[2] A *private blockchain* originally developed by JP Morgan and acquired in 2020 by ConsenSys. A *permissioned blockchain platform*.

quotation currency In a *foreign exchange* context, the second currency in a *currency pair*.

Notes

1 Conjugate Coding. ACM Digital Library, Stephen Wiesner, 1 January 1983. Conjugate coding | ACM SIGACT News (Accessed 25 January 2024)
2 What Is Consensys Quorum? Consensys, 8 June 2021. What is Consensys Quorum? | Consensys (Accessed 25 January 2024)

R

R IS FOR...

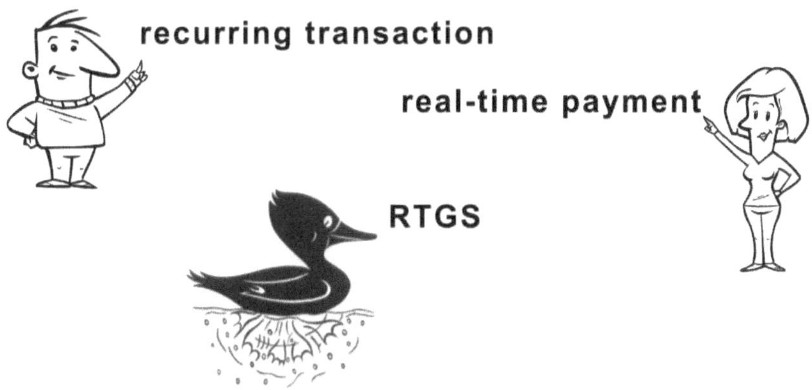

R3 Corda[1] An *open-source* blockchain platform designed for businesses, particularly in the financial services sector. It enables the creation of interoperable *blockchain* networks with a focus on privacy, scalability, and seamless integration with existing systems. Corda uses a unique *consensus protocol* and supports *smart contracts* written in Java or Kotlin.

DOI: 10.4324/9781003571131-19

RAAST[2] A *real-time payment system* (*RTP system*), *retail payment system* (*RPS*) in Pakistan.

Radix See *Tempo*.

RAISP Registered AISP. See *Account Information Service Provider*.

ransomware A type of *malware* whereby cyber criminals block access to the victim's (which may be a person or a business) personal data unless a ransom is paid. Whilst some simple ransomware may lock the system without damaging any files, more advanced versions may delete the files or cause other damage. A form of extortion. Perpetrators usually request the ransom to be paid in *cryptocurrency*, especially *privacy coins*.

RBA See *risk-based authentication*.

RC4 Rivest Cipher. A *symmetric cryptography* algorithm.

real-time The processing of instructions on an individual basis as they are received rather than at some point in the future. Used interchangeably with "real time" or "realtime".

real-time bank transfer A *payment method* that allows users to make online payments in real-time or near real-time using the bank rails. Usually for online and mobile banking. Examples include iDeal in The Netherlands, Sofort in Germany, and SafetyPay in Latin America.

Real-Time Clearing (RTC) A *real-time payment system* (*RTP system*), *retail payment system* (RPS) in South Africa, operated by BankServAfrica.

Real-Time Gross Settlement (RTGS) See *settlement cycle*.

Real-Time Gross Settlement account (RTGS account) An account held by a bank or authorised non-bank institution at a *central bank* or central monetary authority. Referred to as an RTGS account.

real-time payment A broad term used to describe a payment that appears instantaneous or quasi-instantaneous to the user, regardless of the underlying *settlement* mechanism. Also referred to as "instant payment".

real-time payment system (RTP system) A bank *payment scheme* where settlement happens in real-time or near real-time. See also *retail payment system*, *large value payment system*, and *settlement cycle*.

Real-Time Rail (RTR)[3] A *real-time payment system* (*RTP system*), *retail payment system* (RPS) in Canada, operated by Payments Canada.

real-world asset (RWA) Digital *tokens* that represent ownership of tangible or traditional assets, such as real estate, commodities, or financial instruments, on a *blockchain*. *Tokenisation* of these assets enhances liquidity, accessibility, and the ability to trade them in a decentralised manner. See also *security token exchange*.

recurring payment See *recurring transaction*.

recurring transaction A type of payment transaction where the payment account holder gives a payee (e.g. merchant) their payment account details (e.g. card account details) so that they can take regular payments from them. Also referred to as "recurring payment". The payment will be made at a regular frequency, for example, once a year or once a month, without account holder intervention. On the *card rails*, recurring transactions are also known as *card-on-file* transactions, subscription transactions, and *Continuous Payment Authority* (*CPA*) transactions. For this type of transaction, the merchant stores the card details on their system. A type of *Merchant-Initiated Transaction* (MIT). On the bank rails, *direct debits*, *standing orders*, and *Variable Recurring Payments* can be considered recurring transactions. In blockchain infrastructures, a recurring payment may be implemented through *smart contracts*.

reentrancy attack A security vulnerability in *smart contracts* that exploits the way transactions are processed on a *blockchain*. It specifically targets smart contracts that interact with external functions or calls (often to other smart contracts) during a single transaction. As blockchains process transactions in blocks, there's a delay between a transaction being submitted and it being finalised in a block, creating a window of opportunity for attackers. Before the transaction finishes, the attacker tricks the contract into repeating that action, essentially stealing those funds or manipulating the system a second time. Careful coding practices and security audits can help prevent these attacks. See also *replay attack*.

refund A type of payment transaction which is effectively a purchase process in reverse and is invoked by the payer. After clearing and settlement, the amount of the refund is credited to the payer's account, and a corresponding debit will be made to the payee's account.

refund fraud A type of fraud that occurs when a fraudster exploits a merchant's refund policies for financial gain. This includes falsely claiming a product was never delivered, returning a counterfeit item instead of the original, or purchasing an item with the intention of returning it for a refund after using it for a period of time. Also referred to as "refund abuse".

Reference Fraud Rate (RFR) A fraud indicator used in the context of the PSD2 *Transaction Risk Analysis* (*TRA*) exemption to *Strong Customer Authentication* (*SCA*), which specifies threshold fraud rates for specific transaction values (i.e. 0.13% for up to €100, 0.06% for up to €250, and 0.01%

for up to €500). A transaction may qualify for the TRA *exemption* if the business can demonstrate, for that transaction type, that they maintain an overall quarterly fraud rate, as specified by the RFR for the *Exemption Threshold Value*, as set by the PSD2 regulations.

regtech Refers to any business that uses technology to improve, digitise, automate, or provide enablers to help organisations manage their increasing regulatory compliance commitments. It is most usefully applied to heavily regulated sectors such as financial services, healthcare, or gaming.

Regulated Liability Network (RLN)[4] A financial infrastructure concept that uses *Distributed Ledger Technology* (*DLT*) to integrate various forms of regulated money onto a shared platform. It aims to facilitate real-time, programmable settlement of financial transactions across different institutions and jurisdictions, potentially improving interoperability, efficiency, and security in the financial system.

regulatory sandbox A safe environment provided by regulators to enable the testing of new, innovative technologies, services, or approaches that are not fully compliant with the existing legal and regulatory frameworks. This can take place using near-real-life data (i.e. *synthetic data*) or real-life data.

Regulatory Technical Standard (RTS) Technical standard specifications published by the European Banking Authority in support of the deployment of European regulations. Abbreviated as RTS.

relay chain The primary *blockchain* in a multichain network architecture that coordinates communication and consensus between connected chains. It serves as the central hub for cross-chain interoperability, shared security, and governance. Prominent examples include Polkadot's relay chain and Cosmos Hub in the Cosmos ecosystem. See also *bridge* and *cross-chain bridge*.

remittance See *money remittance*.

Remitly[5] A *peer-to-peer money exchange*.

remote payment A payment transaction other than a physical face-to-face transaction. Examples of remote payments include payments over the phone, the internet, and mail order. Also referred to as remote transaction. See *Card Not Present (CNP)*.

replay attack A form of network attack in which a valid data transmission is maliciously or fraudulently retransmitted or delayed. The attacker would intercept a valid transaction and retransmit it, often multiple times, in view of deceiving the recipient or gaining unauthorised access. In *blockchain* infrastructures, this is a type of attack where a valid transaction is fraudulently retransmitted, which may occur when an attacker intercepts and records a legitimate transaction between two parties and then later replays that transaction to one or more nodes on the blockchain network in view of manipulating the system. In traditional centralised financial systems, replay attacks are unlikely to succeed as these systems usually have security and robust security and *fraud prevention* measures, such as authentication, transaction verification, security standards, stringent regulations, and of course, centralised control. In decentralised systems, such as blockchain networks, replay attacks can be particularly problematic because of the distributed nature of the trust framework. See also *double-spending* and *reentrancy attack*.

Report on Compliance (ROC) Produced by a *Qualified Security Assessor (QSA)* or an Internal Security Assessor (ISA) when they validate the *PCI DSS* compliance of a business. An ROC must be renewed annually for businesses in scope (see *merchant level*). ROC templates can be found on the *PCI SSC* website.

representment See *chargeback defence*.

Request for Information See *retrieval*.

Request-to-Pay (RtP) An *overlay service* on the bank rails; it is similar in intent to sending an invoice. RtP involves a payee (e.g. a supplier of goods or services) initiating a digital payment request from a payer, without having to send an invoice. It caters for modern behaviours. For example, the payer can receive the request through their mobile device, or their banking app, or via a *Third Party PSP (TPP)*. But RtP is not just about digital invoicing: it gives more flexibility to payers. For each payment request, a payer may choose to pay in full, in part (asking for more time), or decline to pay altogether. A payer can also communicate with the payee through this service. Because of this flexibility, and the hoped-for outcome that it would help people avoid falling into debt, it could save money at a national level. Not all bank payment schemes can support RtP, and of course banks and other *Payment Service Providers (PSPs)* need to deploy it for it to be available to bank account holders. A type of *pull payment*.

reserve account On the *card rails*, an account holding funds that an *acquirer* requires a merchant to maintain to support the provision of card services and for risk management purposes. The amount of funds for the reserve account depends on a number of factors including transaction volumes, business type, and channel. Also refers to a non-interest-bearing account held at a *central bank* (or correspondent bank) by a financial services institution. A central bank requires banks to hold a certain amount of cash in reserve so that they never run short and have to refuse a customer's withdrawal, possibly triggering a *bank run*. A central bank may also use bank reserve levels as a tool in *monetary policy*.

respondent bank See *correspondent banking*.

retail CBDC (rCBDC) A type of *Central Bank Digital Currency* (CBDC) for general-purpose domestic use, including B2C, B2B, P2P, and G2C. Several architecture models can be used for retail CBDCs, such as *direct CBDC*, *intermediated CBDC*, and *Multi-CBDC* (mCBDC). There are also hybrid CBDC models that incorporate features of other models.

retail payments A term used to describe payments between consumers, businesses, and public authorities. They can be everyday consumer transactions but also include higher-value payments such as payroll and tax payments made by businesses. Often referred to as "consumer payments", they are characterised by high volumes of transactions. Examples are card transactions, *direct debit*, *standing orders*, *cheque* transactions, etc. Also see *Business-to-Consumer* (B2C), *Business-to-Business* (B2B), *Government-to-Consumer* (G2C), and *wholesale payments*.

retail payment system (RPS) A term used to describe bank payment schemes that typically handle high volumes of *retail payments*.

retailer card A card issued by retailers. These can take many forms, such as *closed loop cards* and *co-branded-cards*.

retail settlement A subset of *interbank settlement* referring to the *settlement* of *retail payments* and used on the *bank rails* to describe how funds will be moved to/from a bank accounts. This is the equivalent of *merchant settlement* on the *card rails* and happens after interbank settlement. However, whereas merchant settlement is contingent to contractual arrangements, retail settlement times apply to everyone in the same way according to the bank *payment scheme rules*. See also *wholesale settlement*.

retrieval A process on the *card rails* to request information about a transaction. This process can be invoked by a cardholder when they don't recognise a transaction on their card statement. The process can also be invoked directly by the *issuer* of the card if a transaction is flagged by their *fraud prevention* systems. Sometimes called a "request for information" or "retrieval request".

retrieval request See *retrieval*.

retrieval request fee (RRF) A fee charged to merchants for a retrieval originating from a cardholder or their *issuer*. An example of *card scheme fee*.

Rholang Reflective Higher-Order Language. A programming language specifically designed for writing *smart contracts* on the RChain platform. It is a concurrent, functional language that uses a process calculus model for communication and computation. Rholang features built-in support for concurrency, allowing smart contracts to execute in parallel, which enhances scalability and efficiency. It also incorporates formal verification capabilities, reflective operations, and a communication process model, making it well-suited for creating complex, secure, and flexible smart contracts in *blockchain* environments.

RIPEMD-160 RACE Integrity Primitives Evaluation Message Digest is an established *hashing* algorithm. See also *cryptography*, *encryption*, and *hash*.

Ripple[6] A *Real-Time Gross Settlement* system, currency exchange, and *remittance* network based on a *private blockchain* that is open to financial institutions worldwide and used to transfer funds across borders at a low cost. Created by Ripple Labs Inc. See also *settlement cycle*.

risk-based authentication (RBA) A dynamic security approach that assesses the risk level of each login attempt based on various contextual factors such as user behaviour, device information, location, and transaction details. The system calculates a risk score in real-time and adjusts the *authentication* requirements accordingly. Low-risk attempts may only require basic credentials, whilst higher-risk scenarios trigger additional verification steps, such as *multi-factor authentication*. This adaptive method enhances security by applying stringent measures only when necessary, balancing robust protection with user convenience. See also *biometrics*, *knowledge-based authentication*.

RIX-INST[7] A *real-time payment system (RTP system)*, *retail payment system (RPS)* in Sweden, operated by Riksbank.

RLN See *Regulated Liability Network*.

Robotic Process Automation (RPA) A technology that uses *bots* to automate repetitive, rule-based digital tasks by mimicking human actions within computer systems. These bots interact with applications and data through user interfaces, performing actions like data entry, file manipulation, and form filling without altering the existing IT infrastructure. In the payments industry, RPA is applied to streamline processes such as invoice processing, account reconciliation, payment initiation, *fraud detection*, and compliance checks. It helps reduce errors, increase processing speed, enhance accuracy in financial transactions, and allows human workers to focus on more complex, value-added tasks in the payments ecosystem.

Robux[8] A *virtual currency* used in the game Roblox.

ROC See *Report on Compliance.*

rollup In a *blockchain* context, a *layer 2 scaling solution* similar to *plasma chains* in principle, inasmuch as processing is offloaded from the *layer 1 blockchain* to the adjacent chain (rollup chain), but with some important differences. There are two types of rollups: optimistic rollups (ORU) and zero-knowledge rollups (zk-rollups). An ORU assumes that all transactions are valid by default (hence the optimism), and therefore fraud proofs are a crucial element of their design (similarly to plasma chains), and the main chain verifies them and may potentially reverse and the entire set of transactions if the fraud is proven. A zk-rollup includes a *validity proof* for every transaction in the batch, which is implemented through *zero-knowledge proofs* (ZKP). See also *side chain, state channel*, and *validium*.

Routing transit number (RTN) See *ABA routing number.*

RPA See *Robotic Process Automation.*

RPS See *retail payment system.*

RSA Rivest–Shamir–Adleman. A *public key cryptography* algorithm. By far the most popular.

RT1[9] A *real-time payment system* (*RTP system*), *retail payment system* (*RPS*) in Europe, operated by EBA Clearing.

RTGS Real-Time Gross Settlement. A payment system that enables the immediate transfer of funds between banks or financial institutions on a gross basis, meaning that transactions are settled individually in real-time without netting debits against credits. This system is typically used for high-value transactions, ensuring that payments are completed instantly and securely, thereby reducing *settlement risk*. Increasingly, this method is also used for retail real-time payments. See also *settlement cycle.*

RTGS account See *Real-Time Gross Settlement account.*

RTC See *Real-Time Clearing.*

RTN See *ABA routing number.*

RtP See *Request-to-Pay.*

RTP See *real-time payment system.*

RTP®[10] A US A *real-time payment system* (*RTP system*), *retail payment system* (RPS) privately operated by The Clearing House.

RTR See *Real-Time Rail.*

RTS See *Regulatory Technical Standard.*

Ruby A dynamic, object-oriented programming language created by Yukihiro Matsumoto in the mid-1990s, known for its simplicity and productivity. It emphasises human-friendly syntax, making it easy to read and write, which promotes rapid development. Ruby supports multiple programming paradigms, including functional and imperative styles, and is particularly famous for its use in web development through the Ruby on Rails framework. Its rich set of built-in functions and extensive libraries contribute to its versatility, making it suitable for various applications ranging from web services to data processing.

Rust A systems programming language developed by Mozilla Research, focusing on safety, concurrency, and performance. It features a unique ownership model and borrow checker that ensure memory safety and thread safety without a garbage collector. Rust combines low-level control over hardware with high-level abstractions, making it suitable for a wide range of applications from operating systems to web services. The language emphasises zero-cost abstractions, safe concurrency, and memory efficiency, whilst providing modern developer tools and a supportive community. Rust's compiler enforces strict rules at compile-time, helping developers catch and prevent common programming errors before runtime.

RWA See *Real-World Asset.*

Notes

1 R3 Corda. https://developer.r3.com/next-gen-corda/ (Accessed 21 September 2024)

2 State Bank of Pakistan (RAAST). https://www.sbp.org.pk/dfs/Raast.html (Accessed 21 November 2023)

3 Payments Canada (Real-Time Rail). https://www.payments.ca/systems-services/payment-systems/real-time-rail-payment-system (Accessed 21 November 2023)

4 Regulated Liability Network. https://regulatedliabilitynetwork.org/ (Accessed 21 September 2024)

5 Remitly. https://www.remitly.com/ (Accessed 21 November 2023)

6 Ripple. https://ripple.com/ (Accessed 21 November 2023)

7 Riksbank (RIX-INST). https://www.riksbank.se/en-gb/payments--cash/the-payment-system---rix/ (Accessed 21 November 2023)

8 Roblox (Buy Robux). https://www.roblox.com/upgrades/robux (Accessed 21 November 2023)

9 EBA Clearing (RT1). https://www.ebaclearing.eu/services/rt1/overview/ (Accessed 21 November 2023)

10 The Clearing House (RTP). https://www.theclearinghouse.org/payment-systems/rtp (Accessed 21 November 2023)

S

SaaS See *Software-as-a-Service*.

SAFE System to Avoid Fraud Effectively. A report sent by *issuers* to Mastercard containing information on claims of fraud made by cardholders. For each report of fraud, SAFE data may include information about the merchant, the issuer, the *acquirer*, and the transaction itself. The Visa equivalent is TC40.

DOI: 10.4324/9781003571131-20

safeguarding A requirement on regulated firms to keep clients' funds completely separate from their operational funds. The bank account where customer funds are kept is referred to as a "safeguarding account" provided by a *custodian*. (Please note that the term "safeguarding" can be used more generically to mean "securing").

SafeKey [1] The *American Express* implementation of *3D Secure*.

Samsung Pay[2] A *mobile wallet* provided by Samsung. A *pass-through digital wallet*.

Samsung Wallet[3] A multipurpose *digital wallet* provided by Samsung. Enables users to store and use payment cards, bank accounts, passwords, tickets, keys, passes, keys, and identities.

Sanction In an *Anti-Money Laundering (AML)* context, this is the imposition of trade or financial restrictions and penalties by one or more countries against another country, entity, or individual with the purpose of changing a behaviour in order to reduce *financial crime*. Economic sanctions can include actions such as tariffs, trade restrictions, and financial limitations. See also *Financial Action Task Force (FATF)*, Politically Exposed Person (PEP), *derisking*, and *debanking*.

Sand Dollar The *Central Bank Digital Currency* (CBDC) of The Bahamas.

SAQ See *Self-Assessment Questionnaire*.

SAR See *Suspicious Activity Reporting*.

SARIE[4] A *real-time payment system* (RTP system), *retail payment system* (RPS) in Saudi Arabia, operated by SAMA.

Satoshi The smallest subdivision of a *Bitcoin* where 100,000,000 Satoshis represent one Bitcoin. The unit of measurement for Bitcoin transaction costs. See also *gas price*.

Satoshi Nakamoto Satoshi Nakamoto is the pseudonymous person or group of people who created *Bitcoin* in 2008. Nakamoto authored the Bitcoin *whitepaper*, deployed Bitcoin's original reference implementation, and devised the first *blockchain* database. Nakamoto was active in Bitcoin's development until December 2010, but their true identity remains unknown. Speculation about Nakamoto's identity has focused on various *cryptography* and computer science experts, but no conclusive evidence has emerged. Nakamoto's chosen name is Japanese, but their nationality and background remain a mystery.

Sberbank[5] A Russian *acquiring bank*.

SCA See *Strong Customer Authentication*.

scaling solution In a *blockchain* context, these are improvements to a blockchain aimed at solving the *blockchain trilemma*. There are two types of blockchain scaling solutions: layer 1 and layer 2. Layer-1 scaling solutions augment the base layer of the *blockchain protocol* itself in order to improve scalability. They change the rules of the protocol directly to increase transaction capacity and speed, whilst accommodating more users and data (e.g. changing block data, changing *consensus protocol*, and sharding). Layer 2 scaling solutions involve shifting a portion of a blockchain protocol's transactional burden to an adjacent system architecture, which then handles the brunt of the network's processing and only subsequently reports back to the main blockchain to finalise its results.

sCBDC Synthetic CBDC. See *intermediated CBDC*.

scheme membership The permissions necessary for a *Payment Service Provider (PSP)* or *Account Servicing PSP (ASPSP)* to participate in a given *card scheme*. There are two types of memberships: principal (settling) and affiliate (non-settling). Affiliate members must be sponsored by principal members. Prospective members must have the appropriate regulatory credentials from their competent authority.

Scilla A *smart contract* programming language specifically designed for the *Zilliqa* blockchain, where its name stands for "Smart Contract Intermediate-Level Language". It aims to enhance security and reduce vulnerabilities in smart contracts by imposing a structured approach that separates computations from external communications. Scilla allows developers to write safer contracts with formal verification capabilities, ensuring mathematical correctness and minimising risks associated with traditional smart contract languages. Its design focuses on facilitating secure *Decentralised Finance (DeFi)* applications whilst providing tools for efficient contract analysis and development.

screen scraping A method of accessing data by which an account holder shares their account login credentials with a *Third-Party PSP (TPP)*. The TPP then uses the account holder's credentials to access the account and copies or "scrapes" the data for use outside of the account holder's account facility (e.g. online banking portal). This is, outside of Europe, still a popular method. Apart from the fact that bank account holders would most probably be in breach of their bank's terms and conditions (i.e. sharing of credentials with outside parties), this method is not very secure, especially in financial services. In Europe, PSD2 banned screen scraping. Screen scraping is sometimes referred to as "direct access".

SCT See *SEPA Credit Transfer.*

SCT Inst See *SEPA Instant Credit Transfer.*

SDD B2B See *SEPA Direct Debit B2B.*

SDD Core See *SEPA Direct Debit.*

SDK See *Software Development Kit.*

SE See *Secure Element.*

Second Payment Services Directive (PSD2)[6] A regulatory framework that came into force in 2018 and was the catalyst for *Open Banking* worldwide.

Secure Element (SE) A *tamper-resistant* chip containing a microprocessor capable of storing sensitive data and running secure applications which can be embedded in any mobile device (such as a smartphone, IoT device, or crypto hardware wallet). The content of the SE is protected from malware attacks on the host (i.e. the mobile device operating system) and unauthorised access as the SE acts as a secure vault. Typical applications that would use the SE are *authentication*, digital signature, mobile payments, IoT, secure and encrypted communications, etc. The SE can also be cloud-based, which is referred to as *Host Card Emulation* (HCE). See also *encryption*, *cryptography*, and *Trusted Execution Environment (TEE)*.

Secure Code The Mastercard implementation of *3D Secure* version 1.

secure multi-party computation (SMPC) A *cryptography* protocol that allows multiple parties to collaboratively compute a function over their inputs, whilst ensuring that these inputs remain private. This means that each party can contribute data to a computation without revealing their individual data to others involved. SMPC is designed to protect the privacy of each participant's data through advanced cryptographic techniques, ensuring that the final result is obtained without compromising individual input confidentiality. In the context of *Central Bank Digital Currencies* (CBDCs), particularly *wholesale CBDCs*, SMPC plays a crucial role in maintaining the delicate balance between privacy and transparency. Wholesale CBDCs involve large-scale transactions between financial institutions, where safeguarding sensitive financial data is paramount. SMPC ensures that whilst the overall system remains transparent and auditable, individual transaction details remain confidential. This is particularly important in *distributed ledger technology* (*DLT*) systems, where data privacy must be preserved even as transaction records are shared across a network. By employing SMPC, central banks and financial institutions can perform necessary computations, such as transaction verification and balance calculations, without exposing sensitive underlying data, thus complying with privacy regulations and mitigating the risk of data breaches. SMPC may also be used by blockchain *oracles*.

Secure Remote Commerce (SRC)[7] An *EMVCo* implementation of *One Click Payment*.

security A financial instrument that represents an ownership position in a publicly traded corporation (stock), a creditor relationship with a governmental body or a corporation (bond), or rights to ownership as represented by an option. Securities are broadly categorised into two types: equity securities, such as stocks, and debt securities, such as bonds and debentures. They can be traded on financial markets and are subject to regulatory oversight to protect investors and ensure market integrity.

security token A type of *crypto asset* that is an investment contract representing the legal ownership of a digital, physical, or intangible asset. Security token investors aim to generate a profit (e.g. dividend payments, interest, profit share, and residual rights). Security tokens are regulated under applicable securities regulations and can only be traded on regulated platforms.

security token exchange A regulated *crypto exchange* that facilitates the buying, selling, and trading of *security tokens*, which are digital representations of ownership in an asset or company, typically backed by real-world assets. These exchanges ensure compliance with relevant securities laws and regulations, providing a secure environment for investors to trade tokenised securities. See also *tokenisation*.

Security Token Offering (STO) A regulated form of fundraising where digital tokens representing ownership in real-world assets (such as stocks, bonds, or real estate) are issued and sold to investors. STOs combine *blockchain* technology with traditional securities, offering increased liquidity and accessibility whilst complying with relevant securities laws and regulations. Unlike *Initial Coin Offerings* (*ICOs*) and *Initial Exchange Offerings* (*IEOs*), STOs provide investors with legal rights and protections associated with conventional securities. See also *tokenomics*.

seigniorage The profit a government or central bank makes from issuing currency, typically calculated as the difference between the face value of money and the cost to produce it. In traditional finance, this occurs when the production cost of coins or banknotes is less than their monetary value. In the context of *blockchain*, seigniorage refers to the revenue generated by a *blockchain protocol* through the creation and distribution of new tokens. This can include block rewards for miners or validators, as well as the profits from selling newly minted tokens. Blockchain seigniorage is often used to fund protocol development, incentivise network participants, or maintain the stability of algorithmic stablecoins. See also *minting*, *burning*, and *tokenomics*.

Self-Assessment Questionnaire (SAQ) A form that businesses may use to self-validate *PCI DSS* compliance, and there are several options depending on the type and size of the merchant (see *merchant Level*). SAQs are found in the *PCI SSC* Document Library.[8] Not all merchants are allowed to self-validate as this depends on their merchant level.

Self-Sovereign Identity (SSI) A specific implementation of *decentralised identity* that gives individuals full control over their digital identity credentials. In SSI systems, users store their identity data in a *digital wallet* and selectively share it as needed, without relying on a centralised authority. SSI leverages decentralised identifiers (DIDs) and verifiable credentials (VCs) to enhance privacy and security whilst enabling user autonomy in identity management.

semantic web See *Web 3.0*.

SEMI Small Electronic Money Institution. See *Electronic Money Institution*.

semi-closed wallet See *staged digital wallet*.

sensitive authentication data (SAD) In *PCI DSS* terms, sensitive authentication data consists of the *CVV1*, *CVV2*, *CVV3*, PIN/PIN block, and the other data elements contained in the *discretionary data* on the *magnetic stripe* or *EMV* chip.

SEPA See *Single Euro Payment Area*.

SEPA Credit Transfer (SCT) An *EPC payment scheme*.

SEPA Direct Debit (SDD Core) An *EPC payment scheme*.

SEPA Direct Debit B2B (SDD B2B) An *EPC payment scheme*.

SEPA Instant Credit Transfer (SCT Inst) An *EPC payment scheme*.

SEPA One-Leg-Out Instant Credit Transfer (OCT Inst) An *EPC payment scheme* for transfers between SEPA and non-SEPA countries.

SEPA Payment Account Access (SPAA) An EPC payment-related scheme that specifies a service giving *Account Servicing PSPs (ASPSPs)* the ability to offer value-added services to *Third Party PSPs (TPPs)* by capitalising on the account data they hold (Proxy Lookup Scheme). This could potentially lead to a new surge of *Open Finance* services based on data sharing.

SEPA Proxy Lookup (SPL) An EPC payment-related scheme that provides a data look-up function to be used before initiating a payment, and it covers mobile payments where the mobile number or associated email address is used as a proxy to an IBAN. This scheme may evolve over time to include additional proxy types and identifiers. This may lead to the development of a *Confirmation-of-Payee* (CoP) service. See also *overlay service*.

SEPA Request-to-Pay (SRTP) An EPC payment-related scheme that provides a *Request-to-Pay* (RtP) functionality.

service code A three-digit number contained in the *magnetic stripe* or the *EMV* chip. It is used by *issuers* to tell merchants about the usage characteristics of the card (i.e. how the card can and can't be used) – for example, whether the card is for international use or domestic only, or whether a PIN is required for all transactions, or whether it's only to be used at *an Automated Teller Machine (ATM)*, and the applicable interchange.

service provider level This term is used in the context of PCI standards and dictates the obligations and compliance validation requirements of service providers. Service providers have two levels:

Level 1: those who process and/or transmit more than 300,000 transactions annually per scheme.

Level 2: those who process and/or transmit less than 300,000 transactions annually per scheme.

See also *Payment Card Industry Data Security Standard (PCI DSS)*.

settlement The last step in the transfer of value between a *payer* and a *payee*. After settlement, the obligations of all the parties are fulfilled, and the transaction is considered complete. Settlement brings transaction *finality*. The settlement process will be different for centralised (e.g. *card rail* and *bank rail*) and decentralised infrastructures (e.g. *blockchain*).

settlement agent A bank which orchestrates the *finality* of the transfer of value between parties that hold accounts with them. On the *card rails*, settlement agents are usually commercial banks chosen by the *card schemes* according to their reputation, size, and geographic coverage (but may be a *central bank*). On the bank rails, the settlement agent is a central bank. This concept doesn't exist in *blockchain* infrastructures as the trust framework is distributed.

settlement cycle Refers to the time it takes for payment transactions to be settled. On the bank rails, the settlement cycle is dependent on the bank payment scheme and can be performed in three ways:

In real-time: **Real-Time Gross Settlement** (RTGS) where each payment is presented and settled immediately. This is used by most *large-value payment systems (LVPS)* and also by modern *retail payment systems (RPS)*; or

In near real-time: **deferred net settlement several times a day** where banks batch their transactions at several points during the day and submit the batch each time. This is used by a number or mature real-time RPS. To a payer, the settlement process is transparent as the payments take place within seconds and look as though in "real-time"; or

In batch at the end of the day: **deferred net settlement**, where banks use transaction *batch processing* at the end of the day and submit them in one go, and this is used by (older) retail *ACH schemes*, and it usually takes a few days.

On the *card rails*, the clearing and settlement processes are described in the *card scheme operating regulations*, and the settlement cycle is contingent to the contractual arrangements between parties. The settlement process on the card rails has two stages, *interbank settlement* (between *acquirers* and *issuers*), and *merchant settlement* (between the *acquirer* and the *merchant*). Merchant settlement can be deferred by the acquirer as a risk management tool for specific industries with longer purchase cycles (e.g. airline and hospitality).

In blockchain infrastructures, the concept of settlement cycle is known as the *block interval*.

settlement risk A type of risk that may occur if one party of a financial transaction is not able to hold their end of the deal by failing to deliver the funds or the security required to complete a transaction after the other party (the counterparty) has already delivered the security or funds as per the transaction agreement. Settlement risk may also occur when there is a time lag in payment from one party, usually due to time zones. Also known as "counterparty risk". Also see *Delivery-versus Payment* and *Payment-versus-Payment*, *settlement*, and *settlement cycle*.

set-up fee A one-off fee that may be levied on merchants by some merchant services providers (e.g. *acquirer* and ISO) at the *onboarding* stage.

SHA Secure Hash Algorithm (e.g. SHA-3) is an established family of *hashing* algorithms. See also *cryptography*, *encryption*, and *hash*.

shadow economy Economic activities and transactions that occur outside the purview of government regulation, taxation, and observation. This encompasses a wide range of activities, from unreported income and black market transactions to illegal operations, and *barter systems*. Participants in the shadow economy may include individuals and businesses engaging in legal activities but avoiding taxes or regulations, as well as those involved in explicitly illegal endeavours. The shadow economy's size can vary significantly between countries and is often substantial in developing nations. Whilst it can provide income opportunities for marginalised groups, it also poses challenges for economic policy, tax collection, and fair competition in the formal sector. Also known as "informal economy" or "underground economy". See also *underground banking*.

sharding A layer 1 *scaling solution* involving breaking the state of an entire *blockchain* network into distinct datasets called "shards" which are simultaneously processed in parallel by the network, allowing for sequential work on numerous transactions. Aimed to address the *blockchain trilemma*.

shell company A shell company is a business that usually has financial assets and holds funds but has no active business operations, no employees, and will not engage in trade on a public market or generate any money. They typically hold assets on behalf of other business entities or wealthy individuals. Shell companies may be used for *money laundering* purposes and determining *beneficial ownership* of a company forms part of regulatory obligations for payments businesses.

shim See *shimmer*.

shimmer (shim) A device used by fraudsters to capture data from the *EMV* chip. A shimmer fits inside the card payment terminal, *unattended payment terminal*, or ATM, directly between the card and the card reader, and is therefore difficult to detect (and needs to be less than 0.1 mm thick to enable the card reader to accommodate a card).

shopping cart A software facility on a merchant's e-commerce website that enables customers to make purchases. A virtual terminal should be capable of supporting multiple shopping carts.

SIC See *Standard Industry Code.*

SIBS[9] Portugal's domestic bank *payment scheme.*

SIC-IP[10] A *real-time payment system* (RTP system), *retail payment system* (RPS) in Switzerland, operated by SIX.

side chain In a *blockchain* context, a layer 2 *scaling solution* involving separate blockchains with their own consensus mechanism (e.g. PoS and PoA) that connect to a *layer 1 blockchain* through a gateway called a "bridge", which is usually implemented through a *smart contract.* See also *plasma chain, rollup, state channel,* and *validium.*

signature panel An area on the back of a card containing two elements: the cardholder signature and a printed three-digit code. On some modern cards, you may also find the whole PAN printed on the signature strip, just before the three-digit code. This acts as a visual reminder for the cardholder when the PAN is not present on the front of the card. The cardholder's signature is used to authenticate the cardholder for face-to-face transactions in *EMV* chip and signature or non-EMV markets. Also called "signature strip".

signature strip See *signature panel.*

SIM swap fraud A type of fraud where e fraudster convinces an *agent* of a mobile network carrier to transfer a customer's account to a new SIM card. The fraudster can then use this to bypass *multi-factor authentication* checks, gain access to personal information, and compromise other more secure accounts.

Simplicity A programming language designed for creating *smart contracts* on *blockchain* platforms, particularly focused on *Bitcoin* and its derivatives. It emphasises a minimalist and secure approach, allowing developers to express complex logic in a clear and concise manner whilst ensuring formal verification of contract behaviour. Simplicity operates with a functional programming paradigm and is designed to be more understandable and less error-prone than traditional smart contract languages, thereby enhancing security and reliability in decentralised applications. Its architecture supports the development of complex financial instruments whilst maintaining compatibility with existing blockchain systems.

Single Euro Payment Area (SEPA)[11] An initiative that aims to enable payers anywhere in the EU (as well as in a number of other countries) to make fast, safe, and efficient cashless Euro credit transfers (introduced in 2008) and direct debits (introduced in 2009) to anywhere within the area, just like national payments.

Siirto[12] An *account-to-account payment* service in Finland.

skimmer A device used by fraudsters to read information from the Magnetic Stripe. Skimmers are most often found at *ATMs* and petrol stations and other unattended terminals, but shops and restaurants are not immune (although more difficult to compromise, unless the merchant colludes with the fraudster or is negligent). Skimmers are devices overlaied on top of the card payment terminals and sometimes combined with small cameras to capture cardholder *PINs*.

slashing A penalty mechanism deployed in some *blockchain* infrastructures (mostly *Proof of Stake*) by which validators are punished for misbehaving (e.g. creating invalid blocks and voting twice) by slashing a portion of their *cryptocurrency* stake, meaning they permanently lose those funds. This discourages bad behaviour by making it financially risky for validators to cheat the system. Slashing helps maintain the integrity and security of the blockchain network. See also *staking*.

smart card A historical term for a *EMV chip card* or any card containing a chip.

smart contract Code stored on a *blockchain* that automatically executes when its predefined conditions are met. Based on the "If, Then" principle, they are typically used to automate the execution of an agreement between participants in a trustless environment, without the need for intermediaries. One of the building blocks of *DeFi* and many other blockchain applications.

Smart POS A type of Electronic Point-of-Sale (EPOS). Smart POS terminals support standard card payments but also a range of applications to support the merchant's business. They are usually cloud-based and use operating systems such as Android (making them much more flexible) but are still proprietary to their manufacturers.

S/MIME Secure/Multipurpose Internet Mail Extensions. A protocol for securing email communications through *encryption* and *digital signatures*. It uses *public key cryptography* to provide end-to-end security, ensuring message confidentiality, integrity, and *authentication*. S/MIME allows users to encrypt email contents and attachments, verify the sender's identity, and confirm that messages haven't been altered during transmission. This standard is widely supported by modern email clients and is commonly used in corporate environments to protect sensitive information sent via email.

smishing A contraction of "SMS phishing". A *phishing* technique used by fraudsters involving sending text messages impersonating trusted entities (e.g. a bank or law enforcement) to induce victims to reveal personal information such as bank or card details, and passwords.

SMPC See *secure multi-party computation.*

SMS Short Message Service. A way of sending text only messages of up to 160 characters between phones, commonly known as texting.

SMS verification A type of *two-factor authentication* (2FA) involving sending the customer a *one-time passcode* (OTP) via text message to confirm their identity.

SNCE[13] A *real-time payment system (RTP system), retail payment system (RPS)* in Spain, operated by Iberpay.

social commerce The process by which the whole shopping experience is embedded into a social media platform. Customers can browse through a merchant's shop and view their goods and services, as well as completing purchases without leaving the social media platform.

social engineering A technique used by fraudsters and cyber criminals to psychologically manipulate victims into performing actions or divulging confidential information. Social engineering is more effective than compromising computer systems because it relies on human vulnerabilities rather than finding and exploiting technical vulnerabilities. See also *phishing, vishing, smishing,* and *ransomware.*

social scoring A system that evaluates the trustworthiness and behaviour of individuals, organisations, or entities based on various data points, including financial history, social interactions, and compliance with laws. This concept is most notably exemplified by China's Social Credit System, which assigns scores that can influence access to services and privileges, such as loans and travel. Whilst intended to promote good behaviour and societal trust, social scoring systems raise concerns about *privacy*, surveillance, and the potential for discrimination against those with lower scores.

Society for Worldwide Interbank Financial Telecommunications (SWIFT)[14] A membership organisation that specifies a set of standard messages and formats that the financial services industry agrees on, thus minimising translation and counterparty verification costs, as well as improving security. SWIFT doesn't actually move funds; the bank *payment schemes* do that.

SoFi[15] A *neo-bank*.

Sofort[16] An *account-to-account payment* service in Germany. Acquired by Klarna in 2014.

soft decline A temporary rejection of a payment transaction by the *issuer* that allows for the possibility of approval upon resubmission. Unlike a *hard decline*, which indicates a permanent issue, a soft decline suggests that the transaction may be approved if certain conditions are met or if it is retried. Common reasons for soft declines include temporary insufficient funds, suspected fraud that requires verification, or technical issues. Merchants and payment processors often use automated retry logic or customer communication strategies to resolve soft declines and complete the transaction.

soft fork See *fork*.

soft peg See *peg*.

SoftPOS A modern iteration of *Mobile Point-of-Sale* (mPOS) which doesn't rely on additional hardware and allows merchants to accept card payments directly on a standard consumer smart phone or tablet (i.e. Android or iOS).

Software-as-a-Service (SaaS) A software licensing and delivery model in which software is licensed on a subscription basis and is centrally hosted in the cloud. A category of *cloud computing*.

Software Development Kit (SDK) A collection of software development tools provided in one installable package. An example is *SoftPOS* virtual card terminals which can be deployed on a merchant's own device (e.g. smart phone or tablet).

Solana (SOL)[17] A *layer 1 blockchain*. A *permissionless blockchain*. Also refers to the Solana *cryptocurrency* SOL. See also *blockchain*.

Solidity A statically typed, contract-oriented programming language designed specifically for developing *smart contracts* on *blockchain* platforms, primarily *Ethereum*. Created in 2014, it draws inspiration from C++, *Python*, and *JavaScript*, featuring a syntax similar to that of JavaScript. Solidity enables developers to implement complex, self-executing contracts that can handle digital assets, enforce rules, and interact with other contracts on the blockchain. It supports inheritance, libraries, and complex user-defined types, whilst emphasising security features to prevent common vulnerabilities in smart contracts. Solidity code is compiled into *bytecode* that runs on the *Ethereum Virtual Machine (EVM)*, allowing for *decentralised applications (dApps)* and *Decentralised Autonomous Organisations (DAOs)* to be built on blockchain technology.

sort code A six-digit number used to identity banks in the UK. It's usually split in pairs (e.g. 01–02–03): the first two digits identify the bank and the last four identify the bank branch. Similar to the *ABA routing number* in the US.

SPEI[18] A *real-time payment system (RTP system)*, *retail payment system (RPS)* in Mexico, operated by Banxico.

SPI Small payment institution. See *payment institution*.

split payment A payment transaction for which the full amount of the transaction is split in two or more payment transactions made using different *payment methods* and/or where several individuals may jointly contribute part of the total transaction amount until the full amount is paid. This term is sometimes used interchangeably with *deferred payments*, which also split the total cost into several smaller portions, but these are spread out into instalments and paid off over time, unlike split payments. See also *group payment*.

SQL Structured Query Language. A specialised programming language used for managing and manipulating relational databases. It serves as the standard language for relational database management systems (RDBMS), enabling users to perform a variety of tasks such as querying data, updating records, and defining database structures. SQL is crucial for data analysis and application development, allowing efficient retrieval and organisation of data across large datasets. Its syntax closely resembles English, making it relatively accessible for users to learn and implement in various database environments.

SRC See *Secure Remote Commerce*.

SSI See *Self-Sovereign Identity*.

SSL/TLS Secure Sockets Layer/Transport Layer Security. A cryptographic protocol that provides secure communication over a computer network. It establishes an encrypted link between a client (typically a web browser) and a server, ensuring *data privacy*, integrity, and *authentication*. SSL/TLS uses *digital certificates* to verify the identity of the server and employs both asymmetric and symmetric encryption to protect data in transit. This protocol is widely used to secure web browsing, email, instant messaging, and other internet communications.

StaaS See *Staking-as-a-Service*.

stablecoin A type of *crypto asset* with the intended purpose to facilitate trades on *crypto exchanges*. Stablecoins were created to address the *volatility* risks associated with cryptocurrencies and can be either pegged to a collateral (e.g. *fiat currency*, commodity, and another *cryptocurrency*), or rely on a "mint and burn" stabilising mechanism to control the supply. The former is referred to as a "collateralised stablecoin" and the latter as "non-collateralised" or "algorithmic". Stablecoins are becoming increasingly regulated. See also *coin*, *token*, *fiat-backed stablecoin*, *crypto-collateralised stablecoin*, *commodity-collateralised stablecoin*, and *algorithmic stablecoin*.

staged digital wallet A digital wallet that uses two stages (called back-to-back funding) to complete a payment transaction: the "funding" stage where the wallet collects funds from the payer's payment instrument (e.g. a card or a bank account) and the "payment" stage where the wallet provider pays out the funds to the payer. Wallet holders can transfer funds to other wallet holders on the same wallet network or make payments at merchants with which the wallet holder has an agreement. A staged wallet doesn't necessarily transmit information to the card *issuer*. Examples are PayPal, Square Cash, Bizum, Vipps, Amazon Pay, and Google Wallet. Historically called a "semi-closed wallet". (Note: PayPal also operates as a *stored value digital wallet* since PayPal account holders can have a balance on their account). See also *pass-through digital wallet*.

stake delegation In a *Proof-of-Stake (PoS) blockchain* context, a *staking* model by which coin/ token holders may delegate their stake (voting power and staking rights) to other validators or entities of their choice if they don't have the resources or expertise to run a validator node and still want to participate in the *consensus protocol* and earn staking rewards. Delegators retain control of their stake and can withdraw delegation at any time. Coin/ token holders running validator nodes may also self-delegate to their own node to enhance their reputation and probability of being chosen.

stakeholder In a payments *ecosystem*, these are the parties involved whose interests are affected by the operation of the *value chain*.

staking In a *blockchain* context, the process of reserving an amount of *cryptocurrency* for a particular purpose. In the *Proof of Stake* (PoS) blockchain *consensus protocol*, this is the governance process by which *validators* are governed on a particular blockchain (see also *cross-chain staking*). Another definition applies to *crypto debit cards* and *crypto credit cards*, where some issuers may require cardholders to stake a cryptocurrency amount to be able to use the card.

Staking-as-a-Service (StaaS) StaaS providers may offer infrastructure, node management, validator hosting, etc. to those unable to run their own *validator* node on *Proof of Stake* (PoS) networks who may leverage the infrastructure and expertise of these providers by delegating their stake to them to increase their chance of earning staking rewards. Participants have more flexibility and control over their stake when compared to *staking pools*. They typically charge a fee which is deducted from the staking rewards which are distributed amongst participants according to their contribution. Increasingly attracting regulatory scrutiny.

staking farm In a *Proof of Stake* (PoS) context, this is a large-scale *staking* operation, and validators may delegate their stake to the farm's infrastructure in exchange for professional infrastructure management, security, risk management, optimisation services, and even portfolio management across multiple blockchains. Staking farms will charge a fee which is deducted from the staking rewards, which are distributed amongst participants according to their contribution.

staking pool In a *Proof of Stake* (PoS) *blockchain* context, this is a concept similar to a *mining pool* in *Proof of Work* (PoW) blockchains, whereby validators can join or create staking pools where the pool operator aggregates the delegated stakes to operate a *validator node* on behalf of the pool members. An alternative model is where staking pools function as intermediaries, allowing users to delegate their stakes to validators chosen by the pool operator as the pool doesn't operate a validator node itself. Regardless, staking pools share rewards proportionally to their member's contribution and typically charge fees which are deducted from the staking rewards. These pools can be small (targeted at individual investors or validators) or large-scale operations (targeted at institutional investors) and depending on size may offer professional infrastructure management, security, risk management, optimisation services, and even portfolio management across multiple blockchains.

Participants in a staking pool have limited control over their staked assets as they delegate their tokens to the pool.

Standard Industry Code (SIC) An identifier used to classify a business by the types of goods or services they provide. This is different from the *Merchant Category Code* (MCC) and may be used in some geographies to assess merchant risk. SIC codes may vary across geographies.

Stand-In Processing (STIP) A process by which a *card scheme* would step in on behalf of an *issuer* when that issuer is unable to provide a real-time response during the *authorisation* process. An issuer may face this situation during planned or unplanned outages or network problems. The card scheme would "stand in" on behalf of the issuer to approve or decline a transaction using predefined rules set by the issuer. Whilst this type of service has long been established, card schemes continue to innovate by incorporating new technologies, such as *artificial intelligence* or *deep learning* models, into the STIP mechanism. See also *delegated authentication.*

standing order A *payment instruction* from the bank account holder to their bank to transfer funds to a payee for a fixed amount at a fixed frequency. The payee can be the same person as the instructing bank account holder (e.g. a bank account holder moving funds between their own accounts) or a different person. This is a type of *recurring transaction,* albeit completely controlled by the payer, unlike *direct debit.* Examples would be when a bank account holder transfers a fixed sum from their bank account to their savings account at the end of every month, or when they transfer money to their children every month. This type of payment is not supported by all bank *payment schemes.*

Starling Bank[19] A *neo-bank.*

state channel In a *blockchain* context, a layer 2 *scaling solution* involving separate transactional infrastructures (usually not blockchains) where participants can carry out multiple private transactions off-chain on a *peer-to-peer* basis, where only the first (open channel) and final (close channel) transactions are recorded on the underlying *layer 1 blockchain.* As such, they facilitate fast and cheap transactions without relying on the main chain for every transaction. See also *plasma chain, rollup, side chain,* and *validium.*

STET[20] France's domestic bank *payment scheme* operator

STET Standard[21] The French *Open Banking* standard.

stored value card A type of *prepaid card* where the funds can be increased as well as decreased.

stored value digital wallet A type of *e-wallet* similar to a *prepaid card* inasmuch as they allocate a separate account to each wallet holder. Wallet holders can load funds into their wallet account using a funding mechanism (e.g. a card), and once the wallet account is funded, the wallet holder can perform transactions with sellers that are part of the wallet network, as well as transfer funds to other users within the network. Examples are Alipay, Amazon Pay, Paytm, and Venmo. Also referred to as a *closed wallet*. A variation of this model is the retailer-issued stored value wallet, such as provided by Starbucks[22] or Target.[23]

STIP See *Stand-In Processing*.

STP See *Straight-Through Processing*.

Straight-Through Processing (STP) A process by which automation is used to process electronic transfers with as little manual intervention as possible. STP applications are in payment processing as well as securities trading. Any company involved with STP must have the necessary infrastructure in place to facilitate STP efficiency.

Straksclearing[24] A *real-time payment system (RTP system)*, *retail payment system (RPS)* in Denmark.

Strong Customer Authentication (SCA) An EU regulatory requirement brought by the *Second Payment Services Directive* (PSD2). It mandates the implementation of two or more *authentication* factors when authenticating payment transactions. The authentication factors consist of "knowledge" (i.e. something you know such as a password), "ownership" (i.e. something you possess, such as a payment card), and "inherence" (i.e. something you are, such as a fingerprint or retina scan) and an additional factor for remote transaction which must be dynamic (i.e. can't be used twice) and specific to that transaction (e.g. amount payee). Specific requirements and characteristics apply to the authentication factors. A form of *multi-factor authentication* (MFA).

sub-merchant A generic term used on the *card rails* to refer to a small business that uses the services of a *payment aggregator* such as a payfac to accept card payments.

Substrate A modular *blockchain* development framework created by Parity Technologies that enables developers to build custom, application-specific blockchains efficiently. It offers a flexible architecture with pre-built components for consensus mechanisms, runtime modules, and networking protocols, supporting both *Proof-of-Work* and *Proof-of-Stake* systems. Substrate allows for seamless upgrades through forkless runtime updates and serves as the foundation for the Polkadot network, facilitating interoperability between different blockchains. Its customisable features simplify the creation and deployment of blockchain networks for various applications.

subscription transaction A type of *recurring transaction*. A financial arrangement where a customer pays regularly for ongoing access to a product or service, typically at fixed intervals (e.g. monthly or annually), which may include features like tiered pricing or service upgrades. Also referred to as "subscription billing" or "subscription payment".

super app A versatile mobile application that integrates multiple services and functionalities into a single platform, allowing users to perform various tasks without switching between different apps. These tasks can include messaging, social networking, e-commerce, financial transactions, and more. Examples of super apps include WeChat, which combines messaging, social media, and payment services, and Grab, which offers ride-hailing, food delivery, and financial services all within one app.

surcharge fee A fee that may be levied by merchants on consumers using a credit card for payment. Whether merchants are allowed to surcharge credit card holders depends on the jurisdiction and the *card scheme* operating rules. Generally, surcharges are not permitted for debit card transactions. This term also applies to a fee that may be levied on cardholders by *ATM* owners for the cost of deploying and maintaining the ATM network.

surcharging The practice of adding an extra fee to a transaction when a customer chooses to pay with a specific payment method, typically a credit card. This fee is intended to offset the costs incurred by the *merchant* for accepting that particular payment type. Surcharging is regulated in many jurisdictions, with some countries prohibiting it entirely, whilst others allow it under certain conditions. Where permitted, merchants must clearly disclose the surcharge to customers before the transaction is completed. The practice is controversial, as it can impact consumer choice and purchasing behaviour, but proponents argue it helps small businesses manage payment processing costs.

Suspicious Activity Reporting (SAR) The process by which financial crimes are reported to the regulator. See also *money laundering* and *Customer Due Diligence*.

sustainable finance Financial services, products, and decision-making processes that integrate *environmental, social, and governance* (ESG) criteria to promote long-term economic growth whilst ensuring positive impacts on society and the environment. It encompasses activities such as sustainable investing, green bonds, impact investing, and ESG risk assessment in lending and insurance. In the context of payments, sustainable finance manifests through initiatives like green payment cards made from recycled materials, carbon footprint tracking for transactions, rewards programmes incentivising sustainable purchases, and the integration of ESG considerations into payment processing and financial technology solutions. These approaches aim to align payment systems and consumer behaviour with sustainability goals, encouraging responsible consumption and supporting the transition to a low-carbon, socially inclusive economy.

sweeping A process on the *bank rails* by which funds from one bank account can be moved to another account according to a set of rules set by the bank account holder. For example, covering a short-term deficit in a bank account with funds from another account with a positive balance or moving surplus funds from an account to another offering higher savings interest. See also *Open Banking* and *Variable Recurring Payment*.

SWIFT See *Society for Worldwide Interbank Financial Telecommunications*.

Sybil attack A type of security threat in *peer-to-peer* networks where a malicious actor creates multiple fake identities or *nodes* to gain disproportionate influence over the network. Named after the subject of a book about dissociative identity disorder, this attack aims to undermine the network's integrity by overwhelming it with seemingly independent participants that are actually controlled by a single entity. Sybil attacks can compromise the reliability of *consensus protocols*, reputation systems, and voting processes in decentralised systems, potentially leading to network manipulation or disruption.

symmetric cryptography An *encryption* method where both the sender and receiver use the same encryption key, which is used for both encrypting and decrypting the messages. Symmetric cryptography is considered less secure and more difficult to manage (i.e. key distribution and key management) than *public key cryptography* (aka asymmetric cryptography), but faster. Typically used for bulk encryption of large volumes of data, including in centralised payment applications (e.g. card transactions), or for securing data at rest. Also known as "symmetric encryption" or "secret key cryptography". Well-known symmetric cryptography algorithms include Advanced Encryption Standard (AES), Triple Data Encryption Standard (3DES), and Rivest Cipher (RC4).

synthetic data Artificially generated information that mimics the statistical properties and patterns of real-world data without containing any actual personal or sensitive information. Created using algorithms and *machine learning* techniques, synthetic data serves as a *privacy*-preserving alternative to genuine datasets. It is used for various purposes including software testing, AI model training, data analysis, and research, particularly in fields where access to real data is limited due to privacy concerns or regulatory restrictions. Synthetic data allows organisations to develop, test, and validate systems and processes without risking exposure of confidential information, whilst maintaining the statistical relevance and utility of the original data.

synthetic fraud Also known as "synthetic identity fraud", synthetic fraud is a type of *financial crime* where perpetrators create fictitious identities by combining real and fabricated personal information. These synthetic identities typically use a genuine government-issued identifiers (e.g. social security number), often belonging to a child, elderly person, or someone unlikely to monitor their credit, combined with false names, addresses, and other details. Fraudsters cultivate these identities over time, building credit profiles and establishing seemingly legitimate financial histories before exploiting them for significant financial gain. This form of fraud is particularly challenging to detect and combat because it doesn't victimise a specific individual, making it difficult for traditional *fraud detection* systems to flag. Synthetic fraud is considered one of the fastest-growing types of financial crimes, causing substantial losses to financial institutions and businesses.

synthetic stablecoin A synthetic *stablecoin* is a type of *cryptocurrency* designed to maintain a stable value, typically soft-pegged to a *fiat currency* like the US dollar, without relying on traditional banking infrastructure. It achieves this stability through a *delta-hedging* strategy, which involves creating offsetting positions in derivatives to manage risk. This ensures that the value of the synthetic stablecoin remains stable despite market volatility by balancing gains and losses between the spot and derivative markets. See also *peg*.

Systemically Important Payment System (SIPS) A systemically important payment system is one where a failure due to insufficient protection against risk or disruption could endanger the whole economy. This includes systems that are the sole (or dominant) payment system in a jurisdiction, large value payment systems, etc.

systemic risk See *contagion risk*.

Notes

1 American Express (SafeKey). https://www.americanexpress.com/uk/security/safekey/ (Accessed 5 December 2023)
2 Samsung (Samsung Pay). https://www.samsung.com/uk/samsung-pay/ (Accessed 21 November 2023)
3 Samsung (Samsung Wallet). https://www.samsung.com/uk/apps/samsung-wallet/ (Accessed 21 November 2023)
4 Saudi Central Bank (SARIE) https://www.sama.gov.sa/en-US/payment/pages/sariee.aspx (Accessed 21 November 2023)
5 Sberbank. http://www.sberbank.ru/en/s_m_business (Accessed 21 November 2023)
6 EUR-Lex (PSD2) https://eur-lex.europa.eu/legal-content/EN/TXT/?uri=celex%3A32015L2366 (Accessed 21 November 2023)
7 EMVCo (Secure Remote Commerce). https://www.emvco.com/emv-technologies/secure-remote-commerce/ (Accessed 21 November 2023)
8 PCI SSC Document Library. https://www.pcisecuritystandards.org/document_library/ (Accessed 21 November 2023)
9 SIBS. https://www.sibs.com/en/onde-estamos/portugal/(Accessed 21 November 2023)
10 SIX. https://www.six-group.com/en/blog/swiss-instant-payments.html (Accessed 21 November 2023)
11 European Central Bank (SEPA). https://www.ecb.europa.eu/paym/integration/retail/sepa/html/index.en.html (Accessed 21 November 2023)
12 Siirto. https://siirto.fi/ (Accessed 21 November 2023)
13 Iberpay (SNCE). https://www.iberpay.com/en/payments/spanishpayment-system-snce/about-the-snce/ (Accessed 21 November 2023)
14 SWIFT. https://www.swift.com/ (Accessed 21 November 2023)
15 SoFi. https://www.sofi.com/ (Accessed 21 November 2023)

16 Sofort (A Klarna Company). https://www.klarna.com/pay-now/ (Accessed 21 November 2023)
17 Solana. https://solana.com/ (Accessed 26 May 2024)
18 Banco de Mexico (SPEI). https://www.banxico.org.mx/services/spei_-transfers-banco-mexico.html (Accessed 21 November 2023)
19 Starling Bank. https://www.starlingbank.com/ (Accessed 21 November 2023)
20 Banque de France (Operators). https://www.banque-france.fr/en/financial-stability/financial-stability-mandate/oversight-paymentsystems-infrastructures/french-operators (Accessed 21 November 2023)
21 STET. https://www.stet.eu/en/psd2/ (Accessed 21 November 2023)
22 Starbucks App. https://www.starbucks.com/rewards/mobileapps/ (Accessed 1 December 2023)
23 Target App. https://www.target.com/c/target-app (Accessed December 2023)
24 Danmarks Nationalbank. https://www.nationalbanken.dk/en/what-we-do/safe-and-efficient-payments/the-payments-infrastructurein-denmark (Accessed 21 November 2023)

T

T IS FOR...

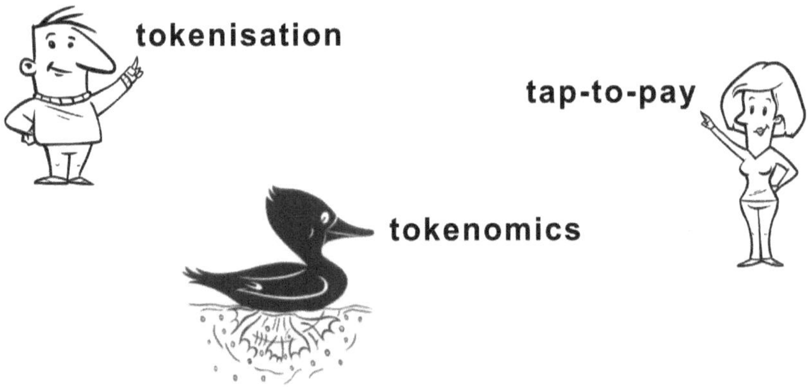

tamper-evident The capacity of a device to show evidence of physical attack.

tamper-proof The proven capacity of a device to resist all attacks.

tamper-resistant The proven capacity of a device to resist physical attacks up to a certain point.

DOI: 10.4324/9781003571131-21

tap-to-pay A *contactless payment* method that allows users to make transactions by simply tapping their payment card, mobile device, or wearable device equipped with *Near Field Communication (NFC)* technology on a compatible *Point-of-Sale terminal*. This method streamlines the checkout process by eliminating the need for physical swiping, inserting, or entering a PIN for small-value transactions, enhancing convenience and speed for both consumers and merchants. Tap-to-pay transactions are typically secure as they often use *tokenisation* and *encryption* to protect sensitive payment information. This technology is widely adopted in retail environments, public transportation systems, and various service industries, contributing to the growth of cashless payments.

TARGET2[1] A real-time gross settlement system owned and operated by the Eurosystem. See *settlement cycle*.

TARGET Instant Payment Settlement (TIPS)[2] A SEPA messaging system specific to the EU. Essentially the EU equivalent to *SWIFT* for Euro-denominated payments. Domestic schemes in the EU completed their migration to TIPS in 2022.

TC40 A report sent by *issuers* to Visa containing information on claims of fraud made by cardholders. For each report of fraud, TC40 data may include information about the *merchant*, the *issuer*, the *acquirer*, and the transaction itself. The Mastercard equivalent is *SAFE*.

TCH See *The Clearing House*.

Technical Service Provider (TSP) A term used in Europe in the context of *Open Banking*. TSPs collaborate with regulated providers to supply financial data that fuels Open Banking. Under *PSD2*, there is a distinction between a TSP and *Payment Initiation Service Providers (PISP)*. Generally, TSPs provide only technical services – they don't gain possession of funds and don't qualify as a *Payment Initiation Service Provider (PISP)* or *Account Information Service Provider (AISP)*.

TEE See *Trusted Execution Environment*.

TEF Transferencias en Linea. A *real-time payment system* (RTP system), *retail payment system* (RPS) in Chile.

Tempo (Radix) An implementation of *Distributed Ledger Technology (DLT)* that uses a data structure called Tempo, where nodes rely upon the passage of logical time to validate transactions. Radix positions itself as a *Web 3.0* platform. See also *blockchain*, *Hashgraph*, and *Directed Acyclic Graph (DAG)*.

Terminal ID (TID) An identifier issued to a merchant by an *acquirer* or *ISO*, usually one per physical or virtual device. The TID ensures that all payment transactions can be linked back to a specific merchant and a specific location for the merchant and, in some cases, a specific device at the specific location. The TID combined with the *Merchant ID* (MID) ensures that the card payment can be traced back to its source.

Terminated Merchant File (TMF) See *MATCH™ list*.

terrorist financing The provision of funds or financial support to terrorists. A form of *financial crime*. See also *money laundering*.

testnet A separate *blockchain* network used for testing and development purposes, allowing developers to deploy and experiment with *smart contracts* and applications without using real *cryptocurrency* or affecting the main blockchain (mainnet). Testnets simulate the mainnet environment, enabling developers to identify bugs, test features, and ensure functionality in a risk-free setting before launching on the main network.

Tether (USDT)[3] A *stablecoin* pegged to the US dollar and issued by Tether Limited.

The Clearing House (TCH)[4] A banking association and payments company owned by the largest commercial banks in the US. It is the operator of the RTP® and EPN bank payment schemes.

The Code is Law A principle in *blockchain* governance asserting that the rules encoded in *smart contracts* and *blockchain protocols* are the ultimate authority within a blockchain system, superseding traditional legal frameworks. This concept emphasises that the programmed rules of a blockchain network automatically enforce agreements and transactions, potentially conflicting with or operating independently of conventional legal systems.

Third-Party PSP (TPP) A payment *ecosystem* actor which provides *Payment Service Users* (PSUs) with access services to payment accounts.

Three-party model An economic model by which there is no separation between card *acquiring* and card *issuing*. This doesn't promote competition, as commercial terms are set unilaterally by the payment scheme, which also operates as an *acquirer* and an *issuer*. This model is also referred to as *closed loop*. Examples of payment schemes operating in this model are American Express and Discover. The three parties referred to are the *cardholder*, the *merchant*, and the *card scheme*.

throughput The rate at which a system processes units of data or completes operations within a given time period. Usually expressed in transactions per second (TPS) and as a performance indicator for transactional systems. In *blockchain* networks, throughput refers to the number of transactions that can be processed and added to the blockchain per second. It's a key indicator of a blockchain's performance and scalability, with higher throughput generally indicating a more efficient network capable of handling a larger volume of transactions. However, throughput often involves trade-offs with other factors like *decentralisation* and security and can be influenced by various elements including *block size* and network congestion.

TID See *Terminal ID.*

time synchronisation attack A malicious attempt to manipulate or disrupt the clock synchronisation process in networked systems. The attacker aims to alter the perceived time of one or more *nodes*, potentially causing communication failures, security vulnerabilities, or system malfunctions. Common techniques include delaying or modifying timing messages, exploiting vulnerabilities in synchronisation protocols, or manipulating local system clocks. These attacks can impact critical operations in various domains, including financial transactions, industrial control systems, and distributed networks (e.g. *blockchain*).

Tink[5] An *API aggregator*, *authorised payment institution (PI)*, *account information service provider (AISP)*, and *payment initiation service provider (PISP)*. Owned by Visa. See also *Open Banking*.

TIPS See *TARGET Instant Payment Settlement.*

TMF See *MATCH™ list.*

token In traditional centralised payments, a token is a representation of a payment account number that has no link with the original payment account number. It is a security measure that prevents fraudsters from gaining access to the real data. The relationship between the token and the account is maintained in token vaults that are provided by *Independent Software Vendors (ISVs)*, referred to as *Token Service Providers (TSPs)*. In decentralised systems (e.g. *blockchain*), a token is a *crypto asset* that is foreign (i.e. not native) to the blockchain it lives on. Examples are Tether (USDT), Uniswap (UNI), or Chainlink (LINK).

token-based CBDC A *CBDC* access model by which users access the CBDC with a password-like digital signature using *public key cryptography*, without requiring personal identification. Both *retail CBDCs* and *wholesale CBDCs* can use this access model.

Token.io[6] An *API aggregator*, Authorised Payment Institution (PI), Account Information Service Provider (AISP), and Payment Initiation Service Provider (PISP) in the UK. See also Open Banking.

tokenisation In traditional financial services, the process of replacing sensitive data with non-sensitive data. On the *card rails*, a process designed to enhance security by which a card *Primary Account Number (PAN)* is replaced with a unique alternative value, or *token*, which can be used for payment transactions instead of the real PAN. This token can be used subsequently in *recurring transactions*. In decentralised systems, tokenisation is the process by which *real-world assets*, or ownership thereof, are represented digitally on a *blockchain*, which is why it is sometimes referred to as "asset tokenisation". Tokenisation service providers typically offer services such as asset evaluation and pricing, regulatory compliance, creation of tokens, investor/ issuer funds management dashboards, Tokenised Asset Offerings (TAO), and listing on security exchanges (see *crypto exchange*).

tokenised asset A digital representation of a *real-world asset* (such as real estate, artwork, or commodities) created through the process of *tokenisation* on a *blockchain*. These digital tokens represent ownership or rights to the underlying asset, allowing for *fractional ownership*, increased *liquidity*, and easier transfer of traditionally illiquid assets. Tokenised assets can be traded on blockchain platforms, potentially reducing transaction costs and increasing market accessibility.

tokenised security A digital representation of a traditional financial *security*, such as stocks, bonds, or real estate, issued and managed on a *blockchain*. These tokens represent ownership rights in the underlying asset and can be traded on specialised platforms. Tokenised securities offer benefits like *fractional ownership*, increased *liquidity*, and automated compliance through *smart contracts*. They are subject to securities regulations in most jurisdictions and aim to bridge traditional finance with blockchain technology.

token migration The process of moving *tokens* from one *blockchain* network to another, often when a project transitions from using tokens on an existing blockchain to launching its own native *coin*. This typically involves exchanging the original tokens for new coins on the new blockchain, whilst maintaining the token holders' balances and rights.

tokenomics A contraction of "token" and "economics". A term used to describe the economic model used by a *blockchain* ecosystem. This includes token/coin supply (e.g. *mining*, *staking*, *burning*, inflation, and deflationary measures), distribution (e.g. *airdrop* and *Initial Coin Offering*), utility (e.g. function, access, governance, and incentives), and governance (e.g. voting and upgrades). To draw a parallel with centralised payment ecosystems, tokenomics encompasses rules and processes related to a particular *payment scheme*, the applicable regulations, and the monetary policy under which it operates.

Token Service Provider (TSP) In the cards world, an *Independent Software Vendor (ISV)* responsible for issuing and managing tokens, including the mapping of cardholder card numbers to payment tokens.

total stake The cumulative amount of *cryptocurrency* locked up as collateral by all validators in a *Proof-of-Stake (PoS) blockchain* network. This metric represents the overall security and decentralisation of the network, as a higher total stake generally indicates greater resistance to attacks and manipulation.

Total Value Locked (TVL) The aggregate amount of *crypto assets* deposited in a *DeFi* protocol, typically expressed in USD. TVL serves as a key metric to measure the overall adoption and *liquidity* of DeFi platforms and the broader ecosystem.

Tornado Cash[7] A *coin mixer*.

TPP See *Third-Party PSP*.

TRA See *Transaction Risk Analysis*.

traceability The degree to which a payment transaction can be traced back to the *payer* or the *payee*.

Track 1 One of the magnetic tracks contained on a card's magnetic stripe. A data container.

Track 2 One of the magnetic tracks contained on a card's magnetic stripe. A data container.

TradFi An abbreviation of "Traditional Finance". A term used to describe the entire traditional financial, centralised, *ecosystems* such as *card rails*, *bank rails*, and traditional centralised *settlement* and financial market infrastructures. Also see *DeFi*, *CeFi*, *CeDeFi*, and *CApp*.

transaction fee There isn't a single definition of a transaction fee. See *acquirer margin*, *address verification fee*, *assessment fee*, *ATM interchange fee*, *authorisation fee*, *card scheme fee*, *early termination fee*, *gas price*, *interchange*, *interest*, *IRS reporting fee*, *Merchant Service Charge*, *retrieval request fee*, *set-up fee*, and *surcharge fee*. This term is also used to describe the fees that users pay to transact on *blockchain* networks.

transaction pruning In a *blockchain* context, a *layer 1 scaling solution* involving the removal of transactions from a *blockchain* after a certain period of time determined by the protocol (meaning that most full nodes won't have to store an entire copy of the blockchain, thus increasing scalability). If a blockchain implements transaction pruning, most full nodes will be pruned nodes, whilst a number of archival nodes will still store an entire copy of the blockchain. Bitcoin introduces this option in release 0.11.0,[8] and Zcash may also have introduced this option.

Transaction Risk Analysis (TRA) An *exemption* to *Strong Customer Authentication (SCA)* that can be applied by PSPs instead of SCA, as directed by the *EU Second Payment Services Directive* (PSD2). See *Exemption Threshold Value* and *Reference Fraud Rate*.

Transfiya[9] A *real-time payment system (RTP system)*, *retail payment system (RPS)* in Colombia.

Transunion[10] A *credit bureau*.

travel rule A *Financial Action Task Force (FATF)* recommendation by which *Virtual Asset Service Providers (VASPs)* and other financial service institutions are required to share accurate *payer* and *payee* information. The FATF recommendations were updated in November 2023.[11]

Trezor [12] A *crypto wallet*.

TrueLayer[13] An *API aggregator*, *Authorised Electronic Money Institution (EMI)*, *Account Information Service Provider (AISP)*, and *Payment Initiation Service Provider (PISP)*. See also *Open Banking*.

Truffle A comprehensive development environment, testing framework, and asset pipeline for Ethereum *blockchain* development. It provides tools for compiling, deploying, and testing *smart contracts* written in *Solidity* or *Vyper*. Truffle features a built-in smart contract compilation, linking, deployment, and binary management system, as well as automated contract testing using Mocha and Chai. It also offers network management for deploying to public and private networks and an interactive console for direct contract communication. Truffle simplifies the development process, making it easier for developers to build, test, and deploy *Decentralised Applications (dApps)* on *Ethereum* and other *Ethereum Virtual Machine*-compatible blockchains.

Trusted Execution Environment (TEE) A secure zone within a computer specifically designed to safeguard the confidentiality and integrity of code and data. Isolated from the main system, it prevents unauthorised access or modification of the information processed within. Even during a system breach, cryptographic techniques and hardware security features keep the data hidden. Additionally, TEEs ensure data integrity, acting as guardians against tampering. This guarantees the authenticity and trustworthiness of computations performed within. In a *blockchain* context, TEEs are relevant for decentralised *oracles* handling sensitive data. TEEs provide a secure space for decentralised oracles to process confidential information before feeding it to *smart contracts*, even within a decentralised network. See also *Secure Element*.

TSP See *Token Service Provider* and *Technical Service Provider*.

tulip mania A period during the Dutch Golden Age in the early 17th century when the prices of some tulip bulbs reached extraordinarily high levels and then dramatically collapsed. It is often cited as one of the first recorded speculative bubbles.

TUPAS A *digital identity* framework in Finland, which is a partnership between all Finnish banks. It expired in September 2019 to be replaced by the Finish Trust Network (FTN).

TVL See *Total Value Locked*.

Twint[14] A *real-time payment system (RTP system)*, *retail payment system (RPS)* in Switzerland, operated by Twint Ltd.

two-factor authentication (2FA) A type of *multi-factor authentication* that uses two factors. The first factor is usually a password, and the second commonly includes a text with a code sent to a smartphone, or *biometrics*.

Two-party model An economic model in which the merchant is both the *issuer* and the *acquirer*. Cardholders for these schemes can only use the card for payments at the issuer, which in this case is the merchant itself. Examples include some store cards (e.g. Target REDcard™ Debit), some fuel cards (e.g. Shell Fuel Card), some public transport cards (e.g. Oyster for Transport for London), and gift cards. These are true *closed-loop* networks.

Notes

1 European Central Bank (TARGET2). https://www.ecb.europa.eu/paym/target/target2/html/index.en.html (Accessed 21 November 2023)

2 European Central Bank (TIPS). https://www.ecb.europa.eu/paym/target/tips/html/index.en.html (Accessed 21 November 2023)

3 Tether. https://tether.to/en/ (Accessed 21 November 2023)
4 The Clearing House. https://www.theclearinghouse.org/ (Accessed 21 November 2023)
5 Tink. https://tink.com/ (Accessed 21 November 2023)
6 Token.io. https://token.io/ (Accessed 21 November 2023)
7 Tornado Cash. https://tornado.ws/ (Accessed 16 December 2023)
8 Bitcoin Core 0.11.00. https://bitcoincore.org/en/releases/0.11.0/ (Accessed 10 May 2024)
9 Transfiya. https://www.transfiya.com.co/home (Accessed 21 November 2023)
10 Transunion. https://www.transunion.com/ (Accessed 28 November 2023)
11 FATF Recommendations. https://www.fatf-gafi.org/content/dam/fatfgafi/recommendations/FATF%20Recommendations%202012.pdf.coredownload.inline.pdf (Accessed 21 November 2023)
12 Trezor. https://trezor.io/ (Accessed 21 November 2023)
13 TrueLayer. https://truelayer.com/ (Accessed 21 November 2023)
14 Twint. https://www.twint.ch/en/ (Accessed 21 November 2023)

U

U IS FOR...

UCoF See Unscheduled Card on File.

UK Open Banking[1] The UK *Open Banking* standard.

unattended payment terminal (UPT) A self-service payment terminal where the customer interacts directly with the device to pay for and obtain goods or services. Examples are self-service terminals at petrol stations, toll booths, vending machines, kiosks, etc.

DOI: 10.4324/9781003571131-22

unauthorised fraud A type of fraud involving the misuse of someone else's financial resources. It may involve malicious third parties where the account holder hasn't provided authorisation for the payment and the transaction is carried out by a criminal (e.g. the victim's card details are used without their knowledge or consent, as in *account takeover fraud*), or when the account holders themselves act fraudulently (e.g. a *money mule* and *first-party fraud*), and also includes employee embezzlement and family member fraud. See also *third-party fraud* and *authorised fraud*.

unauthorised push payment A type of *unauthorised fraud* where a *push payment* is made through a payment account by a person other than the genuine payment account holder. This may happen in the case of *account takeover fraud (ATO)*.

unauthorised transaction Any payment transaction that has not been authorised by the payment account holder.

uCommerce See *universal commerce*.

underground banking Informal financial systems that operate outside of traditional regulated banking channels. These systems facilitate the transfer of money or value between parties, often across borders, without the physical movement of cash or use of formal financial institutions. Also known as alternative remittance systems or *informal value transfer systems (IVTS)*, underground banking relies on trust-based networks and can include methods like *hawala*, *hundi*, and *fei ch'ien*. Whilst sometimes used for legitimate purposes, underground banking's lack of oversight makes it vulnerable to exploitation for *money laundering*, *terrorist financing*, and other illicit activities. See also *shadow economy*.

underwriting The process by which the potential risks that are associated with a potential payment account holder are evaluated. Risk factors may include finances, industry sector, business model, and transaction volumes. See also *onboarding* and *cashflow underwriting*.

unified commerce A retail strategy that goes beyond *omnichannel* and integrates all sales channels, customer touchpoints, and backend systems into a single, cohesive platform, focusing specifically on creating a seamless experience within a retailer's existing ecosystem. Unlike *universal commerce*, which aims to enable transactions anywhere and on any device, unified commerce emphasises the internal integration of a retailer's own channels and systems. It creates a centralised data ecosystem providing real-time visibility across inventory, orders, customer information, and operations, allowing for consistent interactions and personalised service across a retailer's online and offline touchpoints. This approach enables retailers to streamline operations, make data-driven decisions, and deliver a cohesive shopping experience within their own brand environment, rather than expanding into new, universal commerce spaces.

Unified Payment Interface (UPI)[2] Unified Payment Interface. A *real-time payment system (RTP system)*, *retail payment system* (RPS) in India, operated by NPCI. Also see *Aadhaar*.

UnionPay[3] A *card scheme* operating on the *four-party model*. The large majority of cards are used in China, but this scheme is starting to challenge Europe. Also known as China UnionPay or UnionPay International.

Uniswap[4] A decentralised *crypto exchange*.

universal commerce (uCommerce) A comprehensive approach to commerce that enables seamless transactions and interactions between buyers and sellers across all channels, devices, and touchpoints. It integrates online and offline retail experiences, unifying inventory, pricing, and promotions to create a cohesive ecosystem. uCommerce leverages advanced technologies like *artificial intelligence*, *Internet of Things*, and data analytics to provide personalised experiences, real-time inventory visibility, and flexible fulfilment options. This model aims to meet evolving consumer expectations for convenience, choice, and consistency, allowing businesses to adapt quickly to market changes and deliver a unified brand experience regardless of how, when, or where customers choose to engage. See also *unified commerce*.

Unscheduled Card on File (UCoF) On the *card rails*, a type of *recurring transaction* that occurs on a variable schedule and/ or has a variable amount, such as automatic top-ups when a cardholder's balance drops below a certain limit.

Unspent Transaction Output (UTXO) A *double-spending* prevention model in *blockchain* infrastructures where each output from an unspent (i.e. not settled) transaction becomes a UTXO associated with the address of the transaction initiation user. Users initiating transactions will reference one or more UTXOs as inputs to a new transaction to prove that they have funds available. The sum of the UTXOs must cover the amount being spent, and the excess is then sent back as change to the sender's address, creating new UTXOs. The UTXO model, commonly used in

Proof-of-work blockchains (e.g. Bitcoin and Bitcoin-based blockchains) and some PoS blockchains (e.g. Cardano, Zilliqa, and Tezos), enables the blockchain to keep a consistent and unbroken chain of ownership through the tracking of UTXOs where every transaction can be traced back to its origin through the series of unspent outputs. The UTXO model is generally preferred by blockchain projects with a focus on privacy. This is in contrast to account-based models (e.g. *Ethereum*, *Solana*, and *Polygon*) which primarily consider the account balance rather than individual unspent outputs.

UPI See *Unified Payment Interface.*

UPT See *unattended payment terminal.*

USD Coin (USDC)[5] A *stablecoin* pegged to the US dollar and issued by Circle.

USDT See *Tether.*

utility In economics and finance, utility refers to the measure of satisfaction or benefit derived from consuming goods or services. It represents the value that an individual assigns to a product based on its ability to fulfil needs or desires. In the context of *cryptocurrency* and *blockchain*, utility often describes the practical uses of a *token* within a specific ecosystem, such as enabling transactions, accessing services, or participating in governance, distinguishing it from speculative or investment purposes.

utility token A type of *crypto asset* with the intended purpose of giving crypto-project developers the ability to raise interest in their project, encourage developers to create applications, and generally create value in a blockchain *ecosystem*. These tokens can be used to redeem a special service or receive special treatment and are often given out for free to promote the project. Utility tokens are unregulated. Also see *airdrop*.

UTXO See *Unspent Transaction Output*.

UX An abbreviation for "user experience".

Notes

1 UK Open Banking. https://www.openbanking.org.uk/ (Accessed 21 November 2023)

2 NPCI (UPI). https://www.npci.org.in/what-we-do/upi/productoverview (Accessed 21 November 2023)

3 UnionPay. https://www.unionpayintl.com/en/ (Accessed 21 November 2023)
4 Uniswap. https://app.uniswap.org/swap (Accessed 5 December 2023)
5 Circle (USDC). https://www.circle.com/en/usdc (Accessed 21 November 2023)

V

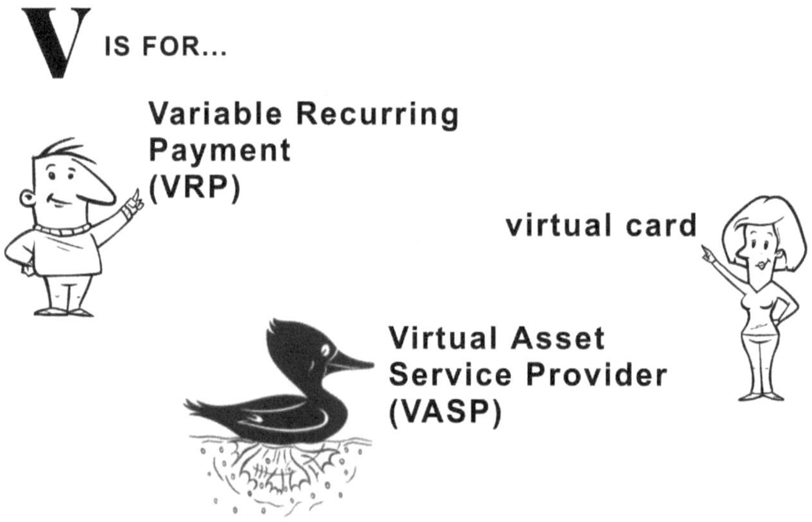

validating node In a *blockchain* context, a node who participates in the transaction validation process. See also *mining*, *miner*, *validator*, *staking*, and *mempool*.

validation A catch-all term referred to a processed of verifying validity. In a *blockchain* context, it may refer to transaction or block validation. See also *staking*, *mining*, and *mempool*.

DOI: 10.4324/9781003571131-23

validator A *validator node* in a *Proof-of-Stake (PoS) blockchain* network who listens and gathers valid transactions to fit in a block (e.g. no *double-spending*). Validators are chosen according to the consensus protocol through *staking* and participate in securing the blockchain in exchange for rewards. This term may be used interchangeably to refer to a *validating node* (i.e. not specifically referring to PoS blockchains). See also *miner, mining,* and *mempool.*

validator node A type of *full node* in a *blockchain* network that actively participates in the consensus process to propose, validate, and add new blocks to the chain. In *Proof of Stake (PoS)* systems, *validators* are responsible for verifying transactions, creating new blocks, and maintaining the integrity of the blockchain. They typically stake cryptocurrency to participate in this process. In *Proof-of-Work (PoW)* systems, *miners* perform a similar role by solving computational puzzles to create new blocks. See also *authority node* and *masternode.*

validity proof A cryptographic mechanism used in *blockchain* networks, particularly in *layer 2 scaling solutions*, to verify the correctness of *off-chain* computations without re-executing them *on-chain*. It allows a prover to demonstrate that a large batch of transactions or state transitions is valid, enabling the main blockchain to accept these changes as correct without processing each transaction individually. Validity proofs provide immediate finality and enhanced security compared to other scaling approaches as they mathematically guarantee the accuracy of the proposed state update. See also *fraud proof* and *Zero-Knowledge Proof.*

validium A *blockchain layer 2 scaling solution*. A validium processes transactions *off-chain* for faster processing and relies on the *layer 1 blockchain* for security but stores transaction data *off-chain* using Data Availability Committees (DACs) or Data Availability Providers (DAPs). Validiums use cryptographic proofs to verify the validity of these off-chain transactions before submitting the proofs to layer 1 for finalisation. See also *plasma chain, side chain, state channel,* and *rollup.*

Value-Added Tax (VAT) A type of consumption tax that is applied on the value of goods and services. It applies to the majority of good and services that are traded in the UK, EU, and the US, as well as several countries globally. Also known as Goods and Services Tax (GST).

value chain A business model describing the steps involved in bringing a product or service to market, from design to distribution, and everything in between.

Valued-Added Reseller (VAR) A business that enhances the value of other companies' products by adding customised products or services to the core product for resale to their customers.

VAR See *Valued-Added Reseller.*

Variable Recurring Payment (VRP) A *payment instruction* issued by a bank account holder to their bank authorising a biller (e.g. a subscription service) to collect payments from their account at regular intervals (e.g. weekly, monthly, and yearly), within agreed limits, without the bank account holder's intervention after the first instruction. It is a bank payment scheme *overlay service* and is a type of *recurring transaction*, but it offers more flexibility and transparency than alternatives such as *direct debit* and card recurring transactions, as the bank account holder remains in control of the payment limits and the payment instruction's end date is agreed upfront. At any point up to *clearing* and *settlement*, the bank account holder can change any of the agreed parameters, enabling them to respond to changes in circumstances as they happen. See also *push payment*, *recurring payment*, and *Open Banking*.

VASP See *Virtual Asset Service Provider.*

VAT See *Value-Added Tax.*

V-Bucks[1] A *virtual currency* used in the game Fortnite.

VDMP The Visa Dispute Monitoring Program. A *merchant monitoring programme.*

vehicle commerce Also known as in-car or in-vehicle commerce. Refers to the integration of financial technology into connected vehicles, enabling drivers and passengers to make purchases and conduct transactions directly through the car's infotainment system or related mobile apps. This emerging *fintech* application allows for seamless payments for services such as fuel, parking, tolls, food orders, and other goods without leaving the vehicle. A prominent example is General Motors' Marketplace platform, which allows drivers of certain GM vehicles to order and pay for items like coffee or fast food, reserve parking spots, or find nearby gas stations, all through the car's touchscreen interface.

Veisa[2] Barter For A Better Vanua Levu (Veisa). A Facebook *barter system* in Fiji.

velocity check A *fraud prevention* tool that can help online merchants stop fraudsters from using stolen card details to make purchases. The process looks for multiple transactions in rapid succession with certain details in common, such as the same card number or IP address. This can help identify *card testing fraud*.

Venmo[3] A *peer-to-peer* payment app, a *stored value digital wallet*.

Verified by Visa The Visa implementation of *3D Secure* version 1. Has been largely replaced by *Visa Secure*.

Verifone[4] An American multinational corporation providing merchant services technology, including point-of-sale card terminals and value-added services at the point-of-sale.

Vipps[5] An *account-to-account payment* service in Denmark.

virtual asset Refers to any digital representation of value that can be digitally traded, transferred, or used for payment or investment purposes. Also referred to as "digital asset".

Virtual Asset Service Provider (VASP) Defined by the *Financial Action Task Force (FATF)* as a business that conducts one or more of the following actions on behalf of its clients:

Exchange between virtual assets and fiat currencies;

Exchange between one or more forms of virtual assets;

Transfer of virtual assets;

Safekeeping and/or administration or virtual assets or instruments enabling control over virtual assets; or

Participating in and provision of financial services related to an *issuer's* offer and/or sale of a virtual asset.

This encompasses a range of crypto businesses, including *crypto exchanges*, crypto ATM operators, custodial wallets, and hedge funds.

virtual assistant See *chatbot*.

virtual card A card that only exists in digital form (i.e. no physical *form factor*). Virtual cards are similar to physical cards and have their own *Primary Account Number (PAN)*, *CVV*, and expiry date. They are usually stored on a smart phone and may be used to make payments in person using a *mobile wallet*, such as Apple Pay or Google Pay, or online where the card details are entered in the usual way. The card can be created to expire after a single purchase, a number of purchases, a specific amount of time, or when the purchase volume reaches a certain total. In some cases, virtual cards can be set up to only make payments to a single entity.

virtual currency A type of *virtual asset* that is issued, managed, and controlled by private *issuers*, developers, or the founding organisation.

A virtual currency is used in a specific community and relies on a system of trust defined by the private issuer. As such, it is a form of a *closed-loop* medium of exchange. Gaming platforms use virtual currencies, such as *V-Bucks* and *Robux*.

virtual IBAN A virtual *IBAN* is a reconciliation tool that allows businesses to send and receive payments using unique addressable IBANs with payments rolling up in to a master settlement account so they can receive and payout on behalf of multiple customers.

virtual machine (VM) A software abstraction layer designed to simulate a computer system. It provides an isolated environment for running various operating systems and applications, independent of the underlying physical hardware. Common examples include VirtualBox, VMWare Workstation, and *Java* Virtual Machine (JVM). The concept of a VM also exists in *blockchain* infrastructures, as with the Ethereum Virtual Machine (*EVM*). See also *Custom Virtual Machine*.

virtual reality payments (VR payments) Financial transactions conducted within a fully immersive, computer-generated 3D environment. Users, typically wearing VR headsets, can make purchases, transfer funds, or manage accounts by interacting with virtual elements and interfaces without leaving the VR space. This technology allows for seamless integration of payment processes into virtual shopping experiences, games, or other VR applications. VR payments aim to provide a more intuitive and engaging way to conduct financial transactions, potentially incorporating gesture controls, voice commands, or virtual representations of payment methods. Whilst offering novel user experiences, VR payments also present unique challenges in terms of security, user interface design, and integration with existing payment systems.

virtual terminal A payment facility that enables *e-commerce* and other virtual transactions. It is the digital equivalent of a physical card payment terminal.

Visa[6] A *card scheme* operating on the *four-party model*.

Visa Dispute Monitoring Program (VDMP) A *merchant monitoring programme* to control *disputes*. In general, merchants will be included in a *card scheme's chargeback*-monitoring programme if their *chargeback ratio* exceeds the card scheme limit.

VisaNet The *Visa* network infrastructure.

Visa Secure[7] The *Visa* implementation of *3D Secure* v2.

vishing A contraction of "voice phishing". A *phishing* technique used by fraudsters over the telephone to make phone calls or leaving voice messages impersonating trusted entities (e.g. a bank or law enforcement) to induce victims to reveal personal information such as bank or card details and passwords.

Vocalink[8] A technology provider specialising in bank payment systems. Vocalink provides the infrastructure for the UK retail bank payment schemes (FPS and BACS) as well as the ATM network. Vocalink also provides bank payment infrastructures in other geographies. Acquired by Mastercard in 2017.

voice-activated payments A payment method that allows users to initiate and complete financial transactions using voice commands through devices equipped with *voice recognition technology*. This system typically uses *artificial intelligence*, *natural language processing*, and *machine learning* to interpret spoken instructions and execute payment actions, such as transferring money, paying bills, or making purchases. Voice-activated payments can be performed through various devices, including smartphones, smart speakers, *wearables*, and other *Internet-of-Things (IoT)* devices with voice assistants like Siri, Alexa, or Google Assistant. This technology aims to provide a hands-free, convenient, and potentially more accessible payment experience, though it also raises considerations regarding security, privacy, and accuracy in voice recognition.

voice authorisation In the cards world, a voice authorisation is used when a merchants attempts to process a card transaction and receives an error code indicating that the transaction requires voice authorisation (See *Call Center*). When a voice authorisation is initiated by the cardholder's *issuer* or the merchant services provider, the cardholder receives a telephone call used to verify that the customer is the one making the purchase. Also called Voice Auth. A rare occurrence.

void The reversal of a current card transaction that has been authorised but not settled. Settled transactions require processing of a credit in order to be reversed (i.e. cannot be voided).

volatility The rate at which the price of a financial asset increases or decreases over a period of time and refers to both the frequency at which the asset value changes and the degree to which it changes.

Higher volatility often means higher risk. Cryptocurrencies such as Bitcoin are volatile.

Vostro account See *correspondent banking*.

VM See *Virtual Machine*.

VRP See *Variable Recurring Payment (VRP)*.

VR payments See *virtual reality payments*.

VT See *Virtual Terminal*.

Vyper A user-friendly programming language designed for writing *smart contracts* on the *Ethereum* blockchain. With a syntax similar to *Python*, it focuses on simplicity and security, making it easier to read and audit the code. Vyper intentionally leaves out complex features like inheritance and recursion to reduce risks and enhance clarity. This makes it an ideal choice for developers looking to create secure and transparent smart contracts, especially in financial applications.

Notes

1 Fortnite (V-Bucks). https://www.fortnite.com/vbuckscard (Accessed 21 November 2023)
2 Veisa Facebook Page. https://www.facebook.com/groups/282307866133018/ (Accessed 30 November 2023)
3 Venmo. https://venmo.com/ (Accessed 21 November 2023)
4 Verifone. https://www.verifone.com/ (Accessed 21 November 2023)
5 Vipps MobilePay. https://vippsmobilepay.com/ (Accessed 21 November 2023)
6 Visa. https://www.visa.com (Accessed 21 November 2023)
7 Visa (Visa Secure). https://www.visa.co.uk/run-your-business/small-business-tools/payment-technology/visa-secure.html (Accessed 5 December 2023)
8 Vocalink. https://www.vocalink.com/ (Accessed 21 November 2023)

W

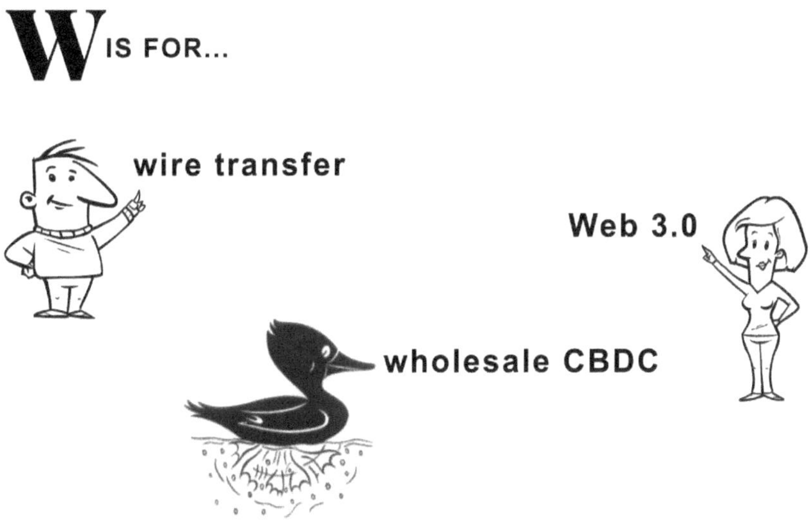

W3C See *Worldwide Web Consortium*.

wash trading A manipulative practice where a trader simultaneously buys and sells the same financial instrument to create artificial market activity. In traditional markets, it's illegal and used to mislead other traders by inflating volumes or manipulating prices. For *crypto assets*, wash trading is common due to less regulation, and it is often employed to

DOI: 10.4324/9781003571131-24

artificially boost trading volumes, create false impressions of liquidity, or manipulate prices of digital assets and *tokens*.

wearables Wearable technology is any technology designed to be used when worn (as clothing or accessories), implanted in the body, tattooed on the skin, overlayed on fingernails, etc. Sometimes referred to as "wearable devices", but the use of "wearables" is the most common. Popular examples are smartwatches, which have a particular relevance in payments. See also *Internet of Things*.

Web 1.0 The first incarnation of the internet characterised by websites that just pushed information to users. It was defined by Tim Berners-Lee in 1989 and provided basic connectivity and hyperlinks. Also referred to as the "static web" or "read-only web".

Web 2.0 The second (current) version of the internet. Instead of just static Web 1.0 websites that pushed information to users, Web 2.0 introduced new forms of interactivity and saw the rise of social media, blogs, and other forms of interactive platforms and technologies (e.g. *Java* and ML).

Web 3.0 The next version of the internet. The exact definition is still loose, but the general consensus is that it has a decentralised infrastructure built on *blockchain* technologies and applications and *artificial intelligence*. Also referred to as the "semantic web" and "Web3". See also *metaverse*.

WebAuthn[1] An *authentication* standard published by the World Wide Web Consortium. See FIDO.

WeChat Pay[2] A *mobile wallet*.

Wero[3] A *staged wallet* solution developed by the *European Payments Initiative* (EPI), a consortium of European banks and financial institutions. Designed to facilitate instant *account-to-account payments* across Europe, it offers features such as peer-to-peer transfers, consumer-to-business transactions, and online shopping payments.

Western Union[4] A *Money Transfer Operator*.

Whirlpool A popular *hashing* algorithm. See also *cryptography*, *encryption*, and *hash*.

white labelling The provision of goods or services to a company where the purchasing company uses their own branding instead of the branding of the supplier to offer the goods or services to their own customers.

white paper A detailed, authoritative report that presents information, analysis, or proposals on a specific topic, often used to inform or persuade stakeholders in business, technology, or policy contexts.

A *blockchain* white paper is a document explaining the primary purpose, technology, current state, and plans for a blockchain project. It should also give information about its participants, utility, and all the potential factors that might give its underlying *coin/ token* economic value. It is meant as a high-level guide that enables investors to ascertain whether a project has future potential and to raise the interest of potential users. The oldest white paper is the Bitcoin white paper, entitled "Bitcoin: A Peer-to-Peer Electronic Cash System", and was written under the pseudonym of Satoshi Nakamoto in October 2008. More recently, the 2014 white paper "Zerocash: Decentralised Anonymous Payments from Bitcoin"[5] that described zk-proofs (see *Zero-Knowledge Proofs*), a cryptographic technique used by many *layer 2 scaling solutions*, received the IEEE "Test of Time" award for its "broad and lasting impact on both research and practice in computer security and privacy".

wholesale CBDC A type of *Central Bank Digital Currency* (CBDC) aimed at financial firms holding reserve deposits with a *central bank* and used for *interbank settlement* and other financial market transactions. Several architecture models can be used for wholesale CBDCs, such as *intermediated CBDC* (sCBDC), *multi-CBDC* (mCBDC), and *direct CBDC*.

wholesale payments A term used to describe transactions between banks or other eligible financial institutions and as being typically large-value payments. Wholesale payments are small in number, but are typically very high in value, and represent most of the value of payments. An example is money market transactions. See also *retail payments*.

wholesale settlement A subset of *interbank settlement* which primarily focusses on high-value transactions between financial services institutions (e.g. banks and investment firms), usually operating on a *Real-Time Gross Settlement* basis. See also *Large Value Payment System (LVPS)*.

wire transfer An electronic method of transferring funds directly from one bank account to another, typically used for quick and secure domestic or international transactions, as well as those using a large-value payment system (LVPS) that generally operates on a Real-Time Gross Settlement (RTGS) basis. See also settlement cycle, real-time payment system (RTP system), and retail payment system (RPS).

Wise[6] A financial services institution, formerly known as TransferWise, that started as a *Peer-to-Peer money exchange* and subsequently obtained further permissions in various geographies, such as the *Electronic Money Institution* (EMI) licence in the EU and the UK.

Worldline[7] An *acquirer*.

Worldpay[8] An *acquirer*.

WorldRemit[9] A *peer-to-peer money exchange*.

Worldwide Web Consortium (W3C) An international community that develops *open standards* to ensure the long-term growth and interoperability of the World Wide Web. Founded in 1994 by Tim Berners-Lee, the inventor of the web, the W3C aims to promote web accessibility, usability, and security through collaborative efforts among member organisations, including businesses, universities, and governmental entities. By creating guidelines and recommendations, the W3C plays a crucial role in shaping the web's architecture and fostering innovation across various technologies and applications.

wrapped token A *cryptocurrency* token that represents a claim on another underlying asset or token, typically from a different blockchain. Wrapped tokens allow assets to be used on non-native blockchains, enabling cross-chain interoperability and liquidity. The original asset is held in custody, whilst an equivalent wrapped version is minted on the target blockchain, maintaining a 1:1 *peg* with the underlying asset.

Notes

1 FIDO Alliance (WebAuthn). https://fidoalliance.org/fido2-2/fido2-web-authentication-webauthn/ (Accessed 21 November 2023)

2 WeChat Pay. https://pay.weixin.qq.com/index.php/public/wechatpay (Accessed 21 November 2023)

3 Wero. https://wero-wallet.eu/ (Accessed 29 September 2024)

4 Western Union. https://www.westernunion.com/ (Accessed 21 November 2023)

5 White Paper That Birthed Crypto ZK-Proofs Receives IEEE 'Test of Time' Award. *Cointelegraph*, 20 May 2024. https://cointelegraph.com/news/whitepaper-birthed-crypto-zk-proofs-receives-ieee-test-of-time-award (Accessed 24 May 2024)

6 Wise. https://wise.com/ (Accessed 21 November 2023)

7 Worldline. https://worldline.com/ (Accessed 21 November 2023)

8 FIS (Worldpay). https://www.fisglobal.com/en-gb/merchantsolutions-worldpay (Accessed 21 November 2023)

9 WorldRemit. https://www.worldremit.com/ (Accessed 21 November 2023)

X

X IS FOR...

X.509 An X.509 certificate is a standardised digital document used in *public key infrastructure (PKI)* to securely associate a *public key* with an entity's identity, such as a website, organisation, or individual. It contains information about the certificate subject, issuer, validity period, and the subject's public key, all digitally signed by a trusted *Certificate Authority (CA)*. X.509 certificates are widely used in various security protocols,

DOI: 10.4324/9781003571131-25

including *SSL/TLS* for secure web communications, S/MIME for email *encryption*, and code signing.

XAI See *explainable AI*.

XaaS Everything-as-a-Service. A collective term for the growing range of cloud-based services, including *Software-as-a -Service (SaaS)*, *Platform-as-a-Service (PaaS)*, and *Banking-as-a-Service (BaaS)*.

x-border payment See *cross-border payment*.

xenocurrency A currency deposited or exchanged in a market outside its country of origin. Today, the term "foreign currency" is more frequently used. These types of currency transactions have become increasingly common, driven by the globalisation of supply chains and financial markets.

XML (Extensible Markup Language) A flexible text-based format for storing and sharing structured data. Unlike its rigid predecessors, such as the fixed-length record format used in *ISO 8583*, XML empowers users to define custom tags. This flexibility allows XML to represent a wide range of data types, from everyday configuration files to complex financial messaging standards like *ISO 20022*. Before XML, data exchange relied on inflexible formats. Imagine fixed-length text files where each data point occupies a specific number of characters, requiring meticulous manual editing for any modifications. Proprietary binary formats, specific to software and often undocumented, further hindered communication. Even early database systems often had their own data formats, creating hurdles when migrating information between databases. XML's structured yet versatile approach addresses these limitations, making it a cornerstone of modern data communication. Its ability to securely and efficiently structure and transport information across various platforms solidifies its prominent role.

Xoom[1] A *PayPal* service for international money transfers.

XRP The *cryptocurrency* issued by *Ripple* on its *private blockchain*. Also a *utility token*.

XS2A See *Access to Account*.

Xuper Chain[2] A *blockchain* infrastructure developed by *Baidu* for various applications, including financial services.

Notes

1 Xoom. https://www.xoom.com/ (Accessed 29 September 2024)
2 Xuper. https://xuper.baidu.com/ (Accessed 29 September 2024)

Y

Y IS FOR...

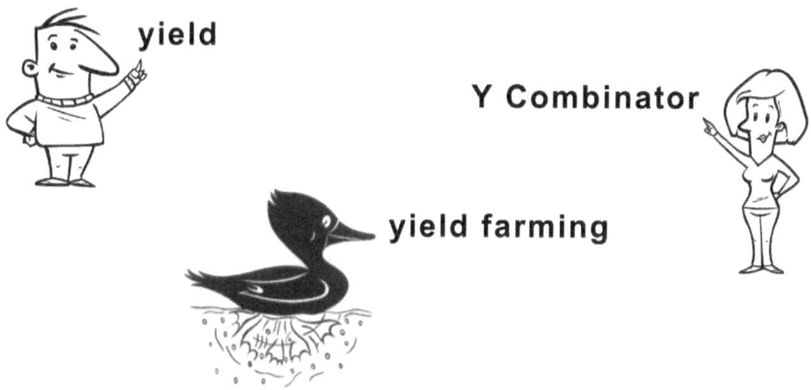

Y2K Year 2000. Y2K refers to the computer programming shortcut that was expected to cause problems at the turn of the millennium.

Yapily[1] An *API aggregator*, *Authorised Payment Institution*, *Account Information Service Provider (AISP)*, and *Payment Initiation Service Provider (PISP)*. See also *Open Banking*.

Y Combinator[2] A prominent startup accelerator that has funded several *fintech* and payment companies.

DOI: 10.4324/9781003571131-26

Yen The official *currency* of Japan. Abbreviated JPY.

yield The income generated from an investment, typically expressed as a percentage of the investment's cost or current market value. It encompasses various forms of returns, including interest payments, dividends, or capital gains, and is used to assess the profitability and performance of financial instruments such as stocks, bonds, and real estate. Yield can be calculated in different ways, including current yield, yield to maturity, and yield on cost, depending on the context of the investment.

yield farming A *DeFi* strategy where users provide *liquidity* to protocols by depositing or lending *crypto assets* in exchange for rewards, typically in the form of the protocol's native tokens or transaction fees. This practice aims to maximise returns on *cryptocurrency* holdings through various incentive mechanisms.

yield management A variable pricing strategy used to maximise revenue from a fixed, perishable resource such as hotel rooms, airline seats, or advertising inventory. It involves analysing and predicting consumer behaviour to optimise product availability and price. Yield management employs various techniques, including *dynamic pricing*, overbooking, and market segmentation, to balance supply and demand efficiently. This approach aims to sell the right product to the right customer at the right time for the right price, often utilising sophisticated algorithms and real-time data analysis.

YOLO (You Only Look Once) A real-time object detection system used in computer vision, with potential applications in financial *fraud detection* and security.

YooMoney[3] An *e-wallet* owned by Sberbank. Formerly known as Yandex. Money and rebranded following its acquisition by *Sberbank*.

Yuan The basic unit of the renminbi, the official *currency* of China, but the word is also used to refer to the Chinese currency generally. Abbreviated CNY.

Notes

1 Yapily. https://www.yapily.com/ (Accessed 21 November 2023)
2 Y Combinator. https://www.ycombinator.com/ (Accessed 29 September 2024)
3 YooMoney. https://yoomoney.ru/ (Accessed 21 November 2023)

Z

Z IS FOR...

Z-score A statistical measure used to assess a company's financial health and predict bankruptcy risk.

Zelle[1] A *peer-to-peer payment* app. A *pass-through digital wallet*. An *A2A* payment app.

Zengin system[2] Japan's domestic funds transfer system.

zero-day vulnerability A software security flaw unknown to the vendor.

DOI: 10.4324/9781003571131-27

Zero-Knowledge Proof (ZKP, zk-proof) In *blockchain* networks, a cryptographic tool allowing a user to prove they are in possession of specific information (e.g. sufficient funds for a transaction) without revealing the information itself to the validator, thus maintaining network integrity whilst protecting user privacy. A commonly used type of ZKP is zk-SNARK (Succinct Non-interactive Argument of Knowledge). Variances of ZKP include zk-SNARK (Succinct Non-interactive Argument of Knowledge) and bulletproof. A *validity proof*.

zero-knowledge rollup (zk-rollup) A *blockchain layer 2 scaling solution*. See *rollup*.

zero-liability A policy that protects cardholders from unauthorised charges.

zero-trust security A *cybersecurity* model that operates on the principle of "never trust, always verify". It assumes no user, device, or network – whether inside or outside the organisation's perimeter – should be automatically trusted. Instead, every access request is rigorously authenticated, authorised, and encrypted before granting access to data or resources. This approach involves continuous verification of user identity, device health, and other contextual factors for each access attempt, implementing least-privilege access, and maintaining strict access controls across all environments. Zero-trust aims to minimise the attack surface, prevent lateral movement within networks, and enhance overall security posture in today's complex, distributed IT landscapes.

zero-value auth An *authorisation request* with a zero value that is used by merchants to either store cardholder details, look up previous purchases, card verification requests, etc.

Zilliqa[3] A high-throughput *public blockchain* platform that uses *sharding* for scalability and employs a hybrid consensus protocol combining *Proof-of-Work (PoW)* for node identity establishment with Practical Byzantine Fault Tolerance (PBFT) for transaction validation.

zip zap machine See *card imprinting machine*.

Notes

1 Zelle. https://www.zellepay.com/ (Accessed 21 November 2023)

2 Zengin System. https://www.zengin-net.jp/en/zengin_net/zengin_system/ (Accessed 29 September 2024)

3 Zilliqa. https://www.zilliqa.com/ (Accessed 29 September 2024)

ACKNOWLEDGEMENTS

Phew! Cross-checking a glossary is a detailed oriented task which took me longer than expected, as I wanted to make sure that this one was practical and useful to the readers. I must put my (virtual) pen down now. I had no idea when I started writing it that this glossary would be more than three times as big as the one I provide in my first book, *Understanding Payments*. This is because the book didn't need that many entries as the readers have both the glossary and the index (to find terms in the book that I didn't put in the glossary). The effort here was to make a standalone, practical, and modern reference. This glossary is not about "finance", or "banking", or "fintech", it is dedicated to "payments", because I believe this industry is worthy of more attention. The fact that it contains more than 1,600 entries proves my point.

As always, I am grateful to all my payments industry friends for their support, encouragement, and endorsements, and for helping democratise payments knowledge.

I am also thankful to everyone at Routledge for once more taking a punt on me!

Finally, I thank you, dear readers, for staying with me. As the payments industry moves so fast, you have my commitment to produce another version in a couple of years' time, and who knows what the payments world will look like then? Did I miss anything in this version? Please let me know. I dedicate this book to all of you.

As for me, on to the next journey...

Neira Jones
September 2024

FSC
www.fsc.org
MIX
Papier | Fördert gute Waldnutzung
FSC® C083411

Kolibri 360 GmbH
Ferdinand-Jühlke-Straße 7
99095 Erfurt, Deutschland
produktsicherheit@kolibri360.de